Effective Change Management Using

Action Learning and Action Research

Concepts
Frameworks
Processes
Applications

Shankar Sankaran
Bob Dick
Ron Passfield and
Pam Swepson (eds)

Southern Cross University Press
PO Box 157
Lismore NSW 2480
Australia
email scupress@scu.edu.au

The National Library of Australia Cataloguing-in-Publication data

Effective Change Management Using Action Learning and Action Research

Bibliography
ISBN 1 875855 55 6

1. Organisational change. I. Passfield, R.M. II. Title.

658.406

Cover Design & Layout: Keenstreet Communications
Cover Photographs: Keenstreet Communications

Foreword

This excellent book represents another significant contribution to applied research in a field where Southern Cross University has achieved a number of successes and aspires to remain a key player. It gives me particular pleasure to note that the publisher is our own Southern Cross University Press, which has already produced works in the area of action research and action learning.

The publication of this book follows our establishment of the Southern Cross Institute of Action Research, SCIAR, in keeping with our commitment to action research as a developing area of research strength, and the formation of a college of research. This volume's editors, and some of its authors, are associated with either SCIAR or the broader University.

I have been made aware that previous centres of action research or action learning in Australia have usually been located within a single discipline – for instance, education at Deakin University, or agriculture at the Hawkesbury campus of the University of Western Sydney. To date, in fact, action learning has been associated mainly with management. In what might be termed a proud break with this tradition, action research and action learning at Southern Cross University have a multi-disciplinary base.

The book itself reflects this diversity. The authors represent different disciplines, different nations, and different action research or action learning traditions. An international flavour is also evident in those chapters that discuss the ways in which action research and action learning, with appropriate minor modifications, can be culturally appropriate in a range of different cultures and settings.

Another unique feature of the book is that most of the applications described are in the Asia-Pacific region where action research and action learning are being increasingly used in the effective management of change – both organisational and personal.

In other respects, the chapters of the book are true to action research and action learning traditions. There is a strong commitment evident in the various chapters to the integration of theory and practice. The early, more theoretical papers pay attention to the application of theory to practice and change. The later, more practical case studies base their changes on the understanding that grows from research.

Participation is emphasised throughout, however: the people in the research situation are involved in the research, which is as it should be.

I note with interest that action research and action learning encourage people to learn from experience, in the process offering a more formal and systematic version of what many good researchers and practitioners do. Perhaps that is part of the multi-disciplinary appeal.

The overall work integrates theory and practice in the true tradition of action research and I am sure it will be used as a valuable source of reference and ideas by both professionals and academics.

Professor John Rickard
Vice Chancellor and President, Southern Cross University
September 2001

About the authors...

Ge Bingfang has been teaching English as a foreign language in high schools in China since 1985 and is now a senior EFL teacher and researcher at Tongxiang High School Teaching and Research Institute, Zhejiang Province, China. He has been using the Action Inquiry Approach in his work since 1994. <bingfang@mail.jxptt.zj.cn>

Assoc Prof Bill Boyd is Associate Professor in Geography within the School of Environmental Science and Management at Southern Cross University. His academic and scholarly interests range broadly, and include cultural heritage and its management. In this field, he views action research as a possible device suitable for studying communities and their relationships with place and the past. <bboyd@scu.edu.au>

Dr Pip Bruce-Ferguson is research leader in her Department and a member of the Professional Development Unit at The Waikato Institute of Technology, NZ. She is interested in contributing positively to the growth of educational organisations and in her recent PhD thesis used Foucauldian analysis to support personal and organisational change in practice. <espmf@wintec.ac.nz>

Dr Stephanie Chee is the General Manager of Parkway Healthcare Foundation, Vice-Chair of Women's and Children's Healthcare Foundation and a Member of the Preparatory Committee of The Foundation for the Needy Elderly in Singapore. Stephanie uses action research and learning to facilitate change and improvement in nursing education, clinical practice and community development. stephani@singnet.com.sg

Emeritus Prof Alan Davies has had a lifelong interest in building learning, personal development and social development into the work and community organisational settings in which we spend much of our waking life. He has found action research and open systems thinking useful in pursuing this interest. <atdavies@bigpond.com>

Adjunct Prof Bob Dick has been an electrician, draftsperson, recruitment officer and psychologist. He is now an academic, publisher and consultant whose academic work primarily helps people learn action research, qualitative evaluation and change management. In these endeavours he helps others to improve their practice while also trying to improve his own. <bdick@scu.edu.au>

Dr Victor J Friedman works to facilitate learning from experience in practice contexts characterised by uniqueness, uncertainty, and/or instability. His research and consulting work is based on an 'action science' paradigm, which integrates theory building and testing with practice. He is a senior faculty member of the Behavioural Sciences Department at the Ruppin Institute. <victorf@ruppin.ac.il>

Susan Goff is Director of CultureShift, a participatory research, learning and evaluation consultancy based in Sydney and Vice President of ALARPM. She has a BA, a PG Dip in Social Ecology, and a Masters of Applied Science and believes that applications of field-generated participatory theories of practice transform the world's sustainability crises to viable resolutions. <cultureshift@bigpond.com>

Dr Goh Moh Heng is the Director of Hibis Consulting in Singapore. His expertise includes business continuity management, disaster recovery planning, contingency planning and crisis management, and he has used action research to develop a methodology for business continuity planning. He is the first elected Asian Board Member with the Disaster Recovery Institute International, US. <moh_heng@hibisasia.com>

Jane Gregg has a Bachelor of Education and Post-Graduate Diploma in Health Promotion. As a teacher and health promotion/public health practitioner with 16 years experience, Jane has maintained a focus on participatory processes for research and practice in education and health development fields. <janegregg@bigpond.com>

Bill Harris, principal of Facilitated Systems, is a consultant, facilitator, and writer. He helps people by helping the organisations in which they work. He draws on action science, action learning, action research and systems dynamics to help organisations integrate their people, processes and strategy. <bill_harris@facilitatedsystems.com>

Assoc Prof Charmine EJ Härtel is an Associate Professor of Human Resource Management at Monash University. Her research and consulting interests include employee, team, leader and organisational development. She is passionate about innovating workplace systems and practices that enable the positive potential within people. <charmine.hartel@buseco.monash.edu.au>

Dr Ian Hughes co-ordinates Action Research on Web and Offshore Facilitated Learning in the School of Behavioural and Community Health at The University of Sydney. He has used action research and learning in indigenous and mainstream Australia, Singapore, West Africa and other parts of the world. He edits Action Research e-Reports. <I.Hughes@cchs.usyd.edu.au>

Dr Deborah Jones is a Senior Lecturer in Organisational Behaviour in the School of Business and Public Management at Victoria University in Wellington, with a focus on communication studies. She is currently very interested in drawing on cultural and creative approaches from the humanities in carrying out organisational research. <Deborah.Jones@vuw.ac.nz>

Dr Richard Kwok enjoys doing anything that is challenging and complex and is passionate about research. He is a Vice-President with Singapore Technology Kinetics, an Adjunct Professor with Southern Cross University, a Member of the Research and Education Advisory Committee of the Parkway Healthcare Foundation and a Co-Chairman of Advanced and Intelligent Mechatronics Laboratory with the Nanyang Technological University. <rkwok@starhub.net.sg>

Deborah Lange works collaboratively with people in organisations to achieve cultural change and improved outcomes from her business, Deborah Lange and Associates. Her intention is to facilitate people to think and act in ways that are better for the world – socially, environmentally, economically, spiritually, and aesthetically. <deblange@ozemail.com.au>

Prof Michael J Marquardt is Professor of Global Human Resource Development and Action Learning at George Washington University. He has authored 14 books including Action Learning in Action and delivered keynotes on action learning at international conferences. He has used action learning to train executives in Boeing, Caterpillar, Alcoa and government officers in Asia, South America, Canada and the US. <MJMQ@aol.com>

Karen May has Community Development experience in Australia and the Philippines. Her approach emphasises participation and experiential learning to inform theory and policy for structures and decisions that support community contexts. Karen believes a sustainable social ecology will be achieved by holistic collaborative investment creating social capital for a 'whole' economy. <cultureshifttoo@yahoo.com.au>

Anne Noble is a senior lecturer in photography at the College of Design, Fine Arts and Music at Massey University in Wellington. She is interested in the development of Fine Art and Design research projects that link research and teaching and place the work of the University at the heart of community life.

<A.Noble@massey.ac.nz>

Dr Ron Passfield is a Director of the Institute of Global Learning and an Adjunct Professor with the Graduate School of Management, Southern Cross University. He specialises in coaching managers and executives in the use of action learning and action research. <ronp@uq.net.au>

Isabel Rimanóczy is a partner in LIM (Leadership in International Management) a global company dedicated to developing global leaders through Action Reflection Learning. She has authored many articles based on her work in Latin America, Europe, USA and Asia. She *co-authored the Learning Coach Handbook, the Leader-*Coach *Handbook*, and the *Mergers and Acquisitions Integration Handbook.* <isabel.rimanoczy@limglobal.net>

Dr Jay Rothman is the President of the ARIA Group, Inc and Research Director of the Action Evaluation Research Institute. Jay has authored many articles on Identity-Based Conflict, Conflict Resolution, and Evaluation. He has led workshops and conducted interventions in more than a dozen countries including South Africa, Israel and Palestine, Northern Ireland, and Sri Lanka. <jrothman@mcgregor.edu>

Dr Shankar Sankaran is the Director of Southern Cross Institute of Action Research (SCIAR). He supervises doctoral students using action research at Southern Cross University and helps organisations using action learning for management development, which was the topic of his doctoral thesis while implementing large-scale change as a Director in Yokogawa, Singapore. <ssankara@scu.edu.au>

Sng Hee Meng is the Senior Vice President of Yokogawa, Singapore. An engineer by training, he has headed various functions including Engineering, Human Resources, Corporate Quality, After-sales Services, Sales and Marketing. He has led various change initiatives within the organisation and has also implemented Action Learning to facilitate change. <hmsng@yas.com.sg>

Dr Pam Swepson has been an organisational psychologist in the Queensland Department of Primary Industries in Australia for many years. Her work involves integrating participatory action research processes into research partnerships between scientists, producers and industry. <p.swepson@uq.net.au>

Israel Sykes is a therapist, consultant, social entrepreneur, and researcher. He co-founded the Unit for Learning from Successes in the Social Welfare Services, at the JDC-Brookdale Institute in Jerusalem. He founded and directs 'Benafshenu – Building Bridges to Recovery', an innovative program staffed by people with mental illness and family members, for bringing about social change in the area of mental health. <israels@jdc.org.il>

Assoc Prof David Tripp is Associate Professor at Murdoch University, working in action inquiry methods in professional and organisational development. He has taught a graduate action research unit and written the SCOPE materials for the Australian National Professional Development Program. He recently produced online action learning materials for the Government of Western Australia, and is currently working in policy and management at the Singapore National Institute of Education. <tripp@central.murdoch.edu.au><dhtripp@nie.edu.sg>

Bob Williams spends most of his time evaluating public sector programs, especially areas such as health, employment and workplace safety. He does this in ways that allow people to gain important insights from the experience – hence his interest in reflection. He is a passionate windsurfer and snowboarder, and never turns down a fine meal, a decent film, or a good argument. <bobwill@actrix.gen.nz>

Jeannie Wilson has a degree in theology and education and worked in the corporate banking and as an accredited Special Religious Educator. She is now broadening her knowledge of effective learning strategies to achieve her ultimate aim of devoting her whole time to the educational needs of young children in state primary schools.

Elisabeth Wilson-Evered is a doctoral candidate in Management at Queensland University and an organisational development consultant. Her research and interests include innovation, leadership and strategic culture change. Her work includes leading organisational change and developing initiatives to implement human resource information systems and design and deliver programs for cultural and systems change. <elisabet@psy.uq.edu.au>

Professor Ortrun Zuber-Skerritt is the Director of OZI (Ortrun Zuber International P/L), specialising in Action Learning & Action Research, Leadership Programs, Postgraduate Research Training and Supervision, including Qualitative Research Methods. She is an Adjunct Professor at Griffith University (Brisbane) and Southern Cross University (Lismore, Australia) and Professor of Professional and Organisational Development in the UK-based International Management Centres (IMC). <o.zuber-skerritt@mailbox.gu.edu.au>

Introduction

Recently several books about conducting action learning and action research have been published, mainly in Europe and the US. However most of these books are either devoted to action learning or action research and contain mostly examples of application of these approaches in the West.

Effective Change Management Using Action Leaning and Action Research attempts to fill a gap in the market by covering both action learning and action research in one book with practical examples of how these approaches have been applied in the Asia Pacific region. The book also covers related approaches such as action science, reflective practice and systems thinking, and how they can be combined with action learning and action research. The applications in this book also discuss how Western approaches such as action learning and action research can be applied to other cultures and in multi-cultural situations with local adaptation.

Initially the book did not have 'change management' in its title. But, after reviewing the chapters contributed to the book as well as the applications, the editors felt that this book has the potential to fill another gap in the market – how to use action learning and action research in successfully implementing change in organisations and communities.

The idea to put together a practical and reasonably priced book on action learning and action research started in Singapore last year, by four managers and their two academic supervisors. They were involved in implementing change in organisations in South East Asia as part of the doctoral programs that the managers completed successfully.

Initially it was difficult to find a publisher for the book to agree to market it at an affordable price for practitioners. The focus for producing this book then shifted to Australia due to the support for the idea from three organisations: Elogue – a virtual 'learning set' of practitioners using action learning/research; Action Learning Action Research and Process Management Association of Australia (ALARPM); and Southern Cross University, who established the Southern Cross Institute of Action Research (SCIAR) as an innovative initiative to create a centre for action research in the Asia Pacific region. Some of the authors decided to contribute to the book when the editors sent out an email – through arlist, the electronic discussion list – to ascertain the market interest in such a book.

The editors are indebted to the following organisations and people who have helped us immensely in our journey in many ways: all the authors of the book who agreed 'in the true spirit of action research' to receive no royalty for the first run of this book so that it could be made available at an affordable price; Professor Peter Baverstock, the Dean of the Graduate Research College at Southern Cross University, who agreed to underwrite the first run of this book; Southern Cross University's Vice Chancellor, Professor John Rickard, for agreeing without hesitation to write a foreword – in spite of being in the midst of implementing changes at the university; Professor Sandra Speedy, Professor Chad Perry and Associate Professor Stewart Hase from the Division of Business for their active support for the book; the families and friends of the editors who gave moral support for the book by not complaining about the time that they gave to get this book together on schedule; Sandra Black and Barbara Bowden of Southern Cross University Press for proofreading the chapters and getting it together in good shape; ALARPM for supporting the efforts to promote the book to its members; and the Directors of Management Learning and

Action Research (MaLAR) in Singapore for their support in contributing chapters to this book.

> '...and most of all the people, too numerous to mention, who unselfishly helped us to develop our own understanding and skills.'

Contents

Part 1

Concepts

Part 1
Concepts

Bob Dick

In this book you are about to embark on an exploration, from many different perspectives, of the two methodologies known as action learning (AL) and action research (AR), and in some chapters their combination (ALAR).

The editors (Shankar, Ron, Pam and myself) have grouped the chapters into four parts: concepts, frameworks, processes, and applications. There are other ways in which we might have grouped them: some of the chapters would fit well into a different part. Consistent with the ALAR methodologies, in many of the chapters the theory and practice is intertwined. In general, however, the sequence of chapters will take you gradually from theory to practice.

This is Part One, on concepts. It introduces you to ALAR primarily at a theoretical level. Even here, though, you will find that users of ALAR pursue both theory and practice. You will find a case study (Swepson), ways of applying the concepts (especially Zuber-Skerritt, Marquardt). In all chapters the concepts translate easily into practice.

This part begins with an overview of both methodologies (Zuber-Skerritt). Following chapters then deal in turn with action research (Dick, Swepson) and action learning (Passfield, Marquardt).

Several of these authors have mentioned the timeliness of these methodologies. Globalisation has been a catalyst for change, as both Marquardt and Zuber-Skerritt mention. Almost all authors mention the way in which ALAR methodologies are responsive to the situation. They are therefore well suited to times of rapid change.

Action research, as I argue, is action *and* research. One might as easily say that action learning is action *and* learning. In fact, most of the chapters at least hint at this. And one might add, as Zuber-Skerritt does, that it is a small step from learning to research.

An emphasis on action is evident throughout this part, and indeed throughout the book. Practical outcomes are valued. ALAR engages with real problems (Marquardt), involves itself in the system being studied (Passfield), and involves those who will use it in the research (Swepson). Marquardt in addition acknowledges that an action orientation is a Western preference, and identifies some of the ways in which it may be approached in different cultures.

At the same time there is a strong commitment to learning and research demonstrated by all five chapters. Passfield and Zuber-Skerritt both comment that learning is often transformational. Passfield continues by mentioning that the transformation is both personal and organisational.

The ALAR methodologies use a cyclic process to integrate action and learning/research (Zuber-Skerritt, Dick, Swepson). The cycle alternates between action and critical reflection. As Marquardt and Passfield state, the asking of appropriate questions is part of this. As befits applied methodologies which engage with live situations, ALAR methodologies are systemic (Swepson, Zuber-Skerritt) rather than reductionist.

A concern for people and their relationships is apparent in all five chapters. It is most evident in Passfield's chapter in the discussion of the importance of collegial support within an action learning group. His emphasis on the need to combine challenge and support mirrors my own experience. In all chapters, egalitarian relationships are favoured.

Marquardt gives attention to the changes that are necessary to achieve participation, and especially egalitarian participation, in non-Western cultures. (Many of the case studies in Part Four of the book demonstrate cross-cultural use.) Dick and Swepson both consider the choices to be made about who will be involved, though all papers mention the importance of participation. Zuber-Skerritt and Passfield both mention the empowering effects of participation. Marquardt's account emphasises the role of the learning group ('learning set') in achieving useful outcomes.

The ALAR methodologies are often seen as distinct from other approaches to research and change. Indeed, as the preceding discussion shows, there are important differences. Action research is distinct both from those approaches often regarded as "scientific" and those related to ethnography.

However, these chapters evidence another side to the story. Swepson discusses some of the similarities between good action research and good agricultural science. She also describes a case study that combines action research and more conventional research. Zuber-Skerritt draws on concepts from grounded theory, personal construct theory, critical theory and systems theory. Dick draws on the literatures of organisation and community development, and community activism, to describe action research. He proposes that action research can serve as a 'metamethodology' within which other methodologies can be accommodated.

In short, these five chapters provide you with an overview of the nature of the ALAR methodologies. Action learning and action research are oriented to both change and learning/research. They are problem-oriented and cyclic. They are usually participative and egalitarian, and often empowering. They are flexible and responsive in ways that allow them to be fitted to the situation in which they are used and integrated with other processes and methodologies.

(Please note that where names are referred to in brackets and no year is quoted, these refer to chapters of this book.)

Action Learning and Action Research: Paradigm, Praxis and Programs

Ortrun Zuber-Skerritt

Introduction

This chapter provides a brief introduction to and framework for Action Learning and Action Research (ALAR). It is informed by my personal perspective drawing on experience over 20 years, mainly within Australia, but also in other countries in Asia-Pacific, Africa and Europe.

Neither Action Learning nor Action Research are absolute or static terms. They emerged in the 1920s and have been developed since then constantly and in a dynamic way. Both gained eminence in times of crisis and enormous change, such as during and after World Wars I and II and in recent years in response to globalisation and rapid technological and socio-economic change.

In future, ALAR will continue to play an important role in R&D (Research and Development) programs in small and corporate businesses, communities and in the public sector. They have proven to be appropriate methodologies and processes for (re)creating change, innovation, leadership and personal, professional and organisational learning. This is because they are more enduring and sustainable than traditional ways of learning, training and research.

The first chapter in this book presents those aspects of philosophy (paradigm) and integrated theory and practice (praxis) that are generally accepted and shared by action learners and action researchers despite their wide-ranging differences in perspectives, processes and practices.

Action Learning and Action Research have been defined in many different ways, so it is useful here to briefly depict the common understanding of these concepts. 'Action' is almost an all-embracing term. In this book its scope includes past, present and future. This means it refers to something that happened in the past that has affected our present insight, learning and knowledge bases, and enables and compels us to plan our future action accordingly.

Thus *'Action Learning' means learning from action or concrete experience, as well as taking action as a result of this learning.* Similarly, *'Action Research' is a cyclical iterative process of action and reflection on and in action.* Through reflection we conceptualise and generalise what happened (action). We can then investigate in new situations whether our conceptions were right; that is, we try to find confirming or disconfirming evidence (see Bob Dick's and Pam Swepson's chapters in this book).

The main difference between 'Action Learning' and 'Action Research' is the same as that between learning and research generally. Both include active learning, searching, problem solving and systematic inquiry. However, Action Research is more systematic, rigorous, scrutinisable, verifiable, *and* is always made public (in publications, oral or written reports).

Figure 1.1 shows where Action Learning and Action Research overlap.

These shared areas provide the structure for this chapter:

-Paradigm
-Theoretical Framework
-Praxis of Action Learning and Action Research
-Programs and Projects.

Figure 1.1: Commonalities of Action Learning and Action Research

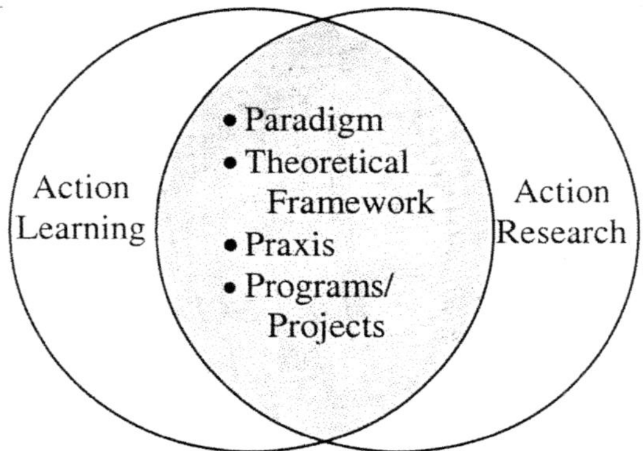

Paradigm

Both Action Learning and Action Research are located in the social sciences, not the natural sciences. This is important to note, because we are not dealing with organic or inorganic matter, but with sentient human beings, groups of people, organisations or societies, whose characteristics, ideas, strategies and behaviour are complex and not easy to predict, if at all.

I recognise two main problems in the social sciences that can be overcome by adapting the ALAR paradigm. One arises from a lack of understanding of what underpins and influences our actions, behaviour and strategies for maintaining or improving our practice. These are, importantly, paradigms, philosophies, values and Weltanschauungen (worldviews). Therefore, this chapter outlines the salient characteristics of the two main competing paradigms in the social sciences, one leading to a technical, reductionist approach, the other to a more holistic, phenomenological approach to learning and knowledge creation (research).

Another problem in the social sciences is the separation between theory and practice, which are conceived as dichotomous. This chapter posits differently, explaining the dialectical relationship of theory and practice as *praxis* in Action Learning and Action Research.

Action researchers have often been criticised by other scientists for not producing 'scientific' research and theory, for producing only action and improved practice. Therefore, in this chapter I explain the difference between a priori 'grand theory' and 'grounded theory', and offer a possible theoretical framework for ALAR.

This framework consists of selected principles borrowed from certain theories and integrated into a new model. As mentioned above, within the social sciences, there are two main competing paradigms: the positivist, mainly quantitative paradigm and the phenomenological, interpretive, mainly qualitative paradigm of inquiry.

The former was first established at the beginning of the twentieth century when social sciences were born and their methodology was adapted to the positivist thinking of the natural sciences. The phenomenological paradigm has gradually emerged since World War II. It is now well established and arguably the predominant paradigm for the new millennium. Evidence for this claim is provided by the many reference books on qualitative methods of inquiry published in recent years (eg. Strauss & Corbin 1997; Denzin & Lincoln 1998; Dey 1999; Glesne 1999; Dick 1999; Gummesson 2000; and in German: Flick 1998; Mayring 1999; Moser 1995 and 1998; Lamnek 1995).

It is useful here to briefly outline the characteristics of and differences between the old and new paradigms.

I have argued elsewhere (Zuber-Skerritt 1992 pp124–42) that it is more appropriate to distinguish between two main research paradigms than to distinguish between quantitative and qualitative methods. Although it is true that in the traditional paradigm the methods used are predominately quantitative, and in the alternative paradigm they are predominately qualitative, both quantitative and qualitative methods may be – and indeed have been – used in both paradigms. However, it is the inquirer's philosophical assumptions that mainly determine which methods s/he will choose, especially when the inquirer is conscious of his or her epistemological framework.

Thus, *methods play a secondary role; the paradigm or theoretical framework is of primary importance and must be made explicit*, so that the reader/examiner can evaluate the process, methods and outcomes, using relevant criteria from the inquirer's particular perspective.

In the literature, the old and new paradigms are often cast in opposition: traditional versus alternative; experimental vs naturalistic; prescriptive vs descriptive; reductionist (reducing phenomena to simplest elements) vs holistic (looking at the totality of the situation); external vs internal (regarding the inquirer's perspective); nomothetic (study of general laws and trends) vs ideographic (study of individual characteristics, case studies); normative vs interpretive; positivist vs non-positivist; using large numbers of 'subjects' and standardised methods to control selected variables vs using a small group of 'participants' and an open-ended communicative approach and multiple methods.

Several points need to be mentioned about this observation. First, there are other paradigms in the social sciences, eg. the critical paradigm. Here I include them in the new paradigm for reasons of necessary brevity and simplicity.

Second, these are observations of paradigms in their pure forms. In practice, such purity does not exist. The oppositions discussed are nonetheless useful as models or mind maps for identifying and justifying our own philosophical position that underpins our R&D strategy.

In their discussion of the theoretical foundation for Action Research, Altrichter et al (1993) have presented a model that is also relevant to Action Learning. They distinguish between a technical/rational view of problem solving and professionalism on the one hand, and a reflective view on the other. In reality most views are somewhere within these two extremes, mixing and using multiple methods (triangulation). Thus we have many choices, so it is important that we explain the rationale for our choice.

I summarise the basic assumptions underlying the two paradigms in Table 1.1 below.

Table 1.1: Basic Assumptions of Opposing Views of Problem Solving (after Altrichter et al 1993)

	Technical Rationality	**Reflective Rationality**
Problem Solution	There are *general* solutions to practical problems	Complex practical problems demand *specific* solutions
Method	These solutions can be developed *outside* practical situations (in laboratories and research centres)	These solutions can be developed only *inside* the context in which the problem arises and in which the practitioner is a crucial and determining element
Application	The solutions can be translated into practitioners actions by means of training, publications, etc.	The solutions cannot be successfully applied to other contexts but they can be made accessible to other practitioners as hypotheses to be tested
Credibility	*Hierarchy* in the institutional power structure: The closer a person is to policy making and theory development, the more credible and powerful s/he is. Separation of theory and practice	New types of communication: networking, *symmetry of communication* and collaboration. Integration of research and development, theory and practice

Action Learning and Action Research are located in the newer, non-positivist paradigm of reflective rationality. It is important to point out that 'validity' and 'rigour' have a different meaning in different paradigms.

Validity in the positivist paradigm is recognised as assured when knowledge is generalisable and when the study is conducted in controlled conditions, using rigorous methods of data collection, analysis and interpretation. The research design is experimental. It starts with the inquirer's predetermined hypothesis that is to be tested and finally either confirmed or refuted. Selected 'subjects' must be recognised as representative of a large cross-section of the relevant population. The sample size must be proportionately large to be valid, and there are normally experimental groups and control groups. This kind of inquiry is useful for statistical purposes, such as population audits, and for predicting future trends, eg. in economics, finance and politics.

On the other hand, phenomenologists believe that knowledge is socially constructed and created from within, and for, a particular group and context. The researcher's role is to describe and explain the situation or case as truthfully as possible. The aim is not to establish generalisable laws for multiple contexts, but to know, understand, improve or change a particular social situation or context for the benefit of the people who are also the 'participants' (not just 'subjects') in the inquiry and who are affected by the results and solutions. Variables are not predetermined and controlled, but are taken on board as they arise from the data. They are multiple and dynamic. Therefore, this kind of inquiry is more complex and difficult to conduct, if it is to be of high quality, systematic and valid to those involved.

Validity in the new paradigm is more personal and interpersonal than methodological, and should be based on an interactive dialectic logic (Reason & Rowan 1981 p244) rather than a dichotomy of 'subjective' or 'objective' truth. This dichotomy can be overcome by the concept of 'perspective' ie. taking a personal view from some distance and *after* an interactive dialectic using multiple data, respondents and co-inquirers. In brief, the action learner/researcher is interested in perspectives, rather than truth per se, and in giving an honest account of how the participants in the project view themselves and their experiences.

Action Learning and Action Research may be informed by many theories of learning and creating new knowledge. Given the length limitations of this chapter, I identify below four important areas of theory that I believe are acceptable to most action learners/researchers in the new paradigm.

Theoretical Framework

I have long maintained that all people – consciously or unconsciously – develop through their life experience a personal theoretical framework or lens through which they see the world. It is determined by their personal values and worldviews (Weltanschauungen) and it determines and guides their strategies and behaviour. Therefore it is important for us personally, professionally, and as members of collective bodies to identify, understand and consciously develop our individual theoretical framework. This can be aided through reflection on practice, personal and organisational learning, and through critical discourse.

I have explained in detail my theoretical framework for Action Research (Zuber-Skerritt 1992), which was confirmed to be relevant and useful in other countries such as Singapore (Murphy 2000), China (Chan 1993), Europe (Zuber-Skerritt 1997, Irvine-Piggot 2001), South Africa (Zuber-Skerritt 2000) and New Zealand (Melrose 1993). My short postgraduate business management courses held annually in Innsbruck (since 1995),Vienna (since 1998) and South Africa (since 1995) yield similar responses. Here I present a revised and briefer version with reference to:

-Grounded Theory
-Personal Construct Theory
-Critical Theory
-Systems Theory.

Grounded Theory

One of the first influential books providing a theoretical framework for ALAR and other methodologies within the non-positivist paradigm was Glaser and Strauss (1967) on *The Discovery of Grounded Theory*.This theory established the notion that theoretical knowledge can be generated from specific contextual information and data collected from people within a certain context (eg. an organisation) by a process of alternating and interacting the phases of discovery and subsequent testing or 'sampling of grounded theory', ie. an iterative process illustrated in Figure 1.2.

Figure 1.2:Testing of Grounded Theory

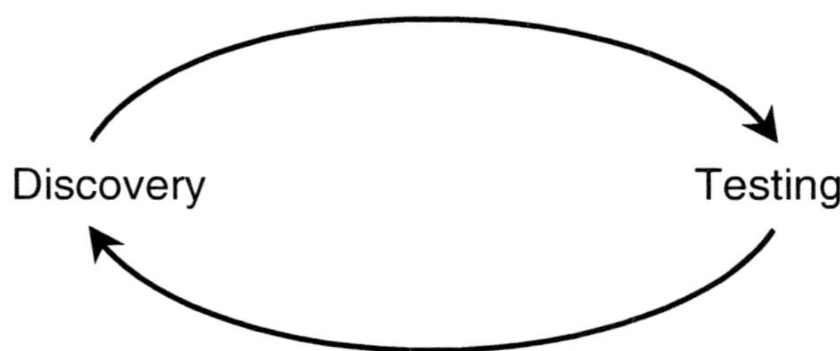

Unlike scientific empirical research aiming at verification of 'grand theories' and placing little value on their discovery, 'grounded theory' emphasises the process of discovery and places value on generating meaningful theories. While empirical research produces 'etic' theory by an outsider who is uninvolved and removed from the object of inquiry, grounded theory is 'emic' with an insider view of the people, groups, organisations or cultures being studied.

The former inquirer tries to establish generalisable (nomothetic) laws; the latter wants to provide knowledge and understanding of a particular, individual (ideographic) case. For the former, generalisations might be statistically purposeful and significant (eg. in population audits, causes of illness and health, national trends), but they often are not applicable or irrelevant to the individual case and specific group.

Personal Construct Theory (PCT)

George Kelly published one of the first books on this topic in 1955. His main message was that everyone is a 'personal scientist'. This means that it is not the privilege of experts and professional scientists to advance knowledge (theories, rules and principles), which we may then accept and apply, but rather that all of us in normal mental health are capable of creating knowledge at various levels. We are not passive receivers of knowledge, but active constructors (or self-instructors) and interpreters of our experiences. Thus, knowledge and theory become personalised, relevant to, and fully integrated into our practice.

Based on this epistemology, Kelly developed his personal construct theory in terms of a fundamental postulate elaborated by eleven corollaries which I have explained in relation to ALAR in Higher Education (Zuber-Skerritt 1992 pp56–66). In particular, I state:

> Kelly's epistemological position is 'constructive alternativism', that is, the assumption that our present constructs or interpretations of the universe are subject to revision or replacement. This means that people understand themselves and their environment, and anticipate future events, by constructing tentative models or personal theories and by evaluating these theories against personal criteria as to whether the prediction and control of events (based upon the models) have been successful or not. All theories are hypotheses created by people; they may be valid at any particular time, but may suddenly be invalid in some unforeseeable respect and replaced by a better theory (p57).
>
> Kelly also believes that people construe reality in an infinite number of different ways. Although he does not deny the importance of childhood experiences or present environmental constraints, he suggests that it is more important to explore people's thinking about their present situation (ie. their current hypotheses structure). He believes

> that people need not be trapped by their early experiences or be impotent in the face of present environmental constraints, but that change can occur if they see their personal theories as open to refutation and not as 'objective truth' (p58).

Relating this to ALAR, I largely agree with PCT that action learners/ researchers are personal scientists, each with an individual system of constructs (individuality corollary) that can be explored by him/herself and by others (sociality corollary). A group of action learners/researchers may be similar in terms of their construction and interpretation of experience (commonality corollary), but their development and conceptual change depends on the 'permeability' corollary, ie. their openness to change and their willingness to search for disconfirming as well as confirming evidence in their research.

However, my constructivist view also acknowledges human feelings, beliefs and values, rather than only a rational construct system in the human mind. Therefore, I refer to 'concepts' and 'conceptions', rather than 'constructs'.

Critical Theory

So far we have established that everyone can be a personal scientist and create contextual knowledge (grounded theory) in an organisation or in any group of people by conducting ALAR projects. Ideally, this kind of problem-solving inquiry is conducted critically *and* collaboratively in a supportive, non-hierarchical environment.

If, however, an organisation is structured and led in a hierarchical manner, it is essential to (1) obtain the approval and support for the program or project(s) from top management and (2) establish team spirit and 'symmetrical communication' among all project team members.

In my experience, it is futile to try to achieve a significant improvement or change in an organisation unless it is fully backed by the chief executive officer and senior management. They must understand and agree with the basic assumptions of ALAR, accept a critical analysis of the problem or 'thematic concern' under investigation and be open for the suggested change(s) resulting from the inquiry.

The Frankfurt School of Critical Theory and its followers have provided useful principles for ALAR, eg. Carr and Kemmis (1986). I mention here just two of these principles: 'symmetrical communication' and 'becoming critical'.

Symmetrical communication demands that everyone in the project team is considered equal – no matter what rank/position – and contributes equally, albeit differently, to solving the research problem at hand. The assumption is that *each member has knowledge, skills, capabilities or talents in a particular area that need to be identified and used effectively.*

Various instruments can be used to identify people's strengths and weaknesses, as well as their work preferences. A good example is the Team Management Systems (TMS) developed by Margerison and McCann (1985, 1992; www.tms.com.au). Team members learn which management types are needed for a 'winning team', how to recognise all types, and to value those who are quite different or even opposite to their own type and work preferences. My experience has led me to believe that this recognition and acceptance of work preferences in a team by means of TMS leads to mutual respect, synergy and symmetrical communication. As such, it is conducive to collaborative inquiry and problem solving.

The second principle of 'becoming critical' was argued and discussed in detail by Carr and Kemmis (1986). They distinguished between technical, practical and critical Action Research. I would add: and Action Learning. I have summarised the characteristics of each type of inquiry in Table 1.2 below with regard to the aims, the facilitator's role and the relationship between facilitator and participants.

Carr and Kemmis maintained that only critical, emancipatory inquiry is true Action Research. However, my experience tells me that emancipatory Action Learning and Action Research are both developmental processes from technical to critical inquiry. Most of us as critical action learners/researchers started with technical, then proceeded to practical, and finally understood and practised critical modes of inquiry. The latter is definitely what we should aim at, in order to achieve far-reaching transformational change, rather than functional or transactional change.

For personal and organisational change to be truly transformational, it is essential that all members of an ALAR group adopt a critical and self-critical attitude. This means critique is never taken as a personal attack (destructive), but accepted as a necessary condition for organisational change, innovation or recreation (constructive). In Action Learning programs, actions and thoughts are submitted to the constructive scrutiny of supportive colleagues as 'critical friends'. We learn from our mistakes and failures as well as successes. We are not merely interested in changing people and organisations; we want them to grow and learn, and we want to learn ourselves within this process.

Table 1.2:Types of Inquiry (after Carr & Kemmis 1986)

Type of inquiry	Aims	Facilitator s role	Relationship between facilitator and participants
1.Technical	- effectiveness/ efficiency of practice - professional development	outside expert	co-option (practitioners depend on facilitator)
2.Practical	- as (1) above - practitioners understanding - transformation of their consciousness	Socratic role, encouraging participation and self-reflection	co-operation (process-consultancy)
3.Emancipatory	- as (1) and (2) above - participants emancipation from the dictates of tradition, self-deception, coercion - their critique of bureaucratic systematisation - transformation of the organisation or system	process moderator (responsibility shared equally by participants)	collaboration

Systems Theory

Again, recognising the brevity required of this chapter, I refer to the two major concepts in systems theory that are important for ALAR: 'interrelatedness' and 'systemic thinking'.For a more detailed account see Alan Davies' chapter in this book.

In this age of global interdependence, systems thinkers understand that everything is interrelated with everything else. As Marquardt (2000) and others before him have pointed out, our worldview has changed from a Newtonian perspective – studying the parts in order to understand the whole – to a Quantum Physics view where the whole organises and even partly defines its parts.

Marquardt (2000) claims that Action Learning builds leaders to be systems thinkers:

> Effective problem solving requires the ability to be a systems thinker... Systems thinkers have the ability to see connections between issues, events and data points – the whole rather than parts... (p234)
>
> During action learning sessions, participants learn how to think in a systemic way and how to handle complex, seemingly unconnected aspects of organizational challenges (p235).

In ALAR sets, members develop system-oriented, holistic resolutions to complex problems in an organisation or other social settings. In this process, participants develop and grow as persons, managers and leaders.

To conclude, within the new paradigm in the social sciences, our theoretical framework for ALAR comprises theories and principles derived from certain aspects of:

- *grounded theory*: enabling action learners/researchers to create knowledge, inductively developed from 'raw data' that has been systematically obtained
- *personal construct theory*: regarding action researchers as personal scientists who share and negotiate meaning to arrive at their individual and group concepts
- *critical theory*: requiring a critical and self-critical attitude in order to achieve real transformational change
- *systems theory*: developing system-oriented, holistic resolutions to complex problems through ALAR.

This framework is by no means complete or static. It is designed to provide a starting point for other people interested and engaged in ALAR to critically reflect and develop their own conceptual framework.

An important point to make is that *established theories may inform us, but we as systems thinkers, personal scientists and critical action learners/researchers develop our own theories as grounded theory* based on our own action and on our data that is systematically collected, analysed and interpreted in the course of our inquiry which is collaborative more often than not. It is this dialectical relationship between action and research that we consider in the next section.

Praxis

There are abundant definitions and ill-defined uses of 'praxis' to be found in the literature. I define praxis as the interdependence and integration – not separation – of theory and practice, research and development, thought and action. I have explained this dialectic relationship between theory and practice and its underpinning philosophy in more detail elsewhere (Zuber-Skerritt 1990).

Here it is important to state that the concepts of both Action Learning and Action Research are conceived as a dialectical relationship between 'action' – activities, concrete experiences, practical trials, explorations, or applications – and 'learning' or 'research' – understanding, creating and advancing knowledge through reflection, inquiry and critical evaluation.

As Figure 1.3 shows, in ALAR we come to know and learn from our action/experience, but whatever we have conceptualised and learnt must lead to action, improvement, development or change. *There is no learning/research without action to follow, and no action without a knowledge foundation based on prior learning/research.* This is the main difference between Action Learning and Action Research on the one hand, and traditional learning/research on the other. The latter may be pursued in its own right (*per se*), in isolation from concrete situations, and not necessarily be of practical use.

Figure 1.3: The Praxis of Action Learning and Action Research

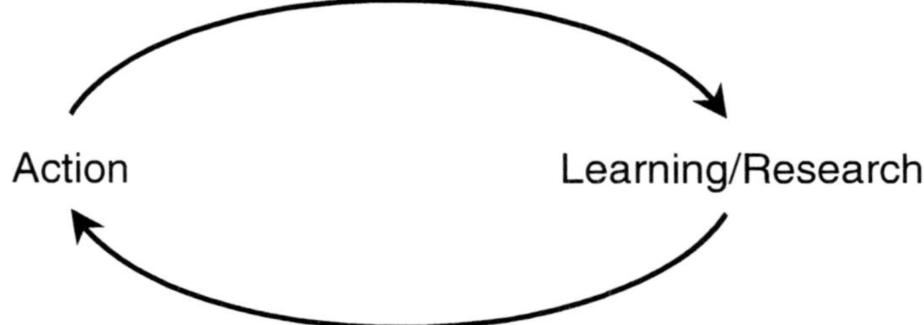

In the following, we consider first the praxis of Action Learning and then of Action Research in more detail.

The praxis of Action Learning is really as old as humankind, but it was first conceptualised as such by Reg Revans in the 1930s and 1940s. Here I discuss two of his concepts, the first relating to 'learning', the second to 'action'.

Revans says on video (1991a) and in his writing (1982, 1991b, 1998) that we learn best by asking fresh questions. This idea is not new and can be traced back to ancient Greek philosophers. For example, Socrates (about 470–399BC) used to ask his disciples probing questions that motivated them to find the answers themselves. He also equated knowledge with ethically correct action and virtue.

I think that one reason why Action Learning has become important, relevant and topical since World War II is the increasingly rapid technological and socio-economic change in our increasingly complex world. *We need to learn faster, more actively and creatively, but also ethically to be sustainable in a global world.*

Another reason might be reaction against the positivist notion of knowledge creation and transmission. According to this view, knowledge is created by scientists using scientific methods. This knowledge is then applied and transmitted from expert to novice in a funnel fashion (*Nürnberger Trichter* in German), as depicted in Figure 1.4 below.

Revans and his followers maintain that such knowledge – established and traditionally taught in universities and schools – is necessary, but not sufficient. What we also need, he termed 'questioning insight'.

Figure 1.4: Traditional Learning Versus Learning Through Discussion and Questioning Insight

Traditional learning

Learning through discussion and questioning insight

Questioning insight develops from asking ourselves fresh and deep-seated questions, including questions of epistemology (eg. how do we come to know?), education (eg. what/how did I learn?), ontology (eg. who am I? and who would I like to be?) and ethics (eg. what is right, fair, sustainable?).

Some of the most important educational principles developed from this holistic philosophy are 'learning through discussion', 'learning by doing' and 'reflective practice', all of which also relate to the second of Revans' concepts of Action Learning: 'action'.

The philosophical assumption underlying this concept of action is that not just the so-called experts, but all of us can create knowledge on the basis of our action and concrete experience by:

- -reflecting on and in action
- -conceptualising, theorising and generalising this action/ experience
- -testing these concepts in new situations, and thus
- -engaging in a new cycle of gaining knowledge through new concrete experience, reflection, conceptualisation, testing, etc.

On the basis of this philosophical assumption, learning is life long and ongoing in cycles of action and reflection, in response to fresh questions that are new and unknown to us and that we seek to resolve. See Figure 1.5 below.

Figure 1.5: The Action Learning Cycle

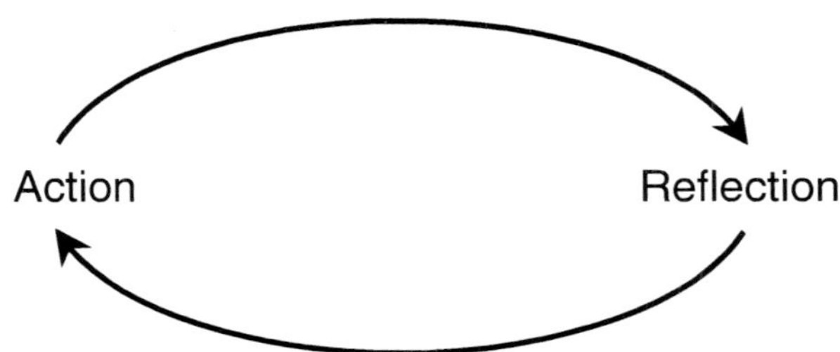

The terms 'Action Learning' and 'Action Research' are often used interchangeably. Indeed, Action Research is based on the same philosophical assumptions and includes Action Learning. However, as mentioned above, the main difference between Action Learning and Action Research is the same as that between learning and research generally. Action Research is more systematic, rigorous in its methodology and use of methods so that it can be scrutinised, and it is always made public (eg. oral presentations, written reports, conference papers, publications in the form of refereed journal articles, book chapters, monographs, books).

It is interesting to note that both Action Learning and Action Research were first conceived by German Jews who started their work in the 1920s, 30s and 40s and migrated to English-speaking countries: Reg Revans to England and Kurt Lewin to America. Whilst Revans worked mainly with managers in industry and business to improve conditions, processes and productivity (eg. in coal mines, banks and hospitals) through Action Learning, Lewin (1926, 1948, 1952) focused mainly on improving social conditions through Action Research in funded research institutions. Therefore, it is understandable that there has been more literature available on educational Action Research than on Action Learning, but this trend is changing, mainly because of the publications on Action Learning in all areas and sectors produced by MCB University Press (http://www.mcb.co.uk; http://www.emeraldinsight.com) and the International Management Centres (http://www.imc.org.uk/imc/harvest/).

I have already mentioned the three types of Action Research: technical, practical and critical or emancipatory. In brief and in line with our theoretical framework outlined above, emancipatory Action Research is collaborative, critical and self-critical inquiry by practitioners (eg. teachers, manager) into a major problem or issue of mutual concern in their organisation. They 'own the problem' and feel responsible and accountable for solving it through teamwork and a cyclical process of (1) strategic planning, (2) implementing the plan (action), (3) observation, evaluation and self-evaluation, (4) critical and self-critical reflection on the results of (1)–(3), and making decisions for the next cycle of action research – that is, a revised plan, followed by action, observation and reflection, and so on, as shown in the classic spiral of Action Research cycles in Figure 1.6 below.

More precisely, Action Research is emancipatory when it aims not only at technical and practical improvement, the participants' transformed consciousness, and change within their organisation's existing boundaries and conditions. It is also emancipatory when it aims to change the system itself or those conditions that impede desired improvement in the organisation. Like critical Action Learning, emancipatory Action Research also aims at the participants' empowerment and self-confidence in their ability to create 'grounded theory' – that is, theory grounded in experience and practice – by solving complex problems in totally new situations, collaboratively as a team, with everyone in the team being a 'personal scientist' contributing in different ways but on an equal footing with everyone else. There is no hierarchy, but instead open and 'symmetrical communication'.

In the next section, I present a model and references to practical examples of ALAR programs and projects within organisations.

Figure 1.6: The Spiral of Action Research Cycles, Programs and Projects

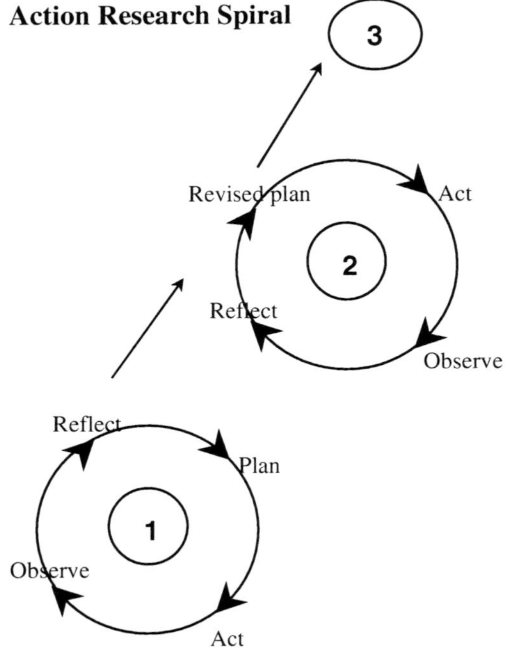

Programs and Projects

There is no prescriptive recipe for conducting Action Learning programs and Action Research projects because of the open-ended nature of solving complex problems in complex situations. However, we have learnt from experience that there are certain processes that can be generalised. For example, I have presented and explained each component of a generic process model for Action Learning programs with Action Research projects conducted within organisations. I refer to my recent article (Zuber-Skerritt 2000a) for a detailed discussion of the model reproduced in Figure 1.7 below.

Figure 1.7:A Generic Process Model

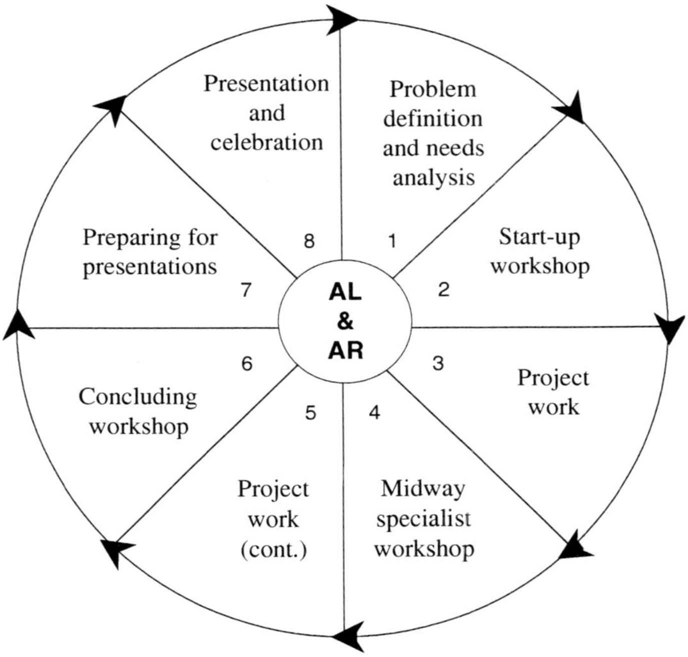

In addition to the examples provided in this book as case studies, I believe it is also useful to refer to major Action Learning programs with Action Research projects in large organisations in industry and higher education, ie. ALAR programs and projects that, in hindsight, followed this generic process model.

Dotlich and Noel (1998) in their Action Research on Action Learning provide the best examples and evidence for success of their programs in large multi-national companies. These companies not only improved their productivity and bottom line, but they also became 'learning organisations', and their leaders and managers developed life-long learning skills which equipped them to deal with change and totally new problems in new situations on a continuing basis.

To the same effect, there are many examples of major Action Learning programs with Action Research team projects in higher education. They include those at Griffith University (Farquhar & McKay 1996; Zuber-Skerritt 1996), the University of Queensland (Passfield 1996; Ryan & Zuber-Skerritt 1994; Zuber-Skerritt 1994 & 1997), and Southern Cross University (Zuber-Skerritt 2000b).

Conclusions

This chapter has tried to provide an introduction to and framework for Action Learning and Action Research. These are approaches that are particularly useful when seeking innovation, change, growth and transformation of organisations and their leaders and managers.

My argument can be summarised as the 3 Ps of ALAR. By this I mean, Action Learning and Action Research (ALAR) have in common the phenomenological *Paradigm* and theoretical assumptions, *Praxis* (integration of action and thought) and a process model for *Programs/projects.*

I have explained the paradigm in terms of ontology (our assumptions about the nature of being/reality), epistemology (our assumptions about the nature of knowledge and knowing) and methodology (our consequent approach to problem solving and inquiry strategy).

I have explained the characteristics of the non-positivist, phenomenological paradigm of ALAR in juxtaposition to the older positivist research paradigm. I have noted that neither are used in their pure form, because they are human constructs. People usually draw selectively from both paradigms. Thus we need to explain and justify our choice so that our findings can be evaluated against our own criteria, rather than against external, positivist criteria.

My revised theoretical framework for ALAR is conceived as an overlap of selected aspects and principles from four existing theories, as shown in Figure 1.8.

Figure 1.8: Theoretical Framework for Action Learning and Action Research

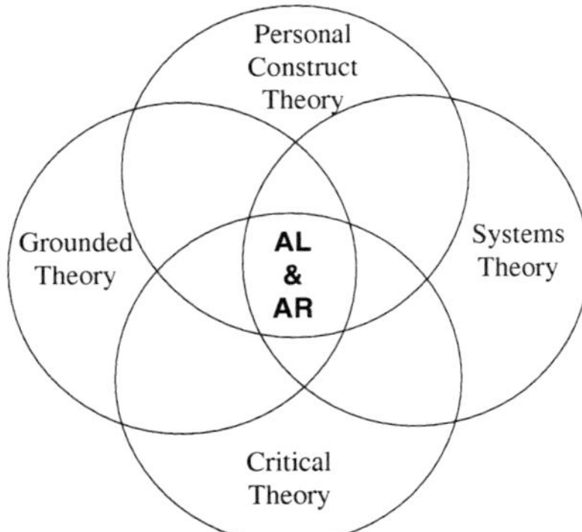

Action learners and action researchers may be informed by these theories, but they are also personal scientists themselves, able to create grounded theory based on their own inquiry. They are open to critique, refutation and change. Their inquiry is emancipatory and system-oriented. They are 'comrades in adversity' (Revans 1991b) or 'critical friends' who support one another in 'symmetrical communication', leading to mutual respect and synergy. Synergy is 'the value that comes when the whole adds up to more than the sum of its parts' (Kanter 1990 p58).

This is the main reason why collaborative Action Learning and Action Research are so powerful and successful in organisational change programs. Usually, the aim of these programs is to solve complex problems in unknown situations during times of rapid change. It is therefore not surprising that ALAR has much to offer as we seek to understand and maximise opportunities for growth and sustainability in the present time of rapid change and unpredictability.

Bibliography

Altrichter H, Posch, P & Somekh, B (1993) *Teachers Investigate Their Work: An introduction to the methods of action research.* London: Routledge

Carr, W & Kemmis, S (1986) *Becoming Critical: Education, Knowledge and Action Research.* Geelong: Deakin University Press

Chan, D (1993) 'A personal view on quality assurance' in *Linkage.* City Polytechnic of Hong Kong, 24 December pp5–6

Denzin, NK & Lincoln, Y (eds) (1998) *Strategies of Qualitative Inquiry.* Thousand Oakes: Sage

Dey, I (1999) *Grounding Grounded Theory: Guidelines for qualitative inquiry.* San Diego: Academic Press

Dick, B (1999) *Rigour Without Numbers: The potential of dialectical processes as qualitative research tools.* 3rd ed, Brisbane: Interchange

Dotlich, DL & Noel, JL (1998) *Action Learning: How the world's top companies are re-creating their leaders and themselves.* San Francisco: Jossey-Bass Publishers

Farquhar, M & McKay, P (eds) (1996) *China Connections: Australian business needs and university language education.* Canberra: National Languages and Literacy Institute of Australia

Flick, U (1998) *Qualitative Forschung: Theorie, Methoden, Anwendung in Psychologie und Sozialwissenschaften.* Reinbek bei Hamburg: Rowohlt

Glaser, B & Strauss, A (eds) (1967) *The Discovery of Grounded Theory.* Chicago: Aldine

Glesne, C (1999) *Becoming Qualitative Researchers: An introduction* 2nd edition, New York: Longman

Gummesson, E (2000) *Qualitative Methods in Management Research.* Thousand Oakes: Sage

Irvine-Piggot, E (2001) *Appraisal: Reducing Control – Enhancing Effectiveness.* PhD thesis. Auckland: Massey University

Kanter, R (1990) *When Giants Learn to Dance.* London: Unwin

Kelly, GA (1955) *The Psychology of Personal Constructs.* New York: Norton

Lamnek, S (1995) *Qualitative Sozialforschung: Methoden und Techniken.* Beltz, Weinheim: Dritte korrigierte Auflage

Lewin, K (1926) *Vorsatz, Wille und Bedürfnis.* Berlin: Springer

Lewin, K (1948) *Resolving Social Conflict: Selected papers on group dynamics.* New York: Harper & Bros

Lewin, K (1952) *Selected Theoretical Papers.* London: Tavistock Publications

Margerison, C & McCann, D (1985) *Team Management Systems: How to lead a winning team.* Bradford: MCB University Press

Marquardt, MJ (2000) 'Action learning and leadership' in *The Learning Organization.* 7 (8), pp233–40

Mayring P (1999) *Einführung in die Qualitative Sozialforschung: Eine Anleitung zum Qualitativen Denken Vierte.* München: Auflage Psychologie Verlags Union

Melrose, MJ (1993) Development and Evaluation of the Certificate in Educational Leadership – PhD thesis. Auckland: University of Auckland

Moser, H (1995) *Grundlagen der Praxisforschung.* Freiburg: Lambertus Verlag

Moser, H (1998) *Instrumentenkoffer für den Praxisforscher.* Freiburg: Lambertus Verlag

Murphy, J (2000) 'An interview with Ortrun Zuber-Skerritt' in *Action Research International – A Refereed Online Journal* http://www.scu.edu.au/schools/gcm/ar/ari/p-jmurphy00.html

Passfield, R (1996) Action Learning for Professional and Organisational Development: An Action Research Case Study in Higher Education – PhD thesis. Brisbane: Griffith University

Reason, P & Rowan, J (eds) (1981) *Human Inquiry: A sourcebook of new paradigm research.* Chichester: John Wiley & Sons

Revans, R (1980) *Action Learning: New techniques for management.* London: Blond & Briggs

Revans, R (1982) *The Origins and Growth of Action Learning.* Bromley: Chartwell-Bratt

Revans, R (1991a) 'The concept, origin and growth of action learning' in Zuber-Skerritt, O (ed) *Action Learning for Improved Performance.* Brisbane: AEBIS Publishing

Revans, R (1991b) Reg Revans Speaks about Action Learning – video program produced by Zuber-Skerritt, O. Brisbane: TV Centre, University of Queensland

Revans, R (1998) *ABC of Action Learning: Empowering managers to act to learn from action* 3rd edition. London: Lemos and Crane

Ryan, Y & Zuber-Skerritt, O (eds) (1994) *Departmental Excellence in University Education (DEUE).* Brisbane: TEDI, University of Queensland

Strauss, A & Corbin, J (eds) (1997) *Grounded Theory in Practice.* Thousand Oakes: Sage

Zuber-Skerritt, O (1990) 'The dialectical relationship between theory and practice in higher education' in Gellert, C, Leitner, E & Schramm, J (eds) *Research and Teaching at Universities: International and comparative perspectives.* Frankfurt am Main, Bern, New York, Paris: Peter Lang. pp165–92

Zuber-Skerritt, O (1992) *Professional Development in Higher Education: A theoretical framework for action research.* London: Kogan Page

Zuber-Skerritt, O (1994) 'Learning and action research' in Nightingale, P & O'Neil, M (eds) *Achieving Quality Learning in Higher Education.* London: Kogan Page. pp99–117

Zuber-Skerritt, O (1996) *Action Research in Higher Education: Examples and reflections.* London: Kogan Page

Zuber-Skerritt, O (1997) 'Die Universität als lernende Organisation. Ein Projekt zur Qualitätsverbesserung in einer australischen Universität' in Altrichter, H, Schratz, M & Pechar, H (eds) *Hochschulen auf dem Prüfstand: Was bringt Evaluation für Entwicklung von Universitäten und Fachhochschulen?* Innsbruck, Wien: Studien Verlag. pp290–305

Zuber-Skerritt, O (2000a) 'A generic model for action learning and action research programs within organisations' in *ALAR Journal.* 5 (1), 41–50

Zuber-Skerritt, O (2000b) Leadership Development of Academic Women through Action Learning and Action Research: Progress Reports No 1 and 2 Canberra: IDP Education Australia.

Action Research: Action *and* Research

Bob Dick

Introduction

Action research (AR) is true to label. It pursues both action (change) and research (understanding) outcomes. It achieves change through its participative approach, often in conjunction with other change processes. The research is achieved by being responsive to the situation and by searching strenuously for disconfirming evidence. At the heart of AR is a cycle that alternates action and critical reflection. Action and research enhance each other.

In the section immediately below I describe AR in a little more detail. I emphasise its flexibility and responsiveness to the situation in which it is being used.

A second section describes how AR can be used to bring about change. I describe some of the benefits that arise from the skilful involvement of people in the change process. I identify some of the difficulties facing researchers who do their work participatively.

Then comes a section in which I explore some ways in which the rigour of AR can be improved. My own view is that, done well, AR offers more rigour in fluid situations than do many other methodologies. This is what it is designed to do.

Finally I examine those features of AR that allow the action and the research components to be mutually enhancing.

Action Research

As the description above implies, AR is a change methodology and research methodology within a single process. It seeks to bring about change – the action – in such a way that more understanding is developed as a parallel outcome. It pursues understanding – the research – in ways which allow the action to be based upon a better understanding of the situation.

There are several varieties. Most of them alternate between action and critical reflection (Figure 2.1). Most are cyclic, participative, and qualitative. These characteristics, and some others, allow AR to pursue its twin goals in such a way that each enhances the other.

Fig 2.1: The AR Cycle Alternates Action and Critical Reflection

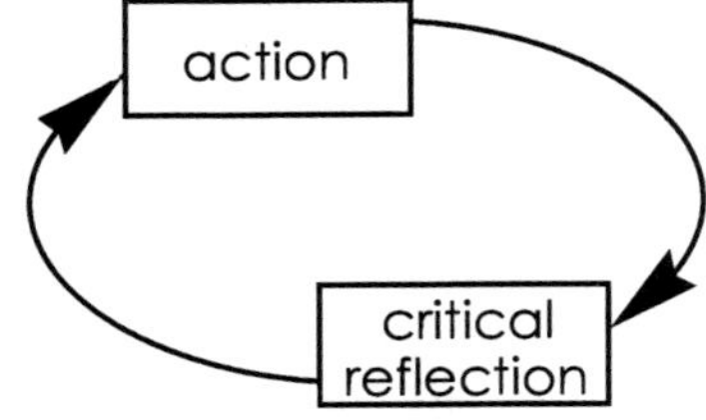

To some extent this is what many practitioners do. They carry out some action. They analyse what worked and what didn't. They try to learn from the experience. AR does not ask you to act very differently from what many of you already do to learn from your experience. It is no accident that the cycle resembles that of experiential learning (Kolb 1964).

The informal AR of many practitioners is often less effective than it might be. Practitioners often engage in reflection that is less regular, systematic and critical than I recommend.

The AR cycle allows AR to be used very flexibly and responsively. There is a valuable consequence. You can begin a change program knowing very little of the situation. You can use AR as an *emergent* process (Glaser 1992). You respond to the situation and the people. As you proceed, you adjust the change process, and the methodology itself, to take account of your growing understanding. Checkland and Holwell (1998) encourage the progressive updating of your philosophy too.

As with grounded theory (Glaser & Strauss 1967) you can begin with as few preconceptions as possible. You can anchor your understanding firmly to the information you collect and the understanding you develop.

Action

In this section I address two main issues. One is the use of participation, both for ideological reasons and to engender greater commitment to the actions. The other is the nature of the action and how actions from other change processes fit well within the AR cycle.

In its action orientation AR is part of the same tradition as community activism and organisation development (OD). Much of the OD literature is set implicitly or explicitly within an AR framework, including French and Bell's (1998) perennial text. Similarly, the key books on AR in organisations, including Cunningham (1993), Coghlan and Brannick (2001) and Gummesson (2001), combine AR and OD. There is a strong tradition of AR and community activism, evident for example in the work of Selener (1998) and Fals Borda and Rahman (1991).

One of the key purposes of AR is to bring about participative change. Those affected by the change decide the change and its implementation. In all three traditions (AR, OD and community activism) participation is valued. For many, the commitment to participation is primarily ideological; for instance Carr and Kemmis (1983), Greenwood and Levin (1998). Participation can also be justified on the grounds of pragmatism. The OD literature in particular draws on the argument that people are more committed to those changes that they have themselves planned and implemented. French and Bell (1998) give some attention to this.

Participation is less easily achieved, however, than much of the literature might imply. Where few people are affected it may appear to be a simple matter. Everyone can be involved. However, that may not be *their* expectation. Even in this less complex situation you may have to establish relationships sensitively and negotiate roles and processes. With few exceptions (eg. Oja & Smulyan 1989) the important early stages in an AR study are often given surprisingly little attention in the literature. Yet it is then that expectations are formed which may continue to influence the study throughout. Other aspects of participation are often well covered, for instance as in Erlich, Rothman and Teresa (1999).

In larger organisations and communities it may be very difficult to involve everyone. Even when those who might be affected are willing the time and budgets may be constraining. It is then often common to set up a representative group of some form. The members of this group may then work closely, perhaps as co-researchers, with you. This still leaves you with the issue of providing involvement for those who are not in this group.

My experience is that maintaining relationships with the wider body of those affected requires at least as much time and attention as the representative group. Elsewhere I discuss some of these issues in the context of community consultation (Dick 1997). My preferred approach is to rely heavily on many small working parties of those directly affected. The representative group then has the responsibility only to resource and coordinate the working parties (Figure 2.2). My intention is to form a communication hierarchy that is not a control hierarchy.

OD from the beginning has provided some large group processes that are intended to involve anyone. These have multiplied in recent years. Both earlier and more recent processes are documented in Bunker and Alban (1997).

This leads us to the second part of this section. A marriage between AR and change processes from other fields is a fruitful one. Descriptions of change processes provide guidance to the novice. The danger is that step-by-step descriptions do not do justice to the complexity of many field situations.

Embedded within an AR cycle the processes gain the flexibility to be more responsive to the situation. Those conducting the AR can follow the description. They can use the critical reflection within each cycle. Before action they can fit the action to the situation. After action they can check if the action has worked as intended. If not, it can be amended and retried.

In other words, within each cycle reflection has two components (Figure 2.3). The first is a critical review of what was done and with what results. The second plans the next action in the light of what has been learned.

Fig 2.2: Small Working Parties Allow a Communication Hierarchy That is Not a Control Hierarchy

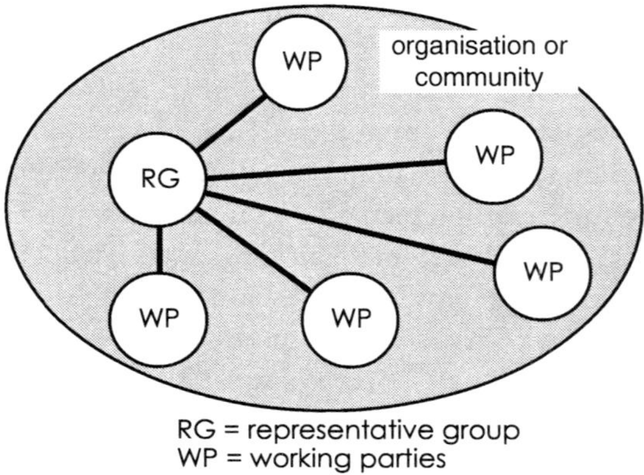

Fig 2.3: Critical Reflection Includes a Critical Review of the Previous Step and Planning for the Next Step

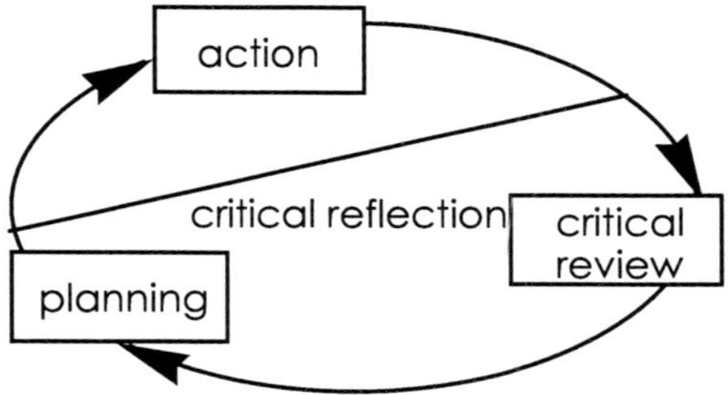

Research

One of the purposes of AR is to research a changing situation. Clearly, this requires an approach that differs greatly from methodologies that can manipulate and control variables under laboratory or near-laboratory conditions. Different sources of rigour must be found. In AR there are several. Here I mention the use of triangulation, maximally diverse samples, a vigorous and ongoing search for disconfirming evidence, and the use of tight AR cycles.

I won't deal in detail with triangulation here. Beginning with Jick's (1979) seminal work it is well covered in other literature. Often referring to the use of multiple methods, it has been extended by other writers.

Fielding and Fielding (1986) give a practical account of using four forms of triangulation: multiple methods; information collected at different times or from different samples; using multiple investigators; and viewing the information through different theories.

(We shortly consider involving a very diverse group of stakeholders in the AR. This clearly contributes to several of these forms of triangulation.)

Peshkin (2001) has recently provided a useful account of the use of different theories, or 'lenses' as he describes them. Alternatively, to make the most of AR's emergent nature, you can first develop your own theories and then compare them to other theories.

When full participation can be achieved then no sampling decisions are required. All of those who are affected by the planned changes can contribute information to the planning. When representative approaches are used, some care may be needed to ensure that all points of view are made available to those who make the decisions. Rather than a random sample, a maximum diversity sample will ensure that all views are available to the decision makers. Patton (1997) in his participative approach to evaluation makes a similar point.

In some communities and organisations there may be no one (and no small group) with enough knowledge to compile a maximum diversity sample. Otherwise, one can usually be put together by a small working party of people who between them know the organisation well. When this is more difficult, a similar working party can compile half a sample. Each person in that half-sample can then be asked to nominate someone else whose position differs from those already selected.

Third is a vigorous and continuous search for disconfirming evidence. In my view this is the most important source of rigour in research, including AR.[1] As well as being effective, it has the added virtue that it is consistent with the views of regular science as influenced by the philosopher Karl Popper (1968). Because of its cyclic nature AR offers multiple opportunities for disconfirmation. Interpretations that survive its multiple cycles can be held tentatively, but with some assurance.

A fourth strategy is to adopt a tight AR cycle. If the cycles are shorter they are more numerous. Each cycle provides another opportunity to seek out disconfirming evidence. Further, the plans that apply the researchers' growing understanding are immediately tested in action. With more cycles there are more tests.

With access to these sources of rigour, AR is not a second-best methodology to be used when other methods don't suit. It is a rigorous alternative in its own right, better for some applications, worse for others. In fact, its research component can be used as a metamethodology that can provide an umbrella for research of almost all flavours. Within an overall AR approach a researcher can choose other methodologies to suit the demands of the research situation.

Action and Research

I have already mentioned that AR can be an emergent methodology. Goals, plans, actions *and methodology* can be revised continuously as the research proceeds. Both theory and practice can be developed through a dual process of continuous improvement. In addition, below I briefly address three further ways in which the theory and practice enhance each other: the use of cycles within cycles; the regular use of quality critical reflection; and planning within each cycle which surfaces assumptions as well as plans.

As already mentioned, brief cycles enhance the effect of a cyclic process. There are also cycles within cycles within cycles. An overall study tends to move through stages of planning, action and review. So does each major phase, and within that each subphase, and so on. AR is partly a mindset in which 'mindful inquiry' (Bentz & Shapiro, 1998), moment by moment, is the aim.

Reflection comes easily to some people, less easily to others. My experience has been that AR often attracts practitioners who value its contribution to change. Having achieved their desired change they are sometimes impatient to move on to the next project.

For those whose action orientation hinders reflection, better planning can compensate. The theories that are of most use to Action Researchers tend to be of the form 'In situation S, to achieve outcomes O, try actions A'. If the plan includes also the assumptions underlying the definition of situation, actions and outcomes (Figure 2.4) it is likely that both action and reflection will be enhanced.

Fig 2.4: Effective Planning Defines the Situation, the Actions, the Outcomes, and the Assumptions Underlying Each

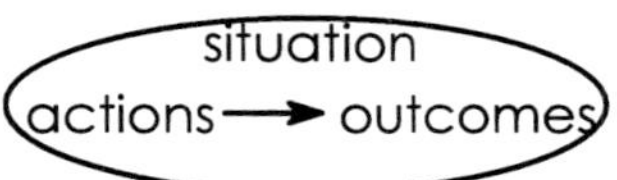

Notes

1. This view may be seen by some as going against the current fashion in qualitative research for a strong constructivism: that reality exists only in people's minds, and there are as many realities as there are people. It seems to me, first, that there would be some irony in an action researcher holding to a strong constructivist position. The purpose of action research is to bring about change – which assumes a world in which that change will occur. A pragmatic philosophy seems to me to be appropriate to action research, as well as being part of action research's tradition. That is the philosophy I implicitly operate from here.

Bibliography

Bentz, VM & Shapiro, JJ (1998) *Mindful Inquiry in Social Research.* Thousand Oaks: Sage

Bunker, BB & Alban, BT (1997) *Large Group Interventions: Engaging the whole system for rapid change.* San Francisco: Jossey-Bass

Carr, W & Kemmis, S (1983) *Becoming Critical: Knowing through action research.* Geelong: Deakin University Press

Checkland, P & Holwell, S (1998) *Information, Systems, and Information Systems: Making sense of the field.* Chichester: Wiley

Coghlan, D & Brannick, T (2001) *Doing Research in Your Own Organization.* London: Sage

Cunningham, JB (1993) *Action Research and Organizational Development.* Westport: Praeger

Dick, B (1997) *Guiding the Consultative Process* [online] http://www.scu.edu.au/schools/gcm/ar/arp/consulpro.html

Erlich, JL, Rothman, J & Teresa, JG (1999) *Taking Action in Organizations and Communities.* 2nd edition. Dubuque: Eddie Bowers Publishing

Fals Borda, O & Rahman, MA. (1991) *Action and Knowledge: Breaking the monopoly with participatory action research.* London: Intermediate Technology Publications

Fielding, NG & Fielding, JL. (1986) *Linking Data: The articulation of qualitative and quantitative methods in social research.* Beverly Hills: Sage

French, W & Bell, CH (1998) *Organization Development: Behavioral Science Interventions for Organizational Improvement.* 6th edition. Englewood Cliffs: Prentice-Hall

Glaser, BG & Strauss, AL (1967) *The Discovery of Grounded Theory: Strategies for qualitative research.* Chicago: Aldine

Glaser, BG (1992) *Basics of Grounded Theory Analysis: Emergence vs forcing.* Mill Valley: Sociology Press

Greenwood, DJ & Levin, M (1998) *Introduction to Action Research: Social research for social change.* Thousand Oaks: Sage

Gummesson, E (2000) *Qualitative Methods in Management Research.* 2nd edition. Thousand Oaks: Sage

Jick, TD (1979) 'Mixing qualitative and quantitative methods: Triangulation in action' in *Administrative Science Quarterly.* 24, pp602–611

Kolb, D (1984) *Experiential Learning: Experience as the source of learning and development.* Englewood Cliffs: Prentice-Hall

Oja, SN & Smulyan, L (1989) *Collaborative Action Research: A developmental approach.* London: Falmer Press

Patton, MQ (1997) *Utilization-focussed Evaluation.* 3rd edition. Thousand Oaks: Sage

Peshkin, A (2001) 'Angles of vision: enhancing perception in qualitative research' in *Qualitative Inquiry.* 7(2), pp238–253

Popper, KR (1968) *The Logic of Scientific Discovery.* New York: Harper & Row

Rogers, EM & Shoemaker, F (1971) *Communication of Innovations: A cross-cultural approach.* New York: Free Press

Selener, D (1998) *Participatory Action Research and Social Change.* 3rd edition. Ithaca: Cornell Participatory Action Research Network, Cornell University.

Action Research as Systematic Inquiry

Pam
Swepson

Overview

It seems to me that we action researchers have appropriately and enthusiastically embraced systemic research problems in complex situations. We have thrown out reductionist methodologies because of their limitations in complex situations. However, it also seems to me that, in throwing out reductionist methods, we might have thrown out 'the baby' with the bath water. I am suggesting that 'the baby' might be the concept of research as systematic inquiry. It seems to me, that whether we use a reductionist research method or a systemic one like action research, or a combination of both, we need to systematically collect and analyse data (whether it is physical, intellectual or emotional data) to justify any information or action claims that we make as a result of our research.

However, I do not think that reductionist research has either a monopoly on systematic methods, nor a prescription for them. I fully recognise that systematically collecting and analysing participatory social data; ie. the conscious thoughts, feelings and actions of co-researchers or stakeholders is quite different from systematically collecting and analysing physical data which to my mind includes the unconscious reactions and behaviours of human beings. However, it seems to me that the issue of systematically marshalling evidence to justify any knowledge or action claim is the same in both cases.

To make my own practice more systematic as well as systemic, I have developed some research guidelines for myself by collecting and analysing case studies of exemplary; ie peer respected action research and agricultural science. And, because I have developed my guidelines from case studies of both scientists and action researchers, they are potentially useful to all researchers; either reductionists or systemic researchers. As my own interest/bias is towards participatory action research, my guidelines are more focussed on validating participatory social research, rather than validating physical knowledge. However, because I have based my guidelines on the general issue of systematic inquiry in all research, these guidelines have the potential to provide a basis for collaboration between action researchers and scientists. I have indeed used them as the basis of a collaborative project with an entomologist colleague and I outline that project at the end of this chapter.

Three Assumptions About the Nature of a Good Research Methodology

My analysis of case studies of exemplary research lead me to make three general assumptions about the nature of a good research methodology which form the basis of my research guidelines. For your consideration, they are:

- -A good research methodology recognises and engages the social system of which it is a part and for whom the research is intended.
- -A good research methodology is systematic inquiry relevant to a particular question.
- -A good research methodology seeks to overcome the inherent human disposition to seek confirming rather than disconfirming evidence.

Below I describe each of these assumptions, offer some suggestions about how they may be achieved in research, and then illustrate them with a case study.

A good methodology includes the social system...

It seem to me that most research is done with and/or for someone else; ie it is done within a social system which involves at least the researcher, the next or end-users, and funders etc.These stakeholders have values and goals for the research and those values and goals are part of the problem definition and, as such, are part of the research data.

I also suggest that involving stakeholders in the research in any way is an intervention into that social system and will fundamentally change it.Therefore, I suggest that it is important to explicitly manage that intervention as part of the research activity. During and after the research, the thoughts and feelings, and possibly even the values and goals, of the stakeholders will change.These changes, which I suggest are changes in data, need to be included and managed as part of the research process to keep the research results valid and to help ensure they are implemented.

The action research community has enthusiastically embraced including the social system with its values and goals as part of the research situation. It also seems to me that bio-physical researchers are, more and more, explicitly involving their social system in their research process.

However, it seems to me that there are few guidelines for choosing which stakeholders to involve for which purpose in a systematic way. It seems to me that it is neither theoretically, nor practically appropriate to involve all stakeholders at all times. Building on Bob Dick's range of participatory options, I wish to make some suggestions for when and why to involve stakeholders. These suggestions may be useful to both participatory action researchers and bio-physical researchers.

A good methodology is systematic inquiry relevant to a particular question...

It seems to me that one of the reasons why action researchers have abandoned reductionist methods is because that methodology is limited to those situations when it is both appropriate and possible to manipulate a few variables in a given situation, while holding all other variables constant. Such a methodology does not have processes for rigorously dealing with all the other variables, when it is *not* possible to hold them constant; eg. in complex social or ecological systems.

One way that a researcher can manage the contingencies of a local research situation is to design a methodology which is relevant to that situation and which has an internal consistency between the research question or hypothesis (I use those terms interchangeably; with an hypothesis just being a more precise question) data collection and analysis; ie it is purpose-built, as indeed a reductionist method is when it is the most appropriate methodology.

Therefore, a method of systematic inquiry will need to have the following elements:

- -A carefully crafted research question/hypothesis relevant to the problem situation that is only as precise as the current knowledge will allow.
- -A method for sampling from the relevant bio-physical or social data, relevant to the question.
- -A systematic collection of valid social and/or bio-physical data
- -Systematic analysis of the data to provide an answer the research question.

To substantiate the results of the research, and to give the reader the maximum opportunity to assess the validity of the research for themselves, it seems to me that the results needs to be supported by clear descriptions of the processes that generated it.

A good research methodology seeks to overcome the inherent human tendency to seek confirming rather than disconfirming evidence...

Alan Musgrave in *Commonsense, science and scepticism* (1993) suggests that human beings are great over-generalisers, rather than great critics. When children are learning their native language, they can amusingly misapply a linguistic rule that they have readily adopted. David Hume in *Treatise of Human Nature* (1739) suggested that tradition is the usual basis for action. Any one who has an idea outside conventional wisdom knows the difficulties in getting that idea accepted, even when the new idea fits the data better than conventional wisdom. Counsellors know how difficult it is for people to break habits and patterns of behaviour, no matter how dysfunctional are these behaviours.

Sir Karl Popper recognised this problem, particularly the potential for scientists to conduct positive testing and search for data to prove the conventional wisdom. Therefore, he developed a method of negative testing as a way to force people to search outside their assumptions. He asks researchers to state what evidence they would need to find if their theory was wrong. Participatory action researches could well ask the same question.

However, action research is also an explicit process to address this problem. There are many definitions of action research and much discussion about the essential elements of action research. For me, the essential element is the process of reflection that actively seeks evidence to disconfirm any emerging theory and to actively critique the limitations of the chosen methodology in terms of the research question.

Whether using a Popperian methodology or an action research methodology, the lack of any disconfirmatory evidence can enhance the knowledge and action claims of the research.

Some Guidelines for Systematic Inquiry

Assumption: All research is done within and for a social system. Therefore a good research methodology manages the intervention into this social system by defining the relevant stakeholders and negotiating their appropriate involvement in it.

It seems to me that managing the social system of the research as an intrinsic part of the methodology will contribute to the end results by:

- -helping to convince the client/stakeholders of the research that it is likely to address their issue
- -if necessary, helping to convince subjects or co-researchers in the inquiry that their input will have impact. Such an assurance can help to maintain the validity and consistency of that input provided by the subjects, and
- -helping to convince the reader that the results can be substantiated.

Defining the stakeholders and their values

I have found Peter Checkland's Soft Systems Methodology, in *Systems Thinking, Systems Practice* (1981) gave me a systematic way of defining and engaging the relevant stakeholders; ie:

- -Define the clients of the research: those who have the power to start or stop the research; eg. funding bodies, communities etc. Consult with the clients to determine what they want the research to achieve, philosophically and practically? (eg. to be seen to be supporting their clients; ie those to whom the problem situation/research is relevant.)
- -Define the other stakeholders including next and end-users of the research. Consult with them to find out what they want the research to achieve, philosophically and practically?
- -Define the researchers? What do they want to achieve, philosophically and practically?

Assumption:A good research methodology is systematic inquiry relevant to a particular research question.

As I have suggested, systematic inquiry can be assisted by internal consistency between research question, data and analysis. Given my own interest in participatory action research, I have given most consideration to collecting and analysing valid social data.

Collecting and analysing valid social data – participatory action research

It seems to me that all researchers intend that the data they collect is relevant to the research question; ie it has internal validity. If the research question is a social one, information about the conscious thoughts, feeling and actions of people is likely to be best represented by qualitative data. I offer some reflection on various processes of collecting social data and how to improve their internal validity.

Questionnaires

I rarely use questionnaires for a number of reasons.The main one is that they are so difficult to design so that they do not confuse the two logical processes of data collection and analysis, induction and deduction, and so collect valid data. If a questionnaire pre-defines the categories of responses *before* the collection of any data, it violates the process of induction that generates general categories of knowledge from specific examples. It is also very difficult to pre-define categories of human thoughts and feelings that will be meaningful to *all* the anticipated respondents. If the questions are not meaningful to the respondent, their responses will be invalid.

If, however, the questionnaire does aims to collect data to validate an interesting theory, then, to avoid collecting only confirmatory, but perhaps, stereotypical data, it will, according to Popper's process of deduction, also need to collect data that could potentially disconfirm the interesting theory. Good questionnaire design is a very complex matter.

The other reason I do not use questionnaires, is that the respondents willingness to give valid data depends to a great extent on their relationship with the researcher and what they see has the purpose of the research – ie. what's in it for them. If there is not a long orientation process to establish this rapport, it is difficult to guarantee the validity of any responses. If the researcher is able to use an orientation process, they might be better to use an interview process.

Interviews

Interviews are my preferred method of collecting social data. However, as an interviewer, I am certainly aware just how easy it is to subtly and not so subtly bias the respondent in the direction of my interests and opinions. Therefore I have used structured processes to overcome this bias; one way of doing this is Dick's method of convergent interviewing (1990). Convergent interviewing allows the interviewer and respondent to generate and analyse data within the interview and for the interviewer to structure the interview in response to the emergent data.

Even with such process, I am also aware of how much I still project myself into the interview data. Therefore, I invite my respondents to validate my interview data. As the convergent interviewing process produces a summary rather than a transcript, the respondents task of reviewing and editing such a summary is feasible.

I have also confronted the issue of respondents wanting to provide second-hand data; what they think some one else thinks or feels. In my opinion, only first hand data is valid data. Obviously the interview design can help overcome this issue, but not always. In these situations, I ask the respondent what they think or feel about the third person's actions. This, then, is first-person data.

I have also confronted the issue of confidentiality of interview material. In some situations, there can be no option and the interviewer needs to do everything to ensure confidentiality. However, I would like to suggest that this is not always possible, nor desirable.

It seems to me that even when the interview data of several people is clumped, the opinions of some strong-minded people will still be evident to some readers. Or worse than that, some readers will *assume* that they know who said what.

It also seems to me sloppy data collection can hide behind an aim of confidentiality. As an interviewee in a research situation, I requested the researchers notes on my interview. Neither my words nor my thoughts were captured in any way that I would have recognised as my own.

It also seems to me that the research process can provide a communication channel between the stakeholders in the research situation and as such, make a positive intervention into that social system. Therefore, where it is appropriate, I now negotiate with my respondents that their interview data will be available to the specified others in the research situation. I offer accuracy of reporting rather than anonymity. This can mean some loss of candour. However, my experience has been that people are more than willing to say with they really think to someone who is really listening.

Observations

And as I have suggested, observations of other people's actions is first-hand, therefore valid data. However, given the frailties of human perceptions, it seems to me to be important to validate the observations, analyses and interpretations of a single observer. However, it will be important to choose the most appropriate other observers. Those who are being observed are not a good choice, because their observations will be coloured by what they intended to do or say. Therefore, should the other observer be one with similar interests to the primarily research/observer? Or someone with different interests? Will the research be enhanced by multiple observations from similar view points or different ones?

Personal reflections

Our thoughts and feelings are certainly first-hand data. However, if we wish to validate them, we might consider ways to make comparisons with this data. Journals offer the opportunity to compare our thoughts and feelings from different times. The observations of others offer us the opportunity to compare our inner world with what other see.

Sampling and validity

An important aspect of valid data collection is the sampling process. Participatory action research is most likely to be aiming for local rather than global relevance and will put its emphasis on internal validity.

One way to assist aims of internal validity is to carefully design a representative sample, relevant to the research question. This is the smallest number of people who can adequately represent the widest range of opinions and interests of the relevant stakeholders.

Data analysis and generalisations

While participatory action researchers usually places an emphasis on processes to validate data in a local situation, it is likely that they would also want to make some extrapolations from that local research to other, but similar situations. This means that they will need a methodology which guarantees some degree of generalisability or external validity.

One of the ways that participatory action researchers can ensure that their results do have some wider implications is to use processes of comparisons in both data collection and analysis. It also seems to me that the process of comparison can be an important element of systematic inquiry. An inductive experimental design method makes a comparison between a control group and a treatment group. A deductive Popperian method makes a comparison between an hypothesis and reality. Ethnography makes a comparison between groups, or between the same group at different times. A personally reflective methodology can make comparisons between a person's thoughts, feelings and action at different times and situation. A participatory methodology can increase both its rigour and its more general relevance if there are processes for comparisons between different stakeholders or the same stakeholders at different times.

Collecting and analysing valid data – bio-physical research

If the research question is a bio-physical one, including reactive human behaviours, it is likely to be best represented by quantitative data. In this case, the researcher is likely to strike the balance to favour external validity and generalisation or global relevance. Assuming that the categories or interest groups are spread over the whole population, the most appropriate sampling process in this case is likely to be a random sample.

The bio-physical researcher will also want to ensure that numeric values given to data do indeed represent the data in a way that is meaningful to stakeholders in the research and that outliers are not unnecessarily discarded.

The internal validity of bio-physical research can be enhanced if the data collection and analysis is either understand or conducted by the stakeholders in the research who then understand the relationship of the metric to the data and the data to the research question.

Assumption: A good research methodology overcomes the inherent human tendency to repeat thoughts and actions and seek confirming evidence of current beliefs rather than to seek evidence to disconfirm them. However, an unsuccessful search for disconfirmatory evidence adds weight to the research results.

As I have suggested, Sir Karl Popper understood this issue and developed the process of negative testing to deal with it.

It also seems to me that the essential element of action research is the process of reflection on planned, systematic action. Such reflections might consider the effectiveness of the planned action and seek data that would disconfirm any emergent theory/or generalisation, rather than seek data to justify both method and assumed results.

One of the ways to do all three things could be to invite relevant stakeholders into the process at this point, especially those who might hold opinions differing from those analysing the data to date.

Participation for a purpose

Given my assumption that all research is done within a social system, it seems to me that some degree of participation is inherent in all research. One might argue that all stakeholders have a 'right' to involvement at all stages. While direct involvement may not be feasible, desirable or necessary for some reason, I think it is important to respect that potential 'right' and to accommodate it by keeping those stakeholders informed.

However, rather than imposing participation on all stakeholder, it seems to me that it would be useful to negotiate appropriate level of participants with potential participants in the research situation. I have suggested various points where a researcher could consider the involvement of specific stakeholders for specific purposes within the research; problem definition, data collection and analysis, interpretation and evaluation.

Conclusions

My reflections on my own practice and that of some exemplary colleagues in both action research and science has lead me to consider action research as systematic inquiry. To make my own practice more systematic, I have developed some guidelines for myself that may be useful to both participatory action researchers and scientists. I also think they can provide a basis for collaboration between action researchers and scientists. To conclude, I will present a case study of such collaboration.

A case study of collaboration: participatory action research and science

My colleague Dr Graham White, an entomologist, and I collaborated in a highly participatory industry funded research project to decide on future research directions for a looming insect pest in the fruit and vegetable industries. We designed an original, purpose-built methodology to address the issue. Instead of inviting geographically spread participants to a problem definition workshop, we conducted an interactive information sharing and decision making process via faxes and emails over a period of four months. Because it was a one-off methodology, we evaluated its effectiveness after we had done the research. Our evaluation suggested that we conducted better research for our client by working together than if we had worked independently and we both improved our own practice by learning from each other's practice.

Our methodology was based on the guidelines that I have outlined.

1. All research is done within and for a social system...
    - We established a steering committee which included the growers of the relevant horticultural crops, national and international scientists and representative of related industries; the nursery industry.
    - The initial contact with the committee negotiated their participation in the electronic information sharing and decision making process and informed the participants of all other participants.
2. Good research is systematic inquiry relevant to a particular question...The initial research question was proposed by the industry body that funded us. What sort of research should they fund, relevant to the looming insect pest? They were not confident of the suggestions of individual researchers with pet research interests.

We systematically collected information in two ways. Graham collated all current scientific information from the literature and current experts and presented them to the whole committee as a series of five short, easy to read papers. Through feedback from the committee we could both validate the scientific data and compare it with the opinion of growers as to its relevance. Secondly, we collected information from growers about their current use of insecticides, via a simple questionnaire of discreet questions, to relate to the relevant scientific information.

Our sample was a representative one – the smallest group of people to cover the diverse range of interests, both as growers and scientists. It needed to be fairly small so that Graham and I could personally follow-up with all participants, as we had negotiated with them, to help them to respond.

We designed a data analysis or decision-making process which was relevant to the situation and actively sought disconfirming data. After we had circulated the five discussion papers, and included feedback from the committee into them, Graham made a series of recommendations, from his expert opinion and based on all the information he and the committee had generated. As a basis for comparison, we invited members of the Steering Committee, who had the same information, to make their recommendations in reaction to Graham's. The Committee was neither fully accepting of fully rejecting of Graham's recommendations, but made its own recommendations.

Our report highlighted the areas of agreement between the expert and the committee as well as the areas of differences. Our client found this report to be useful in that they could estimate which recommendations were likely to be easily adopted by industry growers and those that might need more support.

Finally, to evaluate our methodology for this particular research project, we interviewed a cross section of the Steering Committee. They suggested that the process was much more successful than they expected, especially in terms of time pressure, engagement and quality of information. Graham and I assessed it as an appropriate methodology for information sharing and decision making in this particular situation; ie the stakeholders were disperse and the insect pest was an imminent one rather than an entrenched one. If those conditions had been different, we would have needed a different methodology.

Bibliography

Checkland, P (1981) *Systems Thinking, Systems Practice*. New York: Wiley

Dick, B (1990) *Convergent Interviewing*. Version 3. Chapel Hill: Interchange

Hume, D (1739/2001) *A Treatise of Human Nature: Being an attempt to introduce the experimental method of reasoning into moral subjects.* (reissued by Thoemmes Press)

Musgrave, A (1993) *Commonsense, Science and Scepticism: A historical introduction to the theory of knowledge*. London: Cambridge University Press.

Action Learning for Personal and Organisational Transformation

Ron Passfield

Introduction

Action learning within an organisational context involves learning in and through action while collaborating with others on personal and organisational improvement. It typically involves a learning group (often called a 'learning set') focused on a project or work endeavour.

This chapter is based on my observations of, and reflections on, working with action learning over 25 years in Australia, Singapore and New Guinea. In writing this chapter I have chosen to deal with personal and organisational transformation together because action learning involves learning-in-context. To separate the personal and organisational dimension would involve an arbitrary division.

What is distinctive about action learning in an organisational context is that it involves learning through engagement with the dynamics of the on-going organisation. This means dealing with the realities of politics, power, procedure, culture and systems. It also entails dealing with who we are and how we define ourselves, our role and our capacities within that context.

The transformative power of action learning flows from this real life engagement supported by a form of interpersonal interaction that builds personal and organisational capacity.

Action learning takes people outside their comfort zone, provides supportive challenge, builds relationships, raises personal and group awareness, and builds confidence along with competence. It facilitates personal and organisational learning and builds synergy within organisations.

These characteristics account for the flexibility of action learning and the power to transform the way we do things individually and collectively within organisations.

Moving Beyond Our Comfort Zone

People involved in an action learning project, program or task frequently experience moving outside their comfort zone – moving beyond the familiar to the unknown. We are encouraged to extend ourselves and explore unfamiliar terrain. In one sense this involves breaking out of the shell that surrounds our understanding and locks in our behaviour.

The discomfort we experience during action learning may arise through:

- Trying something that we do not feel competent to do (eg. run a focus group, undertake market research, confront poor behaviour, intervene in a conflict)
- Sharing what is not going well (rather than boasting about how well we are doing)
- Acknowledging what we do not know or understand (instead of maintaining the pretence of expertise)
- Discussing group process (how we are doing things) as well as group task (what we are doing)

-Treating each person in the action learning group as a peer (despite hierarchical differences)
-Discussing our feelings in the group

The norms that underpin action learning challenge ingrained behaviour within organisations that is typically risk-aversive and evasive. Action learning approaches can create a safe environment for self-exploration and experimentation with new behaviours.

This is achieved by finding the balance between support and challenge.

Supportive challenge

The action learning approach combines support with challenge. Participants working in an action learning group are supported by their colleagues who view them as fellow travellers or comrades sharing the same adversity or mess. The challenge comes through asking fresh questions designed to unearth fundamental assumptions about the nature of the problem or the way a participant interprets others' behaviour. It provides a challenge to the way we view our role, the organisation, the world or our competitors.

People in organisations often experience the separation of support and challenge. Support without challenge reinforces the status quo, 'group-think', and perspectives that may have been developed when conditions were different to the prevailing conditions within and around an organisation. Challenge without support can be self-serving (building oneself up by diminishing the other) and damaging to self-esteem (by reinforcing feelings of inadequacy).

Supportive challenge has as its object building the self-esteem of the other while helping them to recognise the limitations that their existing mindset imposes on their potential to realise their full capacity/capability. It is about helping the other person to be the best they are capable of being.

This positive regard for other participants contributes to relationship building and the development of connectedness that forms the glue of effective organisations.

Relationship building

Action learning can produce productivity improvement, new product development, cost savings or other outcome goals, but fundamentally it builds relationships. Relationships enable things to happen within and without organisations. They are the key success factor in alliances and partnerships. It is through relationships that most of the organisational work gets done. It is not the organisational chart that makes things happen but the sense of connection that people have with each other and with the organisation.

Positive relationships facilitate sharing of information and resources, enhance collaboration and engender commitment. In an action learning activity, this is partly achieved through awareness-raising.

Awareness raising

The major contributor to awareness raising within an action learning group is reflection. In action learning, reflection is both an individual and social activity. Group reflection facilitates challenge to existing assumptions that would otherwise go unchecked. The more diverse the group, the greater the likelihood of this challenge occurring.

Reflective processes are built into action learning to aid awareness and understanding. Tools for reflection can include learning logs (Williams & Harris), critical incident analysis (Tripp & Wilson), photography (Jones & Noble), learning partner conversations, feedback meetings (Rimanoczy), one-to-one mentoring, debrief sessions, and journals.

Sharing within an action learning group can aid individual learning through a process of vicarious learning – learning from others and their account of experiences without having to experience the event yourself. This learning occurs in addition to the learning resulting from action and reflection on that action.

Individual and collective awareness grows through:

-making tacit knowledge explicit (Friedman & Rothman)
-understanding how we define ourselves, our role and our capacity (Lange)
-identifying gaps between what we espouse and what we do (Friedman & Rothman)
-understanding where we fit into the overall organisation fabric
-learning about resources, products and processes present within the organisation
-understanding linkages between groups and connections between individuals within the organisation.

As our personal awareness grows, we are better able to learn individually and collectively (Lange). We become more conscious of the barriers to personal and organisational learning and are supported in exploring new behaviours.

Personal and organisational learning

Personal and organisational learning is often impeded because we fail to look at what is actually happening. Even when we look there are many things that we do not see because of our assumptions and the limitations of our perceptions. When we do look and see, we often fail to understand what we have seen because of our interpretative framework, the way we view people and the world. Understanding does not always pass to real learning that influences the way we act.

Action learning, however, builds personal and organisational learning because it enables us to:

-look at what was over-looked
-see what has remained hidden
-discuss the undiscussable
-understand better what we see and hear
-learn to take action with this new in-sight and understanding.

Our increased capacity to understand and work with others, develops a new understanding of who we are and what we are capable of doing and becoming.This new confidence builds competence in an exponential way.

Confidence and competence building

Action learning adds value not only because it develops new process and technical competencies but also because it builds our confidence to use pre-existing knowledge and competence.

Increased self-awareness combined with the acquisition of new knowledge and skills as well as increased visibility, contributes to the development of a stronger 'self-concept'.This growth in self-confidence is enhanced through the experience of working with colleagues who are challenging and supportive (Kwok).

Participants frequently gain an expanded view of what they are capable of and able to achieve.This sense of empowerment comes from:

-freedom from self-limiting assumptions and perspectives
-freedom to access information, people and resources
-freedom to act and create new knowledge.

It is one thing to have the competence to act, it is another to have the confidence to use that competence in a particular organisational context.Action learning builds confidence to use existing competence while developing new competencies.

Synergy emerges within organisations as people growing in confidence and competence form new relationships while collaborating in personal and organisational transformation.

Synergy

Organisations are based on the presumption of synergy – that is that the sum of people who make up the organisation can produce a better result than each of them working individually.The reality, however, is often different.

The synergy that emerges from action learning grows out of a group of people who are more aware, committed to collaboration, motivated to improvement and supported in their endeavours.

Synergy occurs because action learning contributes to:

- -the meaningful exchange of information
- -increased understanding of organisational systems
- -increased awareness of, and utilisation of, resources
- -creation of new linkages
- -closure of information gaps and chasms
- -growth in personal and group confidence, competence and resourcefulness
- -development of change agents committed to organisational improvement
- -closing the gap between what is espoused and what is practised.

The level and breadth of organisational support for action learning activities can place a ceiling on the achievement of synergy. The higher the level of support and the more broadly based, the greater is the chance to realise personal and organisational synergies.

When people in power consciously collaborate with others through action and reflection in the process of personal and organisational transformation, there is real leverage for organisational improvement on multiple fronts (Lange). When the leaders themselves are not open to learning, this stance places real constraints on the flow-on effects of personal and group learning. It acts to block organisational synergy and leverage for change.

Inflexibility on the part of organisational leaders can seriously erode the benefits accruing from the flexibility of the action learning process.

Flexibility of Action Learning

Action learning as a process can be embedded in many other approaches such as action research, action inquiry, action evaluation and participative action research. It is adaptable to cultural differences as is illustrated by Michael Marquardt in this book. It can be used in many contexts and for many purposes.

The flexibility of action learning can be seen from the following projects in which I currently have a mentoring role:

- -Closing the gap between strategy formulation and strategy implementation in a large aged-care facility.
- -Developing parallel learning structures for a global church organisation.
- -Using a values-based approach to build the capacity of an elite, professional sporting team.
- -Developing team learning amongst facilitators of farmer learning.
- -Building information systems within a hospital.
- -Developing a network organisation to provide human resource management services.

- Developing a holistic health clinic using multiple healing modalities.
- Building the flexible learning capability of TAFE organisations.

The impact of action learning can be strengthened when it is combined with action research as is the case in each of these projects.

Action learning is enhanced when it is undertaken in combination with action research because action research builds rigour into observation and interpretation (Dick), facilitates concept development and promotes dissemination of knowledge and learning (Zuber-Skerritt).

Conclusion

Action learning is a flexible, eclectic process that can engage people in organisations in the process of personal and organisational transformation.

The forms of interpersonal interaction encouraged and supported within action learning help people to overcome blockages, extend themselves and build confidence and competence.

Synergies emerge through growth in personal and group awareness, new connections through relationship building and new linkages with people in power.

Action Learning: Does it Work Differently in Different Cultures?

Michael J Marquardt

Abstract

Action learning has quickly emerged in many Western countries as one of the most powerful and effective tools to enable organisations to solve problems, develop leaders, build teams, and create learning organisations. However, since its origins in England in the 1940s, it has been implemented primarily in North America, northern Europe and in former British colonies in Africa, Asia and the South Pacific. Can it work effectively in non-Western cultures? Or does it have to be implemented in a different manner? This chapter briefly presents the cultural dimensions of the six components of action learning and provides guidelines and examples of how it can be successfully adapted to other cultures.

Introduction

Action learning has been implemented with growing frequency and success in the 'Western', Anglo-Saxon cultures of the world (by 'Western', cultural anthropologists generally refer to the United States, Great Britain, Australia, Canada, New Zealand, and parts of northern Europe). Developed by British physicist Reg Revans over 50 years ago, action learning is a prime management development and problem-solving tool for numerous corporations and public agencies in Western countries or in former British colonies (eg. Singapore, Nigeria, Malaysia, South Africa, Hong Kong)

Despite its growing success in Western cultures and Western-headquartered corporations, action learning has been rarely employed in the remaining parts of the world. Why? Is it because people and organisations in the rest of the world are not yet familiar with the basic principles of action learning (although other Western trends and fads such as reengineering, quality management, and 360-degree feedback were quickly discovered and adopted worldwide)? Is it because of the non-Western world's unawareness of the inherent simple power of action learning to change organisations and people?

Or is the limited use of action learning in non-Western cultures the result of the fact that action learning is built on primarily Western cultural values and practices? Are there, in fact, some cultural elements inherent in action learning which discourage the use of action learning in Latin America, much of Asia, the Middle East, Africa, and Southern Europe (Wigglesworth 1987)? And have practitioners been insensitive to the fact that action learning must adapt and adjust to the values, basic assumptions and behaviours of other cultures in order to be successful?

The answers to these questions are important for companies as they go global and employ multicultural workforces and form multicultural alliances. Many of these organisations recognise that solving global problems and the building global leaders and global teams depend on their ability to effectively transfer the power of action learning programs to their multicultural employees and customers.

Can Action Learning Work in Non-Western Cultures?

The fact that there are a growing number of non-Western organisations and communities successfully using action learning indicates that it can be equally valuable and powerful in all parts of the world. Indeed, action learning programs are emerging in non-Western cultures as diverse as Mexico, Colombia, Thailand, Papua New Guinea, Japan, Romania, Mauritius, China, and Egypt (Prestoungrange & Margerison 1999). The author has achieved tremendous results in using action learning in academic programs with multicultural groups of students and with African, Asian and Latin American leaders at the UN Staff College in Turin, Italy. These experiences have led him to conclude that action learning can work anywhere in the world. However, sensitivity to cultural differences as well as modification and adaptation of the elements of action learning are necessary for action learning to be effective in all cultural settings.

Cultural Dimensions of Action Learning

Action learning contains six components, namely:

1. a problem (project, opportunity, task, challenge, issue)
2. an action learning group or team or set
3. a process that emphasising insightful questioning and reflective listening
4. a promise of taking action
5. a commitment to learning.
6. facilitation of the learning process with the assistance of a learning coach (Marquardt 1999)

Each of these components is built upon some basic assumptions and values inherent in Western cultures. Let's briefly explore the cultural implications embedded in the six components and how and why they may prove challenging to implement in action learning programs involving participants from other cultures.

1. Problem (project, opportunity, challenge, task)

a. Basic principles

An action learning program requires having a project or task that gives the group a meaningful challenge on which to focus. There are several criteria to determine if the problem is appropriate for an action learning group:

- -The problem chosen by/for the group must be a real organisational problem, task or issue that needs to be addressed and exists in a real timeframe.
- -It must be feasible; ie. within the competence of the group.

-It should either be within the group's sphere of responsibility or the group must be given the authority to do something about the problem

-It should provide learning opportunities for members as well as have possible applications to other parts of the organisation.

b. Western basic assumptions, values inherent in the determination of problem or task

Western culture encourages sharing and the discussion of personal as well as organisational problems in a public setting (frankness). It is okay for a Western manager to admit difficulties in solving a problem and thus be willing to turn it over to outsiders or subordinates. It is less difficult for him to trust subordinates and to delegate power to them (egalitarian).

c. Non-Western cultural reactions

In many other cultures, it would be more difficult for a leader or individual to turn over his most critical problems to subordinates. And would it not indicate a loss of face to admit his inability to handle the problem himself? Is it not the role of the managers to solve problems and make decisions while the role of workers is to implement those decisions? Most cultures in Africa and India, for example, would see it as inappropriate for the manager to have others solve his problem?

If a problem cannot be solved, should not the manager accept this as fate and be religious enough to embrace it? In most cultures, the sharing of personal difficulties might be seen as culturally crass if shared. And even if he or she delegated such power, some members of some cultures would still not see real power present in the group without the leader being physically there.

2. Action learning group

a. Basic principles

The core entity in action learning is the action learning group (also called a set or team). The group is composed of 4-8 individuals who examine an organisational problem that has no easily identifiable solution. Ideally, the make-up of the group is diverse so as to maximise various perspectives and to obtain fresh viewpoints. Depending upon the type of action learning problem, groups can be made up of individuals from across functions or departments. In some situations, groups are comprised of individuals from other organisations or professions; for example, the company's suppliers or customers. The dynamics of the group and the diversity of its participants are the keys to success of the action learning set. The group should include people who care about the problem, who know something about the problem, and who have the power to carry out the recommendations of the group.

To be effective the group members should possess the following attributes:

-commitment to solving the problem
-ability to listen, to question self and others
-willingness to be open and to learn from group members
-value and respect for others
-commitment to taking action and achieving success
-awareness of own and others' ability to learn and develop.

b. Western basic assumptions, values and practices inherent in composition of action learning set

The mixing of people of differing ages, genders, roles, etc. fits in with the Western values of egalitarianism, equality and informality. Western cultures like variety, different perspectives, new ideas, and the give-and-take among differing groups. Competence of fellow group members is more important than rank or status.

c. Non-Western cultural reactions

In most other cultures, however, the mixing people of differing status groups opposes their sense of hierarchy and respect/acceptance of differences. Mixing may be seen as a means of undermining authority and power in the workplace. It may cause embarrassment, confusion and loss of face.

In Asian countries, young people in a group will hesitate to speak out if older people are in the group. A person's status is important in determining the degree to which a person can state his opinion (Brake, Walker & Walker 1995). In many African societies, there is a rigid, hierarchical, bureaucratic structure with great status differences and extreme deference to authority (Jones 1991). In conservative Islamic cultures, men and women cannot even be in the same room, much less exchange ideas on an equal level. Age is almost always above competence when deciding who is to be the most important member in the group.

Cultures that appreciate hierarchy and clear roles find difficulty in bringing together differing interacting groups. Seating arrangements are determined by one's status. The language used requires one to be addressed in a superior or inferior fashion (ie. use of 'you'). Formality, especially among differing status, is absolutely essential.

In addition, who the members are determines the importance of an activity; therefore it will be difficult to 'volunteer' someone who does not wish to (or cannot) be seen (or it would be seen as inappropriate) with a particular group. In addition, many non-Western cultures could never conceive the idea of involving people from outside the organisation working on an internal company problem.

On the other hand, the collectivism of most other cultures encourages the working in action learning teams. These cultures value much more teamwork and solving problems as a group. Thus action learning sets fits better in these cultures than the individualism of Western.

3. Questioning and reflective process

a. Basic principles

By focusing on the right questions rather than the right answers, action learning focuses on what one does not know as well as what one does know. Action learning tackles problems through a process of first asking questions to clarify the exact nature of the problem, reflecting and identifying possible solutions, and only then taking action.

Action learning programs attempt to provide the essential time and space necessary to stand back and reflect, to unfreeze thoughts, to rise above everyday problems, to bring things into perspective, and to listen so as to draw out the experience and practical judgement of the group members. This questioning-reflection process also encourages the viewing of each other as learning resources.

In action learning members should be open to try out new ways of doing things, to experiment, to reflect on experiences, to consider the results or effects of the experience and to repeat the cycle by trying out newly gained knowledge in different situation. At the heart of action learning is the process of reflection that is designed to develop questioning insight, or as Revans (1983) writes, 'the capacity to ask fresh questions in conditions of ignorance, risk, and confusion, when nobody knows what to do next'.

b. Western basic assumptions and values inherent in processes of questioning and reflection

The questioning/reflection process is more comfortable in cultures that value informality and egalitarianism, where people can be more direct and challenging of each other. The Western approach of inductive thinking and problem-solving encourages careful examination of the particular event and developing new ways of responding.

The Western approach of asking questions is built on the Socratic way of learning; it naturally leads to more openness and creativity in handling problems. Discussion tends to be logical and rational, with a moderate show of emotion.

c. Non-Western cultural reactions

Taking time to first question, reflect and discuss would work well in Latin and Arabic cultures where time is flexible and there is less need to rush to results. However, in some cultures, such as Chinese, there is a high impatience in spending too much time in discussion and reflection; there is a great desire for quick results and speed.

Arabic and African cultures, because of their education system, tend to be imitative rather than creative. And African managers regard their authority, professional competence and information as personal possessions rather than part of their organisation role. They are, therefore, reluctant to delegate authority, share information, or to involve subordinates in decision-making process (Al-Faleh 1986).

Questioning one another, especially people of superior status, is very difficult. The questioning of Asians, for example, can result in ritualised behavior, withdrawal, or even resentment.

4. Commitment to action

a. Basic principles

For action learning advocates, there is no real learning unless action is taken, (and no action should occur without learning from it). Therefore members of the action learning group must have the power to take action themselves or be assured that their recommendations will be implemented, (barring any significant change in the environment or the group's lack of essential information). Action enhances learning because it provides a basis and anchor for the critical dimension of reflection described earlier.

Action learning, therefore, requires that action to be taken, not merely the presentation of recommendations (as task forces or quality circles may do). And unless the organisation, group or individual puts into effect the projects or tasks being focused on, there is no evidence that something different or better has or can be done, and consequently no indication of whether any learning or development has taken place.

b. Western basic assumptions and values relative to ability and commitment of action learning set to take action

Western culture is much more action-oriented than most other cultures. We encourage students/workers to make decisions and take action. We enjoy tasks more than relationships, achievement more than discussion. We also like to do things that have immediate utilitarian value. Time is money and should not be wasted on things that do not achieve results.

c. Non-Western cultural reactions

Other cultures may give people much less authority to act. In Arabic cultures, the leader may consult with others for advice, but will then make the decision on his own. Those strongly influenced by the Islamic religion would also be much more aware/respectful of the role of Allah in taking decisions.

In many Asian cultures, people are much more circuitous in selecting a course of action. Social and political sensitivity drive the solution; and the action taken cannot cause someone to lose face. Even if the group thought it a proper decision, they would desert/disavow the decision later on.

In most cultures, in addition, there is a fear of asking dumb questions since it may also cause one to lose face. One avoids exposing one's weakness and faults. Setting a supportive climate may not be sufficient in these cultural environments.

5. Commitment to individual, team and organisation-wide learning

a. Basic principles

Solving the organisational or individual problem provides immediate, short-term benefits to an organisation or individual. The greater, longer-term, multiplier benefit, however, is the learning gained by the group members and how their learnings can be applied on systems-wide basis throughout the organisation.

Therefore, during the action learning process, individuals should take responsibility for their own, the team's, and the organisation's learning and development. Time is set aside to talk about personal learnings and how the team's learning can be utilised in other parts of the organisation.

b. Western basic assumptions and values inherent in commitment to learning within set

The principles of learning cited above coincide much more congruently with the Western way of thinking and doing things. (eg. questioning assumptions, questioning authority or the past; welcoming the urgency and immediate practicality of learning; accepting change and uncertainty; working in a nonhierarchical fashion so as to acquire fresh perspectives, learning from the feedback of others about ourselves, etc.)

c. Non-Western cultural reactions

Asking for feedback and encouraging self-analysis, although fine for Westerners who value frankness and openness, could be disastrous in Asia where a much higher value is placed on hiding one's feelings and thoughts and not prying into the feelings and thoughts of others. One does not offer constructive advice in public settings. Pointing out a weakness is difficult in Spanish cultures since people are not expected to speak negatively of others. For Arabs, 'Allah loveth not the speaking ill of anyone.' Is this focus on self-awareness and learning 'useful feedback' or enforced admission of error?

Although most cultures would appreciate the emphasis on learning, they would have several concerns about the status and quality of learning in action learning programs. Most people equate learning with lectures and rote learning. And doesn't important learning imply a certificate or diploma? The presence of renowned lecturers from Harvard or London Business School is what high quality education is all about.

6. Facilitation (usually with a learning coach)

a. Basic principles

As set members are involved in reframing the problem, actively listening to one another, and intensively seeking to find alternatives and solutions, it is difficult to also be aware of the group processes that are occurring or the dynamics of interaction around them. Members may also lack the skill as well as the time to understand much less focus on the learning opportunities available. Thus a person is appointed to serve this important role so as to optimise the problem-solving and learning efforts of the group.

b. Western basic assumptions and values inherent in set facilitation

The utilization of a facilitator to guide our learning is a term as well as a process often used in training programs in Western societies. In group discussions, we often designate someone to facilitate the dynamics, timing, etc. Learning from and being questioned by peers or external consultants are common Western practices.

c. Non-Western cultural reactions

Being observed and questioned in a group setting among your peers can be very threatening to many cultures. Being asked by the learning coach questions such as 'how did we do as a group?, what did not go so well?, what have you learned?, why did the group fail to...?, why did you not say that then?' may be uncomfortable to respond to, especially if there is an implicit criticism of another or a diminishing of oneself. Some questions may be seen as too personal to be discussed in the presence of the group.

Acculturising the six essential elements of action learning

Action learning, developed and practiced primarily in Western countries, needs to be 'acculturised', that is, conveyed and transferred across cultural boundaries to assure that the action learning program is, to use a computer term, 'user friendly'. This does not mean that the essential elements of action learning are dropped or radically altered; rather they are adjusted to the cultural milieu so as to ensure that the maximum benefits of action learning can be tapped. Without this acculturisation and adaptation, the power and benefits of action learning will not be realised.

Adapting action learning programs to a multicultural or non-Western cultural setting requires a keen sensitivity to the basic assumptions inherent in those cultures, and to the ways in which these people think and act. The following are just a few of the ways to acculturise action learning programs in multicultural settings.

a. Selection of problem or task

- Select problems which are comfortable and appropriate to values and practices of the organisation.
- Identify problems for which manager can delegate power and set members will accept responsibility.

-Appreciate concern of culture for fate and for maintaining face in selection of problem.
-Begin with smaller issues, yet still of importance and value to set members and to the organisation.
-Allow group members, when serving in role of client, to introduce problems that may be somewhat 'external' to their locus of accountability and responsibility.

b. Composition of group
-Recognise hierarchy and status of members.
-Seek balance between authority and non-authority figures.
-Build on the more cultural values of working in groups (collectivism).
-Gradually include diversity into action learning sets.
-Obtain diversity in other ways – different units, technical areas, industries, etc.
-Begin with some team-building activities to assist members in becoming comfortable and supportive of one another.

c. Use of questioning and reflection processes
-Create an environment which encourages asking of questions.
-As a learning coach or facilitator, demonstrate with initial questions that focus on solving the problem rather than on fixing blame.
-Recognise cultural need to save personal face as well as need not to cause others to loose face.
-Allocate set times for reflection.
-Be comfortable with periods of silence (Asian) or outbursts of expression (Hispanic and Arabic).
-Appreciate indirectness and formality.
-Understand non-verbal communication patterns and context of situation.

d. Commitment to taking action
-Assure the group that it has authority and capacity to take action.
-If client is external to the group, ask that he meet with the group to clearly state that he is requesting group to determine the final action steps.
-Distinguish from 'think-tank' or 'recommendations-only' mentality in group.

-Respect status of those, internal and/or external to the set, who are responsible for taking action.
-Recognise social and cultural limitations on actions considered.
-Respect acceptance of fate or inability to control future.
-Understand importance of maintaining harmony.

e. Focusing on the learning
-Identify and recognise learnings gained through action learning programs.
-Respect need for modesty and humility when identifying how one has contributed to group's learning.
-Use set advisors, at least initially, to help group identify and apply learnings.
-Acknowledge action learning as a new form of acquiring knowledge.
-Connect learning to cultural values that support continuous learning.

f. Facilitation with a learning coach/set adviser
-Be sure to introduce self and role in a clear and supportive way so that it will be not seen as too threatening or a source for causing face-loss.
-Identify positive and constructive areas in the earlier stages of the action learning program.
-Pose questions to the group as a whole rather than towards individuals.
-Demonstrate the value and effectiveness of uncovering and sharing the learnings.
-Encourage members to begin asking questions of the group.
-Emphasise that individual and group disclosures and feedback are confidential to the group.

Action Learning Can and Does Work in All Cultures

It is important to recognise that cultural differences need not lessen the immense power of action learning programs to solve problems, develop leaders and create team. Instead of seeing cultural differences as barriers, one should see them as the source of synergy that contribute to a variety of perspectives that can actually augment the power and success of action learning programs. Thus we are beginning to see the successful use of action learning programs all over the world, from North America to the South Pacific, from Argentina to Zambia, from small countries such as Mauritius to heavily populated countries such as China and India. Action learning has indeed become a worldwide tool for problem-solving and individual, team and organisation development.

Bibliography

Al-Faleh, M (1986) 'Cultural influences on Arab management development' in *Journal of Management Development* 6 (3), pp19–33

Brake, T, Walker, D & Walker, T (1995) *Doing Business Internationally: The guide to cross-cultural success.* New York: McGraw-Hill

Hofstede, G (1991) *Culture and Organizations.* London: McGraw-Hill

Jones, ML (1991) 'Management development: An African focus' in *International Human Resource Management.* Boston: Kent Publishing

Marquardt, M (1999) *Action Learning in Action.* Palo Alto: Davies-Black Press

Marquardt, M & Engel, D (1993) *Global Human Resource Development.* Englewood Cliffs: Prentice-Hall

Prestoungrange, G & Margerison, C (1999) *Multinational Action Learning at Work.* Bradford: MCB University Press

Revans, R (ed) *Corporate Cultures: International HRD perspectives.* Alexandria: ASTD Press.

Part 2

Frameworks

Part 2

Frameworks

Ron Passfield

This section of the book illustrates the flexibility and eclectic nature of action learning and action research. These characteristics flow from what Dick describes as the 'responsiveness' of these processes.

Each of the contributors to this section offers their own framework as a way of viewing, understanding and intervening in ongoing social systems. It is as if each presents one side of a prism as a window through which to view the complexity, uncertainty and dynamism of the social systems with which they are engaged. Within their own frameworks, they draw on a wide range of traditions, mechanisms, techniques and processes to engage individuals and groups in the process of collaborative change.

Friedman and Rothman, for example, discuss their action evaluation framework as a process of social experimentation within the context of social education programs. Their experimentation involves integrating program evaluation, conflict resolution and action science. They also draw on organisational development processes such as goal enquiry, stakeholder involvement and team building and support these with web-based research and interaction. A key goal of their data-driven approach is stakeholder education and learning.

Goff, Gregg and May use a strong, constructivist framework within a Participative Action Research (PAR) tradition. They set out to create a change dynamic by building an equitable base for participation through asking fundamental questions about power and management. They seek to create knowledge and build trust and to explore boundaries within and beyond the focal social system. The goal is to achieve equitable participation through engaging participants as co-researchers, co-producers, co-creators and co-designers. A fundamental goal of their approach is the democratisation of knowledge, power and learning so that the participants themselves create and drive the change. The process involves entering the 'no-go' zone – venturing into 'danger zones of unasked questions, feared experiences of change, subtle forms of decision-making and avoided, denied and repressed conflict'. In the final analysis, power is reconstrued as depth, strength and resource efficiency; thought in action; recognisable realities; ecology in action; and whole community.

Davies uses action research within an open-systems framework. He conceptualises the collective as systems within systems, each system – the individual human, family, work group, organisational and political system – being embedded within broader systems. The imperative for this perspective derives from the need of systems to interact with their significant environments. This interaction is impacted by judgments of participants about the environment, the values they hold and their beliefs about the future. In his open systems approach to action research, he draws on a wide range of techniques, including scenario building, environmental analysis and search conference, to build a future-oriented, participative, egalitarian and iterative approach. Responsiveness of the sponsor and of the facilitator to the emergent, evolving participation is a critical dimension of these processes.

Lange uses a Buddhist framework to integrate processes such as action learning, team building, conflict resolution, role clarification and negotiation within a management team context. She stresses awareness of body, mind and spirit through focusing on the present moment and building consciousness of breathing, feeling and thinking. This awareness building involves her clients as well as herself as facilitator. Her processes identify destructive patterns, deepen relationships and open up new avenues for goal achievement. They also create a peaceful sense of being – a sense that permeates her account of a management team meeting, despite the moments of experienced tension.

On reflection, it can be seen that each of the contributors to this section attempts to develop 'mindfulness' but with a different focus and from a different perspective:

-Friedman and Rothman build stakeholders' awareness of their own goals and the program means by which they are pursuing them
-Goff and Associates build awareness about 'power' – its shape, pervasiveness, barriers (real and imagined) and joint negotiability
-Davies builds awareness of the system and its environment and the impact of individual's values and view of the future on that system
-Lange builds consciousness about 'being states' and their impact on goal achievement.

Each of the frameworks, in their own way, is concerned with:

-giving 'voice' to the unspoken, unheard or disenfranchised
-making 'tacit knowledge' explicit
-asking the hard and/or fresh questions
-exploring the gap between what is espoused and what is practised
-conflict engagement
-negotiating reality – the present and the future
-building the capacity of individuals and the collective through an iterative process of research, action and reflection.

The frameworks are windows that serve to help the facilitator and clients to re-view reality and build collaborative endeavour towards the achievement of agreed goals and/or states.

Action Evaluation for Knowledge Creation in Social-Education Programs

Victor J Friedman & Jay Rothman

Introduction

This paper describes 'action evaluation', a method for integrating knowledge production into the design, implementation, and assessment of social-educational programs. Action evaluation builds on an earlier vision of program evaluation as social experimentation but also incorporates concepts from conflict resolution and action science for promoting productive learning. These include program theories of action, goal inquiry, stakeholder deliberation, team building, conflict engagement, and web-based research.

Emergence of Program Evaluation

Program evaluation represented an intentional, systematic attempt at knowledge creation long before the emergence of the now popular concepts of 'organisational learning' and 'knowledge management'. In the 1960s, US government agencies and private foundations developed 'programs' aimed at solving specific social problems through specific means of intervention. Legislators, administrators, and practitioners wanted to know whether programs 'worked' and the academic community, especially social scientists and statisticians, quickly responded to this need for policy and evaluation research. They believed they possessed the methodological tools to provide administrators and legislators with valid information about program effectiveness. Donald Campbell, one of the fathers of the field, envisioned an 'experimental society' in which social scientists and administrators would closely collaborate in using evaluation to gradually build a scientific knowledge-base for social action (Campbell & Russo 1999 p9).

This early promise of program evaluation as knowledge creation ran aground on methodological and political obstacles. Evaluators faced the thorny problem of establishing causality in the 'real world', which rarely lent itself to the laboratory conditions necessary for conducting true experiments. Innovative approaches, such as the 'quasi-experimental' method (Campbell & Stanley 1963), placed high demands on both program and research design, making evaluation a burden or simply not feasible for many programs. Ironically, increased research on an issue led to *less* of an ability to make clear and unambiguous judgements about success or failure (Cohen & Weiss 1977), leading to the growing public impression that 'nothing works' (Patton 1997 p13). Policy research often shifted from a focus on the issues to a focus on methodology and statistics. Most legislators and administrators showed little interest in methodology or in even using evaluation in decision making at all, tending to ignore unwanted evidence or co-opt/manipulate evaluation for their own political purposes (Patton 1997). By the 1970s most program evaluators came to accept their field as inherently political (Weiss 1993) and many were highly sceptical about evaluation utilisation, much less social experimentation and learning (Patton 1997).

Action Evaluation

Action Evaluation (AE) represents a recent attempt to revive the vision of program evaluation as social experimentation. It provides a data-based framework within which project funders, administrators, staff, and participants can collaboratively inquire into and test their goals and action strategies in order to learn from experience as a project unfolds.[1]

Action Evaluation focuses on defining, monitoring, and assessing success at every stage of program development in order to make it a self-fulfilling prophecy. It has much in common with other evaluation approaches such as 'utilisation-focused evaluation' (Patton 1997), 'empowerment evaluation' (Fetterman 1994), 'theory-driven evaluation' (Chen 1990), and 'evaluative inquiry' (Preskill & Torres 1999). It attempts to break new ground, however, by introducing concepts from conflict resolution (Rothman 1997) and action science (Argyris, Putnam & Smith 1985; Friedman 2000; Schon 1983). In addition, it utilises an innovative web-linked, data gathering and processing system that enables it to (1) overcome barriers of time and space in interacting with large numbers of stakeholders and (2) develop a rich data-base from a wide variety of projects.

'Action evaluation' began when the loan officer of a major foundation asked Rothman (1997) if he could determine whether his foundation's multi-year, multi-million dollar conflict resolution program had been successful, or not. Rothman had to answer 'no' because the very meaning of 'success' in conflict resolution is unclear. This puzzled him and led to a study (Ross & Rothman 1999) that found that (1) definitions of success in conflict resolution programs are varied, local, and contingent upon the nature of the conflict and the desires of the stakeholders and (2) conflict resolution programs involve multiple stakeholders (eg. participants, funders, professionals, administrators, evaluators) who themselves define success differently. Furthermore, Rothman (1997a) noted that his own theory of conflict resolution was constantly evolving through a process of conceptualisation and testing in each new situation. In order to address the uniqueness, instability, and uncertainty inherent in programs like his own, Rothman began developing action evaluation (Rothman 1997b).

The Action Evaluation Project Team began its work in 1992 and is located today at the McGregor School of Management of Antioch University. It has conducted over 40 projects, each of which share the following theoretical and practical elements.

Program Theory Building and Testing

Mainstream evaluations tend to focus on the relationship between program inputs and outcomes, treating programs themselves as 'black boxes' (Chen 1990). In order to get inside the black box and to generate useful information, Chen (1990) proposed 'theory-driven evaluation', which looks at the goals, treatments, and contextual factors in both a program's design and its implementation. Chen's approach was based on the observation that project stakeholders are often unaware of a program's implicit logic. The evaluator's role is to make this *tacit knowledge explicit*, providing stakeholders with a more accurate understanding of how a program works and how it can be improved. This approach is reinforced by action science.

Action science makes a fundamental distinction between an 'espoused theory' – what people intend or believe they do, and 'theory-in-use' – what can be inferred from their actual behaviour (Argyris & Schon 1974 pp6–7). Both program theory evaluation and action science aim at improving programs and organisations by discovering gaps between espoused theories and theories-in-use and by bringing this information to the attention of stakeholders. Action science provides an explanation for the gaps between the two theories and the ways in which individuals and systems keep themselves unaware of them (Argyris & Schon 1974, 1996). From the perspective of action science, helping program stakeholders discover their tacit theories also enables them to achieve greater control over the choices they have made in their perceptions, their goals, and their strategies. By discovering their own causal responsibility for outcomes, they possess some leverage for producing change (Argyris et al 1985).

Three Phases of Action Evaluation

Action Evaluation approaches program theory building and testing as an interactive three-phase process. The *baseline* phase of AE focuses on clarifying definitions of success and on making a program's 'theory of action' explicit by asking: *What* are the goals of relevant stakeholders? *Why* are these goals important to them? *How* are these goals to be achieved? Data on these questions are collected, analysed, and fed back to program stakeholders (Rothman & Friedman 1999). The outputs of the baseline are both an explicit statement of program theory and an action plan for putting that theory into practice. The *formative* phase views program implementation as an iterative process of experimentation aimed at testing and self-consciously refining the program's theory of action. Data on program implementation and initial outcomes are collected, analysed, and fed back to stakeholders in order to compare its espoused theory with its theory-in-use. Inquiry at the formative stage follows the logic of the spiral of organisational knowledge creation, making tacit knowledge explicit at the individual, program, and multiple stakeholder levels (Nonaka & Takeuchi 1995 p73), leading to new problem settings, new goals, and new strategies. The *summative phase* focuses on (1) making judgements about the overall merit of a project, and (2) generalising from the program's cumulative experience to other similar situations – not in the sense of establishing general laws, but in the sense of building a *repertoire* of exemplars that enable planners and practitioners to recognise both the similarities and the uniqueness of related problem situations (Schon 1983).

Goal inquiry

Early on, evaluators realised that effective program evaluation depends upon the existence of clear, specific, and measurable goals, but this often led to complex goals clarification processes with all of their well-known pathologies (Patton 1997). Recognising that different stakeholders may have different goals, Chen (1990) made the identification and clarification of goals not just an antecedent, but an object of evaluation itself. Peled and Spiro (1998) advocated a 'goal-focused evaluation' that identifies both a program's 'declared' and 'operative' goals as a means of refocusing programs and rechanneling resources. The common denominator of all these approaches is the assumption that ends are 'out there' to be found and specifically linked with means. AE challenges stakeholders to consider *why* these goals are important, facilitating 'double-loop learning,' which aims at inquiring into and changing underlying assumptions, goals, values, and standards for performance (Argyris & Schon 1974, 1996). Furthermore, it sets the stage for creating greater consistency between program 'espoused theories' and 'theories-in-use'. Goal inquiry is also essential for addressing conflicts that inevitably surface when the goals of multiple stakeholders are taken into account.

Facilitating stakeholder learning

Learning depends upon engaging 'people who want to know something' (Patton 1997 p50) – that is, identifying and involving the stakeholders for whom a program is important and for whom information about it is relevant to their needs (Patton 1997). In addition, program evaluation can function as an *organisational learning* mechanism to the extent that knowledge created for one stakeholder group reaches others and is used by them (Lipshitz, Popper & Oz 1996).

Most social-educational programs are produced through a bureaucratic process in which programs are developed at a centre and implemented by a distributed population of practitioners, ideally with evaluation acting as a feedback loop. Schon, Drake and Miller (1984) advocated 'inductive planning', in which practitioners design, implement, and research their own policies with the centre documenting and disseminating cases of intervention as well as maintaining the network of practitioners. Neither approach, however, takes into account fundamental discontinuities in the institutional structures of the social-educational services (Lipskey 1980). Program effectiveness is often inhibited by gaps between planning and implementation (eg. Bowen 1999) or contradictions between the goals held by different stakeholders (eg. Cohen, Eran & Friedman 1996). In these cases stakeholders were either unaware of these gaps and contradictions or acted as if they did not exist. AE is conflict-engaged, seeking to ensure that internal gaps and contradictions are surfaced and engaged (see below).

Furthermore, AE attempts to deepen stakeholder involvement and awareness through a systematic process of deliberation and consensus building around goal setting, program design, and monitoring. At the baseline, AE inquires into the goals of each stakeholder group separately and then brings the different stakeholder groups together to reach consensus on program goals and strategies. During the formative stage this deliberative process within and among stakeholder groups continues in reflection on the gap between espoused theory and actual practice. Reasoned, reflective deliberation fosters Model II values, which are considered critical for double-loop learning (Argyris & Schon 1996). It promotes 'internal commitment' by giving each individual stakeholder and stakeholder group 'voice' (Hirschmann 1970). It also attempts to maximise the 'free and informed choice' (Argyris & Schon 1996) of all participants regardless of their formal role or position in the hierarchy.

Team Building

The goal of AE is to produce research *in* practice, not research *on* practice (Friedman 2000) with no clear division of labour between those who produce knowledge and those who use it. Team building here means developing the roles, relationships, and norms for making theories explicit, testing them, and generating valid information (Argyris & Schon 1996). Lipshitz, Popper and Friedman (1998) have identified four behavioural norms which promote the production of valid information: transparency (exposing one's actions and the reasoning behind them), integrity (providing and encouraging full and accurate feedback even when it means admitting one's errors or pointing out those of others), an *issue-orientation* (focusing on the relevance of information to the issues regardless of social standing of the recipient or the source), and *inquiry* (asking questions for the purpose of genuinely understanding uncertain or puzzling situations/behaviours). As discussed below, team-building can also result from open and safe inquiry into differences and disagreements within and across stakeholding groups in order to produce learning and change, when useful.

Conflict Engagement

The evaluation community widely accepts those evaluation processes and purposes are often fraught with conflict – politics as a fact of life, but few evaluators address the issue of conflict directly. Patton (1997 pp353–357), for example, advocates the creation of 'evaluation task forces' for putting competing interests on the table, but does not specify how they can be reconciled aside from using empirical evidence for 'reality testing'. There is a price for not fully engaging conflict. Because each stakeholder hopes that a program will meet his/her needs, there is an incentive to seek pragmatic, short-term solutions that enable programs to progress while leaving contradictions unaddressed. Programs often consume valuable resources but fail to get off the ground, fail to meet expectations, and/or explode when conflict can no longer be contained or avoided. It may often be program evaluators who light the match by exposing internal contradictions and who bear the brunt of built-up frustration and disappointment. Thus, evaluators also have an incentive to collude in the cover-up and avoidance of conflict such that programs not only fail, but that conflict (and failure) rarely function as stimuli for learning (Argyris & Schon 1996; Rothman & Friedman, forthcoming; Friedman 2000a).

In this common approach to conflict, it is viewed as a zero-sum game played out through force and/or bargaining. The zero-sum approach has been challenged by conflict theorists who suggest that clarifying and analysing conflicting interests can reveal opportunities for win/win, integrative, or cooperative outcomes (eg. Fisher & Ury 1981). However, many controversies involving social-educational programs *cannot* easily be reduced to interests because they are rooted in deeply held 'frames' involving perception, belief, and individual and collective identity (Schon & Rein 1994; Rothman 1997). Action Evaluation actively engages conflicts within the stakeholders' goals (eg. between their espoused theories and their theories-in-use) and among stakeholders (eg. groups and individuals who have different goals). It views conflict as a resource for learning and seeks to foster a 'conflict-positive' attitude among stakeholders (Tjosvold 1991).

Although AE acknowledges the destructive potential of conflict, it also recognises that seemingly intractable conflicts offer opportunities for growth, adaptation, and learning (Rothman 1997; Schon & Rein 1994). Since social-educational programs are planned and delivered by people, they cannot be reduced to purely technical skills. Knowledge creation in this sector means producing deep changes in personal and professional identity as well as in the relationships among stakeholders. Therefore, rather than focusing on solutions, action evaluators engage *conflict* by creating 'reflexive dialogue' in which stakeholders critically inquire into their frames and underlying identity issues (Rothman 1997). Integrating conflict engagement with program evaluation provides stakeholders with opportunities for 'negotiating reality,' by testing their frames in concrete situations rather than in abstract ideological or political terms.

From the perspective of organisational learning, the ability to engage conflict is also important because evaluation inevitably involves providing information that is embarrassing and threatening. Evaluators need to be prepared to deal effectively with defensiveness, particularly when they themselves are in the position of revealing gaps between espoused theory and theory-in-use (Argyris et al. 1985).

Web-based Data Collection, Analysis, and Dissemination Strategies

From its inception AE has employed a site on the World Wide Web (see www.aepro.org), the heart of which is a database built on a Filemaker Pro platform. At the baseline stage the database has served primarily as means of collecting, organising, analysing, and storing data as well as generating and disseminating findings. In the formative stage, a customised and web-based discussion forum is used as stakeholders monitor and revise their goals and action plans as they seek to implement them.

The use of the Internet enables action evaluators easy access to programs and participants scattered around the world. Each project receives an account with its own password. Project participants log into their project area and enter their baseline data (What? Why? How?). Participant data is aggregated at the individual, stakeholder group, and project level. The results of the analysis are posted on the website, but feedback sessions have mostly been held face-to-face.

In addition to data management, the website serves a number of functions directly related to organisational learning. Firstly, it provides an organised, easily accessible, cumulative record of program development and implementation. Secondly, it offers program participants who rarely meet face to face an opportunity to converse or exchange information either synchronously or asynchronously. Finally, by bringing together detailed evaluation research on programs in conflict resolution, education, and social services, it offers potential for comparative study, cross-fertilisation, and cumulative learning.

Conclusion

Action Evaluation is itself an experimental social technology for creating new knowledge in areas of practice characterised by uniqueness, uncertainty, and instability. It aims at helping program stakeholders make their definitions of success self-fulfilling prophesies by integrating evaluation research into program practice. Action Evaluation was first launched about eight years ago and has been piloted in over 40 projects worldwide in conflict resolution, education, and social services. Although it belongs to a growing family of evaluation approaches that emphasise stakeholder participation, program theory, and/or learning, Action Evaluation is distinguished by a unique three-phase process and its focus on goal inquiry, program theory testing, team-building, and the constructive use of conflict. In addition, its web-based technology not only makes evaluation more easily accessible to practitioners but also provides a rich database for facilitating learning and knowledge creation among programs in a wide variety of fields.

Acknowledgement

The authors would like to thank the William and Flora Hewlett Foundation for its support of the research that led to this paper.

Notes

1. For further definitions and examples of its application, see the AE website: www.aepro.org

Bibliography

Argryis, C, Putnam, R & Smith, D (1985) *Action Science: Concepts, methods, and skills for research and intervention.* San Francisco: Jossey-Bass

Argyris, C & Schon, DA (1974) *Theories in Practice: Increasing professional effectiveness.* San Francisco: Jossey-Bass

Argyris, C & Schon, DA (1996) *Organizational Learning II: Theory, method, and practice.* Reading: Addison-Wesley

Bowen, K (1999) *Development of Local Program Theory: Using theory-oriented evaluation to make a difference* – paper presented at the Annual Conference of the American Evaluation Association, Orlando, Florida

Campbell, D & Russo, J (1999) *Social Experimentation.* Thousand Oaks: Sage

Campbell, D & Stanley, J (1963) 'Experimental and quasi-experimental designs for research' in *Handbook of Research on Teaching.* Skokie: Rand McNally

Chen, H (1990) *Theory-driven Evaluations.* Thousand Oaks: Sage

Cohen, M, Eran, M & Friedman, V (1996). *Evaluation of the 'New Education Environment' Program in Amal Technological Schools: First interim report.* Jerusalem: Brookdale Institute

Cohen, D & Weiss, J (1977) 'Social science and social policy: schools and race' in Weiss, C (ed), *Using Social Research in Public Policy Making.* Lexington: DC Heath, pp67–84

Fetterman, D (1994) 'Empowerment evaluation' in *Evaluation Practice.* 15(1), pp1–15

Fisher, R & Ury, W (1981) *Getting to Yes: Negotiating agreement without giving in.* Boston: Houghton Mifflin

Friedman, V (2000) 'Action science: creating communities of inquiry in communities of practice' in Bradbury, H & Reason, P (eds) *The Handbook of Action Research.* Thousand Oaks: Sage. pp159–170

Friedman, V (2000a) *Designed Blindness: When program theory meets program practice* – paper presented at the Annual Conference of the American Evaluation Association, Honolulu, Hawaii, November 2000

Hirschmann, A (1970) *Exit, Voice, and Loyalty.* Cambridge: Harvard University Press

Lipshitz, R, Popper, M & Friedman, V (1998) *Facets of Organizational Learning* – unpublished paper

Lipshitz, R, Popper, M & Oz, S (1996) 'Building learning organizations: The design and implementation of organizational learning mechanisms' in *Journal of Applied Behavioral Science,* 32, pp292–305

Lipskey, M (1980) *Street-level Bureaucracy: Dilemmas of the individual in public services*. New York: Russel Sage

Morgenthau, H (1948) *Politics Among Nations: The struggle for power and peace*. New York: Knopf

Nonaka, I & Takeuchi, H (1995) *The Knowledge Creating Company*. New York: Oxford University Press

Patton, M (1997) *Utilization-focused Evaluation*. 3rd edition. Thousand Oaks: Sage

Peled, E & Spiro, S (1998) 'Goal-focused evaluation: lessons from a study of a shelter for homeless youth' in *Evaluation*, 4(4), pp455–468

Preskill, Hallie & Torres, RT (1999) *Evaluative Inquiry for Learning in Organizations*. Thousand Oaks: Sage

Ross, M & Rothman J, (eds) (1999) *Theory and Practice in Ethnic Conflict Management: Conceptualizing success and failure*. London: MacMillan

Rothman, J (1997) *Resolving Identity-Based Conflict: in Nations, Organizations and Communities*. San Francisco: Jossey-Bass

Rothman, J (1997a) 'Action Evaluation and conflict resolution in theory and practice' in *Mediation Quarterly*, 15 (2)

Rothman, J (1997b) 'Action Evaluation and conflict resolution training: theory, method and case study' in *The Journal of International Negotiation*, 2(3)

Rothman, J. (1999) 'Articulating goals and monitoring progress in a Cyprus conflict resolution training workshop' in Ross, M & Rothman, J (eds) *Theory and Practice in Ethnic Conflict Resolution: Conceptualizing success and failure*, London: MacMillan

Rothman, J & Friedman, V (forthcoming) 'Conflict, identity, and organizational learning' in Meinolf, D, Antal, A, Child, J & Nonaka, Y (eds) *The Handbook of Organizational Learning*. Oxford: Oxford University Press

Rothman, J & Friedman, V (1999) *Action Evaluation: Helping to define, assess and achieve organizational goals* – presented at the American Association Conference in Orlando, Florida and published on the Action Evaluation Website http://www.aepro.org/inprint/papers/aedayton.html

Rothman, J & Ross, M (1999) 'Integrating Evaluation into the Intervention Process' in Ross, M & Rothman, J (eds) *Theory and Practice in Ethnic Conflict Resolution: Conceptualizing success and failure*. London: MacMillan

Schon, D (1983) *The Reflective Practitioner*. NY: Basic Books

Schon, D, Drake, W & Miller, R (1984) 'Social experimentation as reflection-in-action' in *Knowledge Creation, Diffusion, and Utilization*. 6(1), pp5–36

Schon, D & Rein, M (1994) *Frame Reflection: Towards the resolution of intractable policy controversies*. New York: Basic Books

Tjosvold, D (1991) *The Conflict Positive Organization: Stimulate diversity and create unity*. Reading: Addison-Wesley Publishers

Weiss, C (1993) 'Where politics and evaluation research meet' in *Evaluation Practice*. 14(1), pp93–106. (originally published in 1973).

Participatory Action Research: Change Management in the 'No Go' Zone.

Susan Goff, Jane Gregg & Karen May

Introduction

This chapter discusses strategies for change management that are referenced to Participatory Action Research (PAR) theories of practice as experienced and interpreted by the authors in the Australian context.The chapter proposes that when PAR theories of practice inform change management practices, the phenomenon of'power' transforms both conceptually and experientially. This transformation has a flow-on effect of changing the way power is used as a core dynamic of change management. Being implementers of participatory practices, we avoid making didactic, foundational statements about the definition of PAR. Instead we invite our readers to make their own distinctions particularly in reference to our use of language, the ways in which we formulate questions and the role that questions have in participatory environments as compared to other research and learning environments.

The Authors' Positions

The Task that lies before us in the 21st century cannot be accomplished by strategising around, with or against simplistic concepts of power. Power is a resource on the table for negotiation along with clean air, wealth, health and new paradigm thinking.

PAR theories of practice build and use structures and processes of 'community-building' to form collaborative inquiry partnerships between, 1.those with the recognised power to act in the public interest (the 'co-researchers', eg. Reason 1988) and 2.those who are recipients of such actions (the 'critical reference group', eg. Wadsworth 1984). PAR builds active communities of interest in questions that are equally relevant to all participants, including the facilitator.

Such communities function best by operationalising principles of equity, which continually manifest as unpredictable, multiple forms of equitable *participation* in collaborative inquiry and action. As such, PAR practitioners create environments for learning about new forms of power – power as equity for example, as compared to power as inequity. Such new forms of power become the currency for negotiating rights and responsibilities to act in the public interest.

Reflections on power from the field of practice

In the following sections, we share our reflections on power as depth, strength and resource efficiency; as thought in action; as recognisable realities; as whole community; and as a form of change management focused on equity and accessability.

Power as depth, strength and resource efficiency

PAR utilises a range of schemas, constructs and mindsets with which PAR practitioners reflect, make meaning and act. These ways of functioning facilitate participants' capabilities to travel to territory that is often deemed 'too hard' and left unattended. However such territory is *necessary* if the fundamental managerial, social and ecological issues that present as barriers to change are to be explored. By using rigorous and recognised participatory research practices in this 'no go' zone practitioners can illuminate new forms of power that are accessible to new players for new purposes.

The following excerpt about boundary crossing from Parkes and Panelli's paper (2001 p28) on their use of PAR in a catchment management strategy in the Taieri Catchment, New Zealand, illustrates power as *depth and strength* (added italics draws attention to the definition of power):

> As well as advocating for integrated, participatory and equitable approaches to inquiry and problem solving, researchers and decision-makers also carry a responsibility to recognise, value and develop the tacit skills required for the practice of boundary crossing – both in themselves and others. Not least the skills of listening, critical reflection, humour and humility that are often essential to genuinely reflexive, innovative and evaluative processes.

PAR practitioners see boundary crossing as an essential skill for generating 'indicators of diversity'. Such indicators when approached with principles of equity mark opportunities for questioning the recognised *authority* to build knowledge and apply it, the existing *quality* of knowledge, the *applications* of such knowledge, and the *infrastructure* that currently supports knowledge application and generation in any action research setting.

For example, a recent participatory initiative in the field of domestic violence, enabled consumers to question existing positions and capabilities of community agencies in the light of informal support networks and their ways of responding to family violence issues. The questions that the participants raised, and that agencies engaged with, made visible previously unquestioned assumptions about political leadership, accepted ontologies of the issues being addressed and methodologies of intervention.

PAR makes visible that which is undervalued or invisible: knowledge and experience that old assumptions of power keep hidden from the conscious and public views. Such knowledge is contributed by those who are marginalised from decision-making about their issues due to access impedances such as fear, status, alienation from formality, cultural and/or literal literacy, distance, gender, race etc. The reconstrued functional system that a PAR strategy can develop from the emancipation of such knowledge and its keepers brings reconstrued and energised power – that is, resource efficiency that is built into an existing organisation, strategy or community.

Power as thought in action

PAR operates as a dynamic rather than a mechanism. It provides a flexible and contextually responsive way to experience change rather than a lever for manipulating a predetermined form of change in a predetermined direction. It works with tension between process and outcome by maintaining awareness of one as nested, interchangeably, inside the other rather than one being a consequence of the other.

Valuing interpersonal communication-based knowledge makes it possible for those who are engaged with the change management initiative to interact with the process and respond to what is happening in terms of *relationship building in the process of knowledge construction.* By working so explicitly with trust amidst the volatility of change, PAR methods deploy collective power as 'thought in action' to drive and reflect upon change *as it is happening.* Such a flexible, rapid and creative process accommodates interpersonal communication, grouped values and lightly held propositions. It is a process that does not claim viability of such elements on the grounds of authority or fit to pre-existing theory, but on the grounds of participant-observer evaluation of participant action. Nothing is held as permanent truth, everything is prone to continual change including change itself. Such continual impermanence and resistance of hidden truths generates a quality of action that is as much thought as it is action.

This experience of power as 'thoughtful action' is described in Reason (1994 p36) in reference to the work of Judy Marshall:

> Future participation will use language and concepts as a way of re-visioning our experience without setting it in a new concrete form... to 'hold an idea lightly' – in other words as a potential, a possibility, a plaything which if permitted will illuminate experience without rigidifying it.

To hold an idea 'lightly' one needs the power of collaborative and self-critical analysis, to continually refrain from closure, ownership or defence (see Heron's special inquiry skills, 1996 pp58–59) and to be open to others, even when others are not reciprocating openness (a 'no-go' zone). Thought in action generates co-created and co-owned power – sustaining consciousness of self in relationship to idea, future and others.

Power as recognisable realities

PAR is about building questions and processes generated from resources (capabilities, traditions, time, trust, etc) that exist *within* an organisation and its social and ecological catchment and that thus fit that organisation and its context. It constructs descriptions and understandings that are uniquely recognisable to participants and authentic to their experience: owned by them, trusted and within their range of useability. This sense of 'real world' or, in our sense 'realised world' is usually embedded in interpersonal relationships and often-unexplored beliefs about how the world and others are – or are not.

The phrase 'in the real world' too often implies defeat: the grievous gap between ideal and compliance (a 'no go' zone). In PAR environments 'real world' is a shared construction of experience, not limited to narrative but brought strategically into practice for mutual benefit – a shared history. Truths are expressed as perhaps less grandiose in scale but more powerful in terms of recognisable, accessible and 'doable-by-us' realities.

For example, Weil, Bhandari and Shah (2001 p26), in their concluding reflections on a collaborative inquiry strategy that worked with coronary heart disease interventions in the medical arena, provide an example of how this authenticity avoids the anxiety of the impossible while stimulating the more fascinating 'doable':

> We have certainly come to know better and more deeply that uncertainties cannot be easily resolved, that nothing stays the same and that nurturing alternative forms of dialogue, co-inquiry, attention and action that reveal alternative choices for learning and making pathways through the world may be the best we can do. To assert such things is itself challenging. To live and learn them in ever changing contexts for practice and choice is more so. And as anyone who fishes knows, the same place on the river is never the same place.

Building relationships between lay and professional participants can be strong enough to carry and value simple truths and depth of feeling (emotional intelligence) when the 'real' is spoken, documented and integrated into strategies and criteria for evaluation. This strength of relationship, truth, value and recognised reality, as impermanent as it is, becomes a power for action that reflects this depth of reality. This power, born internal to the research initiative's community and rooting into the 'no go' zone, extends beyond the 'safer house' of the facilitated environment to realise its obligation to make a 'real world' difference beyond the research community. Its extension is through living demonstration, publication, advocacy and strategic partnerships.

Power as whole community

PAR shifts the concept of power away from the familiar 'middle ground' of formal roles, responsibilities and uncritiqued concepts of power within an organisation. It creates a legitimate environment to include the currently perceived polarities of personal dimensions of power and change on the one hand and global dimensions on the other. It involves intense personal immersion in learning and its relevance to a whole world picture. PAR enables the personal and global to inform the middle ground rather than enabling the middle ground to control a change strategy often at the expense of the personal and the global.

Dimensions of change, the personal and the global qualities of power, are often disenfranchised in organisations and community. They lack the place, language, legitimacy and credibility for formal systems to feel confident about relying on them. They seem too complex to be included in commonly used organisational change processes (another 'no-go' zone). However middle ground assumptions of power are not coping with the demands of personal or global (including regional) pressures (as the current discourse on greenhouse gas illustrates – see *New Scientist* Environmental Supplement, March 2001). PAR provides a means of bringing a breadth of interests, resources and traditions together with equity, and reorienting these elements into a change strategy that garners multi-level perspectives creating arenas for change to take place. The change management strategy shifts from being a linear process within an aspect of a community, to a spherical process of a whole community recreating itself from within.

So how do we progress from continuing to accommodate the failures of old forms of power and work through the ambiguities of the new, in the face of accelerating crisis and reducing resources?

PAR as a form of change management

PAR methods solicit voluntary participants on the basis of rights and responsibilities with regard to issues being addressed by the inquiry (Goff 2001a). Change and the issues of power that rights and responsibilities raise, are construed and reconstrued, as are management practices. Participants use their reconstrued elements of power and management to realise self-determined and mutually shared objectives of improving an aspect of an organisation and/or its social-ecological catchment. Participants create and drive change rather than react to change directives from external sources.

The quality of change that results from these repeated reconstructions ever more closely reflects the values of those whose information is being invested in the change strategy. The change energy that is created lies within participants' interrelationships of shared purpose. This provides promise for placing resources where they are needed, builds knowledge about change and develops theories authored by the participants for their use. Even in the throes of essential dissonance, through respect and self-determination, change occurs within personal comfort zones, thus energising, enabling, expressing and inspiring confidence in humanity and self. Individuals are given the means to go to somewhere other than 'business as usual'. By crossing boundaries, and knowing uncertainty more deeply (refer Weil et al, cited above), participants develop capabilities (rather than positions) of new power to confidently ask critical questions with resilience.

The big 'CO' of PAR power

Where knowledge construction is perceived to be a specialist activity in traditional research environments, PAR resists what its practitioners see as the 'elitism' of such claims and democratises research, learning and knowledge construction. Our language includes 'co-researcher, co-creation, co-production, co-design'... to imply the partnership basis of collaboration and the focus on equity and accessibility that such a relationship needs for it to be operable.

Context, values, practices of knowledge construction and tests for truth are open to appraisal by all participants. This strategy enables hard questions to be asked, undervalued capabilities to be identified, unheard voices to be heard and a significant redefinition of resources, critical to our time. Communicating the meaning of research and theory in ways that are meaningful outside of academic environments becomes necessary to bridge the demands of the work with effective and responsible theories of practice. When successful, these efforts are rewarded by statements such as the following from *lay* participants in the domestic violence research strategy completed this year (Evaluation Report, Goff 2001b):

> I learned about the unfolding process – I could see it working: a lot of input from different sources, the awareness of facilitation and knowledge, how it came together and got broken down through analysis – it went into a deeper level – that's the stuff I love;
>
> It's about learning from others and being honest – to hear the truth when you hear it;
>
> Most social research is very unscientific and keeps going down the same road and comes up with the same answers. Your ideas of research go to the real people;
>
> I learned heaps! That research does not have to be statistical. Critical appraisal was new to me; That personal stories are valued – I thought they were just talk; That most people stayed for most of the time. It acknowledged personal experience and did not pretend that personal values don't matter – everything is about personal values and can be worked with as such in a research environment – because research has a basis to it. That 'research' has credibility – and when used with government is seen as powerful. The validity of the process cannot be dismissed.

Taking liabilities and strengths of individual learning capabilities, educational background and current positions into account, PAR builds individual and collective capacity on a 'trans-capability' level in research output in terms of theory *and* practice.

PAR focuses on knowledge construction *and* application rather than just theory and action – and it is the democratisation of knowledge construction that is the fundamental emancipatory distinction of PAR as compared with AR. Knowledge construction is not viewed as a specialist practice: everyone does it all the time. PAR raises collective awareness of the process and the political implications of its consequences, which gives rise to the discourse on power that PAR enables. This capability of PAR is based in a belief that it is essential to democratise learning if individual and collective capacity is to be self-reliant and avoid self-referencing with dangerous consequences. This belief represents the beginnings of a vital, right angle turn in consumerism for the 21st century. Dwindling human, material and ecological resource bases counter-levered by accelerating change rates, broadening impacts and deepening understanding about the nature of change itself, demands doing something other than more of the same in research and management.[1]

To summarise, PAR method is distinguished by:

-its democratisation of research, learning and action

-the explicit and tacit discussion about power that develops from complementary power relationships, and the new constructions of power that emerge from such discussions

-its critical appraisal of knowledge construction, forms of knowledge and every aspect of a PAR initiative

-its cultural meaning as a departure from concepts of research that are based on western notions of consumerism in response to 21century resource issues

-the primacy of human capabilities as the principle research tool

the development and use of collaborative relationships as the primary context for the research endeavour

-the meta-level focus on research method simultaneously with research direction and output

-the use of iterative cycles that equally balance reflective, critical learning with practical action

-the use of the dialectical power relationships to problematise research issues and their questions and generate research methods.

In this chapter we present power as depth, strength and resource efficiency, thought in action, recognisable realities and whole community. These descriptions are but a few of a much richer and more complex portrait – the face of a new author of the journey that awaits human kind in the century before us.

Notes

1.The reality of dwindling resource bases and the efficacy of PAR gives rise to fears of exploitation of PAR participants – however this fear is counterbalanced by the principle of equity that the method both manifests and sustains.

Bibliography

Goff, S (2001a) *Draft Facilitators Participatory Action Research Kit.* Funded by Queensland Health, produced by CultureShift (unpublished)

Goff, S (2001b) *Reclaiming Community: Final report for the Partners for Prevention Strategy.* funded by Partnerships Against Domestic Violence Strategy, Office of the Status of Women, Prime Minister's Dept (unpublished)

Heron, J (1996) *Co-operative Inquiry: Research into the human condition.* London: Sage Publications

Parkes, M & Panelli, R (2001) *Integrating Catchment Ecosystems and Community Health: The value of participatory action research.* (pending publication)

Reason, P (1988) *Human Inquiry in Action.* London: Sage Publications

Reason, P (ed) (1994) *Participation in Human Inquiry: Research with people.* London: Sage Publications

Wadsworth, Y (1984) *Do it Yourself Social Research.* Melbourne: ARIA

Weil, S, Bhandari, J & Shah, S (2002) 'Breaking the mould of traditional science: developing collaborative inquiry-based practice in primary care – and beyond' in McGill, I & Brockbank, A (eds) *Handbook of Reflective Learning.* London: Gower.

Action Research and Systems Thinking

Alan Davies

I have been pressed by the editors to make a contribution to this book, presumably because they think I have something to contribute that is both unique and useful, based on my 40-odd years of reflecting on how others, and I, learn. What follows might be of some use in that it may add weight to what many others have found, and about which no doubt some have written.

However it is very unlikely to be both unique *and* useful, as in my experience of social, organisational and management affairs, any important new insights arising from changing environmental circumstances are sensed independently by many people across the range of human endeavours and quickly put into the public arena by journalists, novelists and academics. Unfortunately I am a flyweight compared with the Bob Dicks, Fred Emerys and Don Schons of this world. In balance, publishing takes more from the environment in the paper it takes to be printed than the light it brings to this subject, or the empowerment it will bring to my remaining praxis. Why then do I begrudgingly consent to my contribution being a part of this book? Because I believe action research is a methodology that can improve our world, and the editors of this book are dedicated to getting this recognised in academic, community, and business establishments. All strength to their collective arm.

I will first set down my understanding of 'action research' (ar), 'Action Research' (AR) and 'Systems Thinking'. Secondly, I will discuss how and why I came to value action research and systems thinking as guiding concepts in my work with organisations. Then I will address what I see as the relationship between the two – action research and systems thinking – which is the topic I was asked to address. Finally, I will list some of the tools that I have found to be useful in applying action research within a systems framework.

'action research' and 'Action Research'

'action research' (ar) is a process of gaining improved information about a situation through a deliberate process of:

-planning to intervene in the situation to find more about it, based on your -current hypothesis (theory) of how it 'works'
-carrying out the intervention you have planned
-observing what happens as a result of your intervention
-reflecting on your observations with a view to reformulating your hypothesis (theory) of what makes it 'work', and
-planning another intervention based on your reformulated hypothesis.

...then repeating (iterating) the process until you understand the processes to your satisfaction, or you run out of puff.

Thus it is about clarifying causality, starting with a hazy or fuzzy understanding and moving progressively to increased clarity. Action Research (AR) involves the same processes, but in addition the findings are published in the refereed journals.

Fred Emery first introduced me to the concept of Action Research (AR) in 1970. He had just come to the Australian National University from the Tavistock Institute where he and colleagues coined the term, and had started the process of legitimising it as a credible research methodology in the human sciences.

At the time I recall thinking that action research described the way I learnt about the things that I could sense – ie. the things I gained through feedback from doing something. Like gravity, inertia and momentum when learning to ride a bike, like peer-group pressure after dobbing in my brother to my parents, and like cauterisation when finding there was, pain, a hole, but no blood, when I poured molten lead on my leg while extracting lead from bullets I had gathered from the rifle range. In fact, action research was so integral to life that it was expressed in many everyday expressions in the English and no doubt other languages. 'Learning from mistakes', 'practice makes perfect', 'try, try, try again', and 'learning by doing' were but some related expressions. In fact, action research seemed to describe the way in which we develop our common sense and even wisdom.

The value of the term *action research* lies in the credence it gives to the learning (informal) we do as a part of growing and living as opposed to that which we do in schools and which is credentialed by the state (formal) or state-backed organisations. The value of *Action Research* is that the findings are subject to the scrutiny of the appropriate international 'guild' of 'recognised social scientists' and hence becomes 'knowledge' rather than common sense. Thus, Action Researchers can be recognised as professionals and be credible in our modern society when they deliver common-sense advice. Whereas the uncredentialed 'Elder', who has forged common sense into wisdom through the same processes, is at best humoured outside his/her face-to-face community.

If we accept that humans are purposeful and even ideal-seeking beings, then at birth the action research cycle is in place and provides the mechanism by which the baby starts to learn, make sense of its world, and slowly becomes certain of the invariances in *our* world. The process is innate and unconscious. The value of focusing on *action research* and *Action Research* is to make the process conscious and so to provide potential for further deliberate improvement and for the checking of one's observations, reflections and plans with others.

I am reminded here of Fred Emery's assertion that 'Schooling pokes your eyes out and university teaches you Braille'. Here he was, I think, referring in particular to school's propensity to progressively undermine a student's confidence in his or her own theory building (which again is innate) at the expense of the theories the teacher is employed to inculcate. Formal teaching is generally a necessary methodology in those aspects of maths and the physical sciences where theory is not based on those things we sense in our evolutionary environment and/or which can be counter-intuitive.

However, it is often unnecessary and destructive in the social sciences where each individual is a finely tuned observer and actor. True, one needs to test one's hypothesis against others and conventional wisdom, but from a position that respects rather than undermines your own observations, reflections and theory building. Fortunately there is a growing acceptance that learning strategies not only vary between individuals, but also that they vary according to the nature of what is being learnt. Action research reinstates our confidence in our own observations and reflections.

Systems Framework

To me, a system is made up of a set of interdependent parts that collectively have identifiable and reproducible properties that distinguish 'the system' from things. One can have systems within systems, each having a different environment. For example we have a vascular system within a human being and an organisation within a nation state. The systems I have found useful to conceptualise in my work with organisations are the individual human, the family, the work group, the organisation and the various political systems. It is also useful to distinguish between closed and open systems – closed systems being ones that do not interact with their environment(s), open systems being ones that transact with their environments. In the social sciences we are inevitably talking about open systems, however, the breadth of, degree of, and intentions about, openness, are usually important considerations in organisational matters.

Just as it is useful to identify structure within a system (interdependent parts), it is also useful to identify textures within environments. Those parts of the environment that impact significantly on the ability of a system to carry out its purposes, I call its 'significant environment'. Fred Emery and Eric Trist characterised different textures in environments. They are placid-random, placid-clustered, disturbed-reactive and turbulent. Oguz Baburoglu added a fifth: vortical.

Understanding the nature of these environments is of particular importance to Boards and managers of organisations because of what they enable or prevent systems from doing. I have found it to be most important also in interventions aimed at bringing about organisational change. Importantly, it should impact on the questions of who should be involved and what intervention strategies and tools should be chosen to enable adaptive organisational change. The best coverage of the impact of environment on organisation I have seen is by Mike Gloster in his unpublished PhD dissertation. He can be contacted through email on gloster@powerup.com.au.

My value framework and range of experience

I started professional life as a science graduate with the desire to provide others with the same opportunity to understand the physical world that I had been given. During my childhood years I had come to value the importance of individuals and church, sporting, school and work organisations in creating opportunities for people (and particularly me) to learn and develop. During my late teens and twenties I learnt about organisations by involvement in the management and leadership of sporting clubs, school P&Cs and work organisations. All of this had given me a great confidence in the value of participation and egalitarian values within organisations, in enabling individuals to grow and develop to their potential.

In my late 20s and early 30s I became openly and actively politicised by the arguments and debates I became involved in as a mature-age research student during the Vietnam War and the ascent of Gough Whitlam. I thought that politics was important in creating the environment in which the opportunities I had received could be secured and extended to others and so I became involved. When that important avenue was closed to me I sought to pursue the social sciences and by chance happened to be at the Centre for Continuing Education (CCE) at the Australian National University (ANU), led by Chris Duke who created a very rich environment for social and organisational experimentation and research. Here my view of the importance of participation in the management of all aspects of one's life, and particularly one's work and community organisations, was strongly reinforced. It was also clothed with concepts and armed with tools to jointly enhance the viability of the enterprise and the knowledge, wisdom and control of its employees. One of the guiding concepts I picked up from Fred Emery was: 'Organisations are at best purposeful, human beings are ideal seeking.' Hence the importance of enabling the members of organisations to share their views about the external environment and its future directions, particularly in a rapidly changing and unpredictable external environment.

During that time I also met Bob Dick, who breathed life into the versatility, practicality and accessibility of action research as a participatory – and more importantly, egalitarian – tool for learning and active organisational adaptation. Since that time I have been involved in several hundreds of projects in which action research and Action Research, within an Open Systems framework, have been the overriding methodologies. I have continually reflected on that experience to improve my understanding of organisations and their members and to improve my facilitation skills and practice. Those activities involved public, private and community organisations in nine countries in four continents; some of these activities were as an employee, while others were as a member of the community involved in the intervention.

Action research and a systems framework

Here I focus on the organisation as the system and organisational problems and puzzles as the presenting issue for my involvement as a facilitator of 'improvement' or change.

Action research is a methodology that is particularly useful where the problem or puzzle you are trying to solve is multi-factorial. This is usually the situation in organisations. Action research allows you to start with a very ill-defined (fuzzy) hypothesis (theory) about the causality and connectedness and then progressively bring focus through an iterative process. On the way various tools are used to progressively clarify and challenge the emerging hypothesis. Once the major variables in the problem become clear, statistical, case study or other methods can be used to home in on, and quantify, the causality.

The use of an open systems framework is important for at least five reasons.

Firstly, planning, as a process, necessarily involves the making of judgments about the future external environment within which the system has to operate. In our daily discourse this 'anticipated future scenario' is normally taken for granted, or is subconscious. This is based on the assumption that we all know the future and we all see it in the same way. In a stable and unchanging, or slowly changing, environment the explication of the environment is of little importance and even seen as time wasting, as over time we get to know indirectly how others see the future. In a rapidly changing environment the normal mechanism of developing a collective 'future scenario' is not rapid enough to enable people to keep up with the changing worldviews of their fellow workers. Thus in planning in turbulent environments it is important to deliberately focus on and share the participants' understandings of the organisation's future environment and to work openly and participatively. If, however, the environment happens to be vortical and, as a consequence, the organisational issue stalemated, then participative methodologies will fail. One has to intervene at a higher systems level to break the stalemate before proceeding to active, adaptive planning. Mike Gloster, once again, can provide a clear and persuasive exposition of this point.

Secondly, human and organisational systems need to transact with their environment at some level to survive and prosper. The nature of that environment and the way in which it changes over time can either help or hinder the organisation achieve particular outcomes. Therefore it should be understood and taken into account in any organisational planning or problem solving. There are various ways of characterising and analysing the environment for this purpose. Scenario building, environmental scanning, environmental analysis and an opportunities-

and-threats analysis are but a sample. There are also various strategic planning methodologies that package these and other tools into a Strategic Planning event that can form one iteration or cycles of an ongoing action research process. One such strategic planning process that I have often used, and which is both open systems oriented and participative in design, is the 'Search Conference'.

Thirdly, we need to have the right people involved in the planning process to ensure that, on the one hand, there is sufficient knowledge of the system and its environment to make informed recommendations, and, on the other hand, sufficiently powerful membership to enable the adoption and implementation of those recommendations. Where possible, I use a stakeholder analysis and a knowledge analysis to determine who should be involved in a particular event or discourse and establish a representative project board to monitor and decide on changes to the action research process during its conduct. The stakeholder analysis should be open-system oriented in that it considers persons, roles and interests, internal or external to the organisation (system), who can enable or prevent (veto) active, adaptive change.

Fourthly, the individuals who make up the organisation and its significant environment, as Board member, employees, shareholders, managers, and clients need to be aware of the external factors influencing the organisation if they are to be able to effectively contribute to the implementation and monitoring of change. This is particularly the case in a modern flat organisation operating in rapidly changing environment(s). To become aware, they need to be involved in the characterisation of the external environment and in an assessment of the opportunities and threats it affords the organisation.

Finally, an open systems framework can improve the communications between those involved in the planning process. I have found people filter communications through their stereotype of the person they are listening to. This may be okay if the current circumstances are the same as those that operated over the period in which the stereotype was formed. This is decreasingly likely given the mobility in the workforce and between roles. Further, the reason for conducting the intervention usually has its origin in the impact of changing external circumstances of the organisation. Also I believe that people hold the positions about organisational questions as a result of both their value base and a view of what the future will hold for them, their family and their organisation. Neither of these is usually made explicit in the communication. I have found that the participative and collective conduct of an environmental scan enables all participants to see where other participants are coming from, their values and their scenario for the future. This knowledge enables participants to better understand what people are saying and why they are saying it and hence to contribute collaboratively and constructively to the planning process.

My Practice

Much of my work has been aimed at helping groups of people with their planning in a more participative way than has traditionally been the case. My involvement arises from the request of somebody (the sponsor) within the organisation/community who has the power/influence to allocate the necessary resources and gather people around their intention. A period of negotiation between the sponsor and myself then occurs about the nature of the problem, the processes to be used and any boundaries or conditions either of us might wish to place on the process. These negotiations can lead either to an ongoing contract or a parting of the ways. I specify up front that I prefer an open-systems, future-oriented, participative, egalitarian and iterative approach.

There are often tensions between the sponsor and myself over the extent of participation and levels of sharing and disclosure of information about the organisation or the information generated in the process. There are also tensions between the sponsor, who often has a pre-existing view of desired outcomes and who largely sets the initial agenda, and the majority of the participants who are largely cynical about the process and the extent to which their views will be heard and/or heeded. Many would prefer the apparent security of their current worldview and to express their concerns and solutions by sniping from the sides rather than taking the risk of accepting a broader responsibility (Type 2 Learning). The processes I use are aimed at enabling all involved to better understanding the open system they have come to review and possibly change. Where this involves iterative or parallel processes that increase the validity/robustness of that collective understanding, we are dealing with an action research process. Through this process of collective comparison and review they may become action research processes and outcomes. If accepted in the refereed literature they become Action Research findings.

My Experience of Outcomes

I have been involved in over 300 facilitations in the last 35 years that I would consider used action research processes within an open-systems framework. I find it useful to think of two types of outcomes that are associated with most organisational interventions.

The first, and in the short term by far the most important, is the achievement of the stated or understood organisational objectives (at its minimal, the objectives of your sponsor in the organisation). Here my success rate over the 35 years would be at best 15 to 20 percent. The rate would be far higher in the small number of interventions (five to 10) where I was a member of the organisation seeking the change. It would be even higher again where I had a longitudinal involvement in the project rather than being hired for only one cycle of the process (five to 10).

The overall success rate would now be in the range of 60 percent as a result of the 35 years of action/reflection/action. Future improvements, I believe, will arise from using a systems perspective, and particularly an analysis of environmental types, as the basis of the planning and negotiation with the organisational sponsors of any intervention. The improvement that has occurred is a series of step functions rather than through an incremental rise. The important steps are set out in the next section.

The second type of outcome is the individual learning that participants undergo in the action research process. Here I would claim a 70 to 80 percent success rate from the start – a figure that has remained largely unchanged through the 35 years. I attribute this largely to the fact that people who go through an environmental scan are opened to Argyris and Schon's Type 2 Learning. They are opened through the environmental scan, to the values of the other participants/antagonists. They come to better understand the worldviews of other participants and hence why they come to their day-to-day decisions and positions. Formerly, these positions would be seen through stereotypes and uncontextualised behaviours.

However individual learning, taken collectively, does not lead to organisational change unless a whole range of other things also pertain. Firstly, the necessary interests are sufficiently involved – decision makers, those with a veto and those who have to implement. Secondly, the process is seen to provide all involved with the opportunity to input their views and concerns and have them fairly considered before being taken up or dropped. The best jury for these views are ones peers. The critical factor we are attempting to counter here involves the high propensity for duplicity in all of us. We say things in private about fellow workers and managers we are not prepared to say to their face. Collectively this forms the *dark side* of the organisation.

While the organisational outcome is critical to the organisation in the short term, the personal learning is important in the long term through the diffusion of an ar/open-systems approach throughout society. I have found that invitations to facilitate organisational planning often come from people (sleepers) who participated in an action research activity I facilitated as long as 10 to 15 years ago and who are now in a position to make decisions about such matters or influence those who do. Such approaches are likely to be the tip of the iceberg of such initiatives. Many of these 'sleepers' act themselves or call on other facilitators within or without their own organisations when the circumstances are appropriate and they are in a position to initiate planning and action. The general acceptance in the language of terms such as continuous improvement, action research, SWOT, search and teaming are an indication of the long term diffusion from the development of these concepts in the 60s and 70s.

Personal lessons arising from using action research processes within a systems framework

Given all of the above, the following are my key conscious learnings.

-There is a need to contract with the sponsor in the organisation to:

—Determine the boundaries of the system they are trying to change. Failing to do this means the recommendations for change that are produced can get into territory beyond the control of the sponsor and participants. In my experience, this invites participants to indulge in fantasy rather than reality and leads to increased cynicism when their feet eventually hit ground and the recommendations fail to be implemented.

—Undertake a textural analysis of the significant environment of the presenting issue.

—Conduct a stakeholder analysis to see who from within and without the system should be involved and at what stages.

—Get agreement with the sponsor about the powers he/she is prepared to give over to those invited to participate.

—Clarify the status of the recommendations. Will the manager accept them regardless (no matter how dangerous)? Will he/she respond 'publicly' to the recommendations with reasons for acceptance, rejection or modification?

—Establish a 'project board' to oversight the intervention. The project board should have sufficient authority to decide on changes to the process that inevitably occur during an action research process. This helps ensure the facilitator is not entirely a captive of the sponsor.

—Gain agreement from the sponsor to be involved over the whole process.

—Agree about the distribution of information generated in the process.

—Agree to make it clear to all involved who you, as a facilitator, are ultimately answerable to.

—Gain clear commitments to the right to information and participation of all stakeholders included in the pantheon.

-Use an open-systems approach to feedback on your own performance. For 30 of the 35 years I was under the delusion that if participants enjoyed and gave positive feedback, the process was a success in organisational terms. I came to the realisation in 1997 (I am a slow learner!) that the feedback I had been using for 30 years to improve my effectiveness as a facilitator was taken from a closed- rather than an open-systems framework. The closed system was made up of the participants and myself. I adjusted my practice primarily in a way that increased their trust that I would not manipulate them through the processes I employed. This may have lead to increased personal learning but it did not necessarily translate into improved organisational outcomes. My change should have been tied to feedback on organisational outcomes as well as trust. This can be more dangerous to the consultant in terms of volume of return business, but it certainly increases the effectiveness of the interventions. Few sponsors can handle a mirror being held to their performance, despite the rhetoric to the contrary. Incidentally, an undue emphasis on increased trust at the expense of organisational outcomes is a major contributing factor to phenomena whereby many facilitators coming out of an action research/open-systems perspective find it difficult to cooperate on large projects. Each has developed a set of tools attuned to their ability to gain trust with the participants and hence an idiosyncratic rather than a generic or genotypical set of tools. Their jargon is common but its meanings differ. The collective identification of the genotypical in the phenotypical is the most important task facing practitioners of action research in an open-systems framework.

-Design the intervention to meet the needs of the situation, not just the skills and processes you have in your kit bag.

-Develop some strategy that can involve the widespread discussion of the dark side of the organisation – sufficiently widespread to prevent the 'organisational ostriches' carrying the day by default.

-Ensure the whole system is involved in any intervention.

-Enable participants to elicit whether factors requiring change are within the control of those participating, totally outside their control or shared with other outside bodies, and plan accordingly:

—Within our control – can proceed to a decision and to the development of implementable action plans.

—Partially within our control – need to negotiate the plans and actions with other stakeholders, therefore the only planning option is to develop strategies for including or working with the other stakeholders, or to develop propositions to put forward for their consideration.

—Outside our control – treat as a given in planning. Elicit whether factors requiring attention are win-win, win-lose or lose-lose for those participating and deal with them in appropriate ways:

—Win-Win – can deal with in an open planning framework involving disclosure and joint planning. If aspects arise that are win/lose they should be set aside and dealt with in a win/lose paradigm.

—Win-Lose – establish Queensbury Rules for dealing with the negotiation (a Zero-Sum game). Disclosure should be in the context of the negotiation.

—Lose-Lose – either try to isolate the issue or push it into a win/lose or win/win framework. Often needs external intervention or conflict to resolve. In effect it has a localised vortical environment.

-The wisdom of the facilitator is in choosing the appropriate tools for the situation. When the situation calls for processes you are not skilled in or which lie outside your comfort zone, either don't take the job or call in others with the necessary skills/confidence to help.

If the above line of logic is accepted then the following processes are in my view some of those that can be called on in appropriate circumstances to facilitate the conduct of action research within an open systems ethic. I list them to give scope to my discussion. Details can be found in many books that discuss facilitation:

-Negotiation with the sponsor
-Project team formation
-Email strengths and weaknesses
-Legitimising strengths and weaknesses by allowing considered judgments about a collective response
-Emailed environmental scan and digest scenario
-Opportunities and threats based on digest
-The use of digests
-Iterative workshops
-Convergent workshops
-Convergent interviewing
-Workshop sampling
-Table mix
-Plenary sessions for collective understanding
-Parallel groups and triangulation to overcome groupthink
-Participants' expectations

-Convenors' expectations
-Facilitator's expectations
-History
-Presentations
-Pre-distributed information
-Synthesis
-Brainstorming
-Nominal group
-Voting
-Valentines
-Johari's window
-Client presentations
-Fishbowls.
-Force-field analysis

A Sense of Being: Action Learning from Eastern and Western Practice

Deborah Lange

An Evolution

In the first stage of my life my learning has been predominantly from Western thinkers. I have turned to Eastern Buddhist practices in more recent times to enable me to be more of what I espouse and this has enabled me to better assist others who also desire to practice what they preach. This paper is a practical example of my work with a management team. I briefly state the simple yet profound Buddhist practices that have been of significance to my work and to me. The practices are fundamental to being a kind, compassionate, peaceful, mindful, human being no matter what culture, religion or political belief. Being 'mindful' here is being more aware of one's own emotional, mental and spiritual states, the effect these have on self and others and the ability to act 'mindfully'.

A few moments in the life of a Management Team

The overall intention of my work with the team was for them to better understand themselves and each other and be able to improve the way they work together for their own satisfaction, the group's satisfaction and ultimately for the organisation and the community which they serve.

My focus in this chapter is not on sharing how the team improved their business strategy, products, services, etc; rather, my intent is to share an understanding of the underlying values and beliefs inherent in the relationships which were hindering the success of their work. This is usually not only undiscussable but also outside of both the individual and the group's awareness. The uncovering of the blind spot has the potential to create a transformative experience.

I had drawn the group's attention to awareness of the mind, body, spirit and awareness itself. We had practiced the following behaviours at previous gatherings:

- -Breathing
- -Awareness of thought and feeling
- -Awareness of attachment and avoidance
- -Silence
- -Being present to the moment, being aware of when our thoughts and feelings are in the past, the present or the future
- -Awareness of projection and assumptions
- -Awareness of defensive states and non-defensive states
- -Kindness and compassion towards oneself and others.

Process

My purpose was to observe the group in action and intervene appropriately. I had permission to stop the meeting and ask the group questions such as: 'What just happened? What triggered the action, word or feeling? Was it a projection based on a previous experience? Was an invalid assumption being made? What was the consequence? Could something be done differently for a better outcome? Could we 'be' more present? What else could we be aware of?'

We had developed a ritual to focus on the present. The group began in silence focusing on their breathing, focusing on the room, the chair they were sitting on, noticing their thoughts and their feelings bringing them into the present moment.

And then to begin the conversation...

Me: 'Well, how is everybody feeling today, right at this moment, as we are about to start our day together?

Generally most people's voices were soft and lilting. There were silences and reflective periods. Questions were predominantly asked in an inquiring mode, sometimes tentatively, to seek further understanding of each other and the group.

The afternoon session

I asked the group to share, any or all of the following:

-What they 'thought' about the group's progress?
-How they 'felt' about the group's progress?
-What they 'imagined' about the group's progress?

The round table... and where it led...

Mike: 'I think we have improved, I feel good about the team and I can imagine we will continue to do better.'

Rachael: 'Hmm, yes, we are now being more focused, our planning is better... I feel more a part of the team now... I still feel a bit tentative, though, that some people don't like my style or something like that.'

Others made similar comments... until...

Bob: 'Well to be perfectly honest I hate these meetings. I do not look forward to them. I feel undervalued. I feel as if my suggestions are discounted, as if you all, especially Mike [the Manager of the group] think I am not doing my job well.

What happened to the group...

The group reacted; some people stopped breathing momentarily, others did not seem surprised. The group looked at me and looked at the Manager to see how we would react. The air was thick with suspense. Had Bob really said that? What would happen next?

What I was thinking...

For Bob to have the courage to be open about how he actually felt was significant. The group had developed a sense of trust so that it was OK to say what you really felt. It was critical that I helped the group create this into a fruitful event and not one where Bob would be alienated for speaking about how he actually felt.

What I did, how I did it, and the consequence for the group...

I focused on being relaxed, I remembered to drop my shoulders momentarily, take a deep breath, and leant forward slightly towards Bob. In that precious moment of time, as I relaxed, the group breathed with me. They felt OK. This was not going to be a slinging match. This was different.

There were some 'hmms' and some 'ahas' – everyone was nodding their heads in agreement that there was a dynamic that occurred between Bob and Mike with an effect on the group that needed to be explored. The entire group was happy to start with Bob's issue. Bob was eager to explore it too.

What I said... and the response...

Me (in a soft, lilting, approachable voice): 'So Bob, you mentioned that you felt put down in these meetings and that you imagine that Mike thinks that you are not doing your job well. What is it that Mike does or says that makes you feel like that?'

Bob looked at me, looked at Mike and looked back again at me. He breathed with a sigh of relief. In a matter-of-fact, credible voice tone, Bob said: 'When Mike tells me that I am not right. When he completes the topic I have raised and I have not got a satisfactory response.'

As Bob spoke he occasionally looked at Mike (the Manager) to check his reaction but he predominantly looked at me. He seemed to be looking for safety, for reassurance – is it OK to talk like this to my Manager?

In an approachable voice I said: 'Can you give me an example of when this has occurred?'

Bob, in an aggressive tone and with his body tense, said (as an attack), 'Yes, today. I said Anne's position was responsible for all of the administration staff. Then Mike said: 'How could I interpret it that way? Anne only has responsibility for four of the administration staff.'

Bob: 'I was only asking a question – just checking out something that I was unclear about.'

What I was doing and how I was doing it...

Using peripheral vision, I could see from the corner of my eye that Mike had a slight smile on his face as if he was finding this interesting.

I could see his chest and shoulders moving rhythmically – he was OK. The rest of the group was silent, curious about what would be said next.

In a soft voice, I asked Bob: 'Bob, could you remember back to that time this morning when you felt that way? Could you get a picture of you and Mike in your head and tell us what you can remember Mike actually did and said? What did you see Mike do, what did you hear Mike say and how did he do this and say this?'

My intention...

I wanted to help Mike and the group increase their observation skills and differentiate observation from judgement, projection and assumption.

What I did...

I encouraged Bob to try to remember the scene as if it was on video, to see the picture, to sharpen the focus, to bring back the colours, to hear the voices and to bring back the feelings.

After a few moments Bob said: 'Well, I remember Mike sitting up straight. He had his shoulders back and his chin was down. He looked as if he could not be moved. He looked strong. I remember he looked down, pointed with his finger at the paper on the desk in front of him, while he spoke and then stopped definitively. He did not look up at me, and then he moved on to the next agenda item and seemed to go on talking to the rest of the group. He did not look at me or check with me how I felt about what he said.'

Me (approachable): 'When Mike did that, how did that make you feel?'

Bob (in a low voice tone, quite flat and depressed): 'I felt put down. I felt that Mike was saying that the topic was closed and he didn't want me to speak anymore.'

Me (approachable, being careful to maintain rapport with Mike and the group. Using peripheral vision to notice where the group was looking and what they were doing, making sure my breathing was relaxed and the group was still breathing in a relaxed manner as well): 'What did you assume were Mike's intentions?'

Bob: 'I assumed that Mike wanted to put me back in my place, that he was questioning my competence, and that he didn't trust me.'

Roger (with enthusiasm and interest spoken in an approachable voice tone): 'Yes, I see this pattern. We have all spoken about it. There is something that goes on between Mike and Bob that gets in the way of the group getting on with what it needs to do. I am glad that Bob spoke about his concerns with his relationship with Mike and I wondered whether he would say anything.'

Others nodded and 'hmmed' agreement.

Mike had been patiently listening and trying to understand Bob. I now gave Mike the opportunity to express his understanding of Bob (to show Bob that he had been deeply listening) and what went on from his own perspective.

Mike: 'Yes, I can understand Bob feels put down but when he tells me something that is not correct, I think he should know I get frustrated.'

What I was thinking…

Oh oh, things could get messy here!

I wanted to connect the whole group, so that the whole group would understand it was not just Bob or not just Mike but it was something that they were doing that they could change if we could only put a finger on it. I also wanted the group to begin to see our behaviour in patterns rather than as isolated events – that there is choice, there is a way out, we do not have to be locked into the way things are. Choice is about responsibility, not blame and a choice to change our habits.

Me: 'When Bob spoke about the administrative position what is your perception of what he said? What did you think, feel and imagine at the time?'

Mike: 'He sat back in his chair. His shoulders were straight, he leaned slightly, he looked straight, he was definitive… I thought it was a statement and I thought he was challenging me.'

What happened…

The rest of the group agreed with Mike's description of Bob's behaviour. I shared with the group my understanding of the non-verbal characteristics associated with sending information and seeking information when at peace with oneself and others. The characteristics when sending information from a peaceful state are perceived as credible and people listen. The characteristics when seeking information from a peaceful state are perceived to be approachable and people trust the questioner and openly share information.

On the other hand, when there is a negative emotion present such as anger, aggression or frustration our voice tone and body changes. The message may be interpreted as being arrogant, aggressive, intimidating or not listened to when a person has a negative emotional state and shares information. A person may be interpreted as interrogating or bullying when there is a negative emotional state when asking a question. When we can become aware of our emotional state and then remember to become aware of our breathing we can let go of the tension and speak from a more relaxed state. When we breathe in a relaxed manner our voice tone and body softens and becomes more respectful.

Bob remembered that he was feeling tense when he spoke to Mike. The emotional tension had changed Bob's voice tone to be more aggressive than respectful, hence the group's interpretation that Bob was 'posturing'. Bob said he wanted to seek clarification from Mike. I suggested to Bob that the non-verbal style that he used was a style for sending information. If his intention was to seek information there was a mismatch and when there is a mismatch between the non-verbals and the message the recipients become confused.

At the time Bob was unconscious of his intentions. However, through becoming more aware of the tension that had arisen and where that had come from he realized that he was tense because he did not feel that he had the respect of his manager and the group. He had wanted to:

-show everyone that he was competent
-show the group that he was just as important as others were
-clarify a misunderstanding.

These multiple intentions were visible in his actions. The group perceived Bob to be 'posturing'.

I asked Bob to ask his question again but this time, breathe deeply, ease any tension from his body and be relaxed. Being relaxed changed his voice tone and his body posture to be highly approachable. His questioning style had changed to respectfully seeking clarity about an issue.

We talked about what we see, hear and feel when someone is at peace with themselves and others and is being respectful. When Bob breathed easily, relaxed and spoke the group's response was unanimous.

A member of the group said: 'Bob, you are a different person.'

The group's analysis...

He changed his 'state of being'. This behaviour was interpreted as softer, approachable, sensitive, and friendly. The muscles in his face, in his shoulders and in his body were relaxed. The tension, pain and suffering from anxiety and fear had been released. Mike, now not feeling under attack or being threatened, unconsciously matched Bob's style and responded naturally in an approachable style. The energy of the group had changed.

Initially there was fear being embodied in behaviours that exhibited competition between Mike and Bob and the group. The group was a battlefield. Bodies were taut and tense, voice tones were aggressive, and language was being used to attack. Bob became aware of his belief that he was in competition with the group.

Then a surprise emerged...
Bob said: 'When I am breathing deeply, relaxed, perhaps sitting forward, using a soft, lilting tone of voice which goes up at the end of the sentence to mark a question with an inquiring demeanour, I think that I am being submissive. Then I think I am not being credible, I am not being a Manager and then I think I am not manly.

I believe that as a result of a need to be credible as a Manager, I think I must know the answers. It is not right for me to ask inquiring questions. I must be indestructible. Questions for interrogation, for investigation in an authoritarian manner are OK, but not questions that are inquiring, I perceive an inquiring tone as submissive, and I think that men must be like that too' [like Managers].

My analysis...
We had now entered the realm of values and beliefs. We had arrived at this place from observable, concrete behaviour. It was as if we were spiralling down a ladder to get to a deeper layer beyond the seen to the unspoken - we created a deeper level of safety at each rung.

This was Bob's interpretation of himself. He had uncovered a blind spot. In this present moment he went through a combination of feelings, thoughts and images from denial – 'Did I really just say that?' 'Was that me?' 'You must have put words into my mouth' – to anger, sadness, and acceptance.

What I did... and the response I received...
I suggested to him that he think about this revelation of his underlying beliefs in the third person as if he was looking back at a part of himself from another part of himself. 'Bob thinks this?' I did this so that he would remain non-defensive about his revelations and he could observe a part of himself that he was unaware of, with the part of himself that is confident and respectful and kind. I asked him to be kind and compassionate to himself. I also asked him to think back to another time when he was relaxed, approachable, credible and successful. My aim here was to help him remain non-defensive and to become conscious of his successful states and experiences.

I asked in an approachable style: 'Do you ever talk in this approachable style to anyone?'

Bob was quietly reflective for a few moments and then he quietly said: 'Yes, to my wife.'

Me: 'So, Bob, if you talk in an approachable style with your wife, what is different about the conversations you have with your wife compared to the conversations you have here?'

Bob: 'I trust her. I know she thinks I am credible. I do not have to prove my worth to her.'

Me: 'You do not have to prove your worth to her? What does that mean about your sense of who you are, your identity with your wife?'

Bob: 'I have a strong sense of who I am in relation to my wife, I trust her, I can express my vulnerability to her, I can make mistakes and be who I am with her.'

Me: 'What does this mean about your relationship with this group in a work setting and your senses of who you are in relation to this group?'

Bob: 'I do not have enough trust in this group to be approachable. I believe I have to prove my worth to everyone here, so I am guarded. I think they would not accept me, or see me as a good manager if I was approachable. I would worry that they would think that I am not competent.'

My analysis…

What emerged was this pattern, a defensive dance that goes on every time they communicated with one another. It is not usually permissible to discuss 'how' they work together or their values and beliefs. It is normally only permissible to discuss what they do, their tasks, programs, strategies, objectives and goals.

Our conversation moved on to others who felt the need to explore their interactions.

Later in the day: Archetypal Pattern from Images…

I asked the group to imagine with the use of images, metaphors, story, heroes or heroines, symbols, etc. what was going on within the conversation. This question led to the following images.

It was revealed that a similar pattern was occurring between Bob and Jenny. One of the participants said that she imagined the group to be acting like a family. Mike was Dad, the other Managers were siblings and sibling rivalry was occurring for Dad's attention. The female Manager described her experience in the group as if she was a child trying to gain attention by competing with her older brothers, just as she did in her childhood. This was very revealing. It showed a deep archetypal pattern in the group. When this pattern was named it was explored in depth and the group continued their conversations about how they wanted to work together and their commitment to principles for working together effectively and with kindness and compassion.

To conclude the process…

I asked the group to elicit the original group operating norms which had been unspoken and out of their awareness. They did this and then I asked them to elicit the new norms based on the 'what' and 'how' of their current conversation. This is what they noticed from their lived experience in the moment:

-A change in the energy or emotional state of the group.

-A change in the group's breathing, from people literally holding their breath, to people breathing slowly and deeply.
-A change in the group's appreciation of one another.
-The old norm: the female speaks assertively, the group looks away, eyes up, sighs of 'here we go again', 'we are tired of the female getting all of the attention'.
-The new norm – the female does not feel the need to compete anymore, she knows she will be listened to, so when she does she can do so matter-of-factly. The response – being listened to, empathy being shown by being looked at, having inquiring questions made to understand her issues and her needs.
-An increased emphasis on maintaining genuine, respectful relationships.
-An increased level of tolerance and understanding.
-An increase in people actually liking one another, as they understood one another better, as people had been prepared to disclose information about themselves.
-An increase in smiling.
-The ambience – reflective, inquiring, appreciative, open, honest; encouraging discussion of feelings; expression of vulnerability, tolerance for difference.
-Members said, 'Now I can say what I really think or feel. Now I can be who I am.'
-A greater connection with others in the group and a sense of the inter-dependencies – we are on the same team, we are working together.

This was now not espoused theory; this was the group's theory in action, being lived in the present moment.

Conclusion

I have not been able to elaborate on all of the theoretical models and skills present in this case study. I have described through practice (and reflection on that practice) simple, yet profound practices based on being mindful from Buddhism and from action learning methods from the West. Increasing our awareness of the dimensions of mind, body, and spirit through being aware of the present moment; allowing ourselves to breathe deeply; and doing so with kindness, compassion and a smile, has the potential to change our sense of being so that we can 'be' the change we desire in the world.

Part 3

Processes

Part 3

Processes

Pam Swepson

Action research and action learning can often be used as frameworks for holding together a collection of methods, in a logical way, to research and improve a situation. The authors in this section present a number of important and helpful methods that may fit the action research framework for the problem you are researching to improve.

They are all methods that involve systematic and critical reflection. For me, this is the element most central to action research and action learning, but most difficult to achieve without the sort of systematic process that these authors offer.

David Tripp describes the process of critical incident reflection to improve a professional's practice. On the surface, the professional achieved a successful outcome in a particular problem situation. However, by reflecting on that incident from different angles she was able to consider a range of alternative actions for that and similar situations in the future.

Stephanie Chee carefully documents and reflects on the crucial issue of entry and contracting that is necessary for the success of any research into a social situation. The amount of care that Chee took in a situation that was not immediately open to action research is a model for all researchers.

Victor Friedman and Israel Sykes describe a process of reflecting on reflection-in-action through a process of dialogue between an exceptional social service professional and her interlocutor. Their joint process made her tacit reflections-in-action explicit enough to form a general theory for her staff.

Anne Noble and Deborah Jones open up the debate about what counts as a knowledge or research outcome. They describe a process whereby a group of workers select and arrange a series of photos to reflect the place of their work in their community. The photos do not just illustrate their work – they give meaning to that work and change how they and others see it.

Bill Harris and Bob Williams give us not only some theories behind successful learning logs, but also the opportunity to try out those theories through carefully structured processes as we read their chapter. I learned a lot about myself *and* learning logs!

The detailed descriptions of these powerful processes for reflection are real tools for any action researcher.

Bob
Williams &
Bill Harris

An Experiment: Plan, Act, Observe, Reflect, Plan, Act...

Plan

Please reach for a piece of paper. Anything will do – the back of an envelope, the back of the train ticket you purchased before reading this chapter this morning, your boarding card. If you have an electronic notepad, that will do fine. There's some space on this page too. Now see if you can get hold of something to write with.

Please now write some notes about what you hope to get out of this chapter.

What are the reasons for reading it, how do you intend to use the material? Where do you intend to read this chapter?

When do you intend to read it? How do you intend to read this chapter – all in one go or a bit at a time? Are you going to read the first couple of paragraphs and skip to the conclusion before you decide whether to read the rest?

You may want to jot things down immediately, or you may want to think about things for a minute or so. You may want to close the book and come back to this at another time. That's fine.

When you have finished the task, please turn the page.

Act

So what did you do? What else did you do? How did you do it? When did you do it? What did it feel like? Did you talk to anyone about it?

What did you not do? How did that feel?

Observe

What else happened whilst you were (or were not) doing this? What didn't happen? What else were other people doing or not doing? Describe your physical, and emotional environment? What other demands were there on your time and energy? How hard was the task? How relevant was the task?

Reflect

Compare what you were asked to do, and what you actually did. How can you explain the similarities and differences? What does that say about the way you like to work on a task?

Plan

Now rewrite the instructions at the beginning of the chapter. Only this time write them based on your answers to the previous paragraph.

…

We have just put you through an action learning cycle. Admittedly it wasn't a very large task, and didn't involve much physical action, but still there was plenty of potential for learning.

You'll probably have noticed that the 'reflection' part was actually quite short compared to the other parts of the task. This may seem odd in a chapter dedicated to learning processes, so why do you think we did this?

You'll have noticed that we also asked you to write things down. You may have done that or done the entire exercise in your mind. You may have decided that you are far too rushed today, skipped the exercise and not done anything at all. Consider for a moment our reasons for asking you to document the process and what your response may say about how you best engage in reflective processes.

Notice how we also distinguished between your actions, and what you also observed happening. For instance, we asked you to describe certain things in your environment. To what extent did you use that data in your reflections?

Notice too how we started your reflective process by posing questions. What was distinctive about those questions?

…

This chapter is about the use of learning logs based on the above 'action learning' cycle. It is written as a conversation between you and the two authors – Bill and Bob. Although we don't always acknowledge who is 'speaking', in general Bill describes the use of the logs and Bob reflects on that use.

In the first half of the chapter we describe a particular learning log that the two authors developed and use. We then explore some of the thinking that went into its development, with some more detailed examples from the log to give you a better feel for it.

In the second half of the chapter we look at the theory and practice of getting the most out of learning logs. We first look at Bill, Bob's and others' experiences. After that, we explore some of the research we think helps to explain what we observed from our own practice. We point out that the trick to using learning logs successfully is often working out when *not* to use them.

An Introduction to a Structured Approach

Why structure reflection? Why include all the other stuff on action, planning and observation?

While in the above exercise we made the valid point that action learning comprises both learning (reflection) *and* action, it does seem that most managers have mastered action but struggle more with effective reflection. (That's not to say that they don't also struggle with effective action; if they didn't, there would be no need for action learning.) Some try to start with a blank notebook or sheet of paper, but, after a long, busy day, it's really quite hard to stop and think deeply about what has occurred and what it all means.

Some find learning sets useful. These are groups of people who meet to ask each other questions about what they experienced, how they interpret their experiences, and what they intend to change in their next cycle of action learning. They provide an independent view and a bit of calm to ask the questions that are obvious to all but those personally engaged. They also come at a cost: you need to find people who want to meet, who have the time to meet, who have the insight to ask good questions, and whom you trust.

What if you can't find or form a learning set because of a lack of people or because of the scheduling inconvenience, but you still want the benefit of such external questioning to help you learn and improve? Bob, based on work by Shankar Sankaran, who was then a director of a Japanese electronics company in Singapore, developed a one-page learning log form that had standard questions a learning set team might ask. Bill added to it, and together they turned it into a learning log package. While you can use individual pieces or tailor it to your needs, it's designed to be used as a system.

The log includes eight individual forms, some trivial, some key:

- -Cover – simple cover sheet, if you want to use this as a book
- -Goal form – a form on which to set forth your goals
- -ELT form – elements of a Learning Theory: a personal user's manual, a form to document lessons you learn
- -Project_sheet – a simple form to organise 'to do' items by project over a longer time horizon
- -Todo – a blank sheet of paper to organise daily 'to do' lists
- -Reflections – a form to record intent, actions, observations, reflections, and future plans
- -Timelog – a rather different sort of way to look at how you invest your time
- -Analysis – a blank sheet of paper for conducting analyses

All are word processing documents, except Timelog, which is a spreadsheet. All but the Cover, Project_sheet, Todo, and Analysis can be found in the appendix to this chapter.

While you may use these forms as you will, Bill has found it handy to carry the Reflections and Timelog forms with him. Unfortunately, that led to a rather complicated routine of carrying those forms plus a daily planning guide and other work materials. By assembling all of these forms into a single monthly book that included the functions of daily planning guide and action learning log, he found it easier to integrate work and learning. http://facilitatedsystems.com/llogs.html contains a ReadMe file that describes one way to assemble that book, as well as all of the individual forms.

The Advantages of Documenting the Process

Why should you go to all the bother of filling in Bill's forms? Why not just sit and think about things?

There's nothing wrong with sitting and thinking. However we believe the process of permanently recording the cycle in some way or other has three main advantages.

Advantage One

It places past and present on an equal footing. Writing is an effective way of viewing the past as clearly as the present.

One of the most common ways we have used learning logs is as part of a periodic reporting system. You write what you plan to do at the beginning of this period, and fill in the 'action' and 'observations' either at the end of the period, or whilst it is actually happening. At the end of the reflection process you write the planned action for the next period

– thus completing the cycle. Recording things in real time, rather than as a recollection, allows you to:

- -Compare what seemed important at the time with what actually was important later
- -Avoid inaccurate memories – especially the sequence in which things happened, or what things were happening in parallel.

Advantage Two

One of the major platforms of the action research process is that action is informed not only by 'research' but by research *and* reflection based on accurate, valid and relevant data. Documentation provides a means of assessing at any stage the accuracy, validity and relevance of the data used in reflection, planning and action.

Peter Drucker (1999) looked at learning from one's own experience in 'Managing Oneself'. He focuses on *feedback analysis* as a tool for understanding one's strengths:

- -Write down what you expect will come of key decisions or actions you take.
- -Wait nine or 12 months, and then compare the actual results with your recorded expectations.

Drucker claims that two or three years are sufficient to see patterns in one's work. We'd probably shorten that period considerably. On the other hand, there are very good reasons for looking at long-term cycles as well as shorter term ones.

He also encourages his readers to observe how they best learn: do we prefer assimilating new information by reading or by listening? Do we learn by reading, by taking notes, by talking, or by writing?

Advantage Three

The last part of this chapter looks at research that explores what prevents effective reflection and use of learning logs. The overall busy-ness of business and our lives is acknowledged as a major factor. A major benefit of the logging approach is that it slows you down. Many argue that reflection needs its own special time – yet the social pressure on us to 'do' something rather than sit 'thinking' is very high. So the act of writing is a socially acceptable means of doing that buys the space to allow us to think without causing too many comments around the water cooler. Indeed Bob tested the log with a group of senior managers. A substantial number of them admitted that the greatest benefit of the log was not insights from the specific questions it posed, but the mere fact that they had to put all the urgent stuff aside for ten minutes or so and just think in a fairly focused way.

Using the core forms: Reflections and Timelog

Back to Bill's set of logs. Which are the critical ones?

Without a doubt, the Reflection Sheet and the Timelog are the two most frequently used forms in the set, so it makes sense to use them well. Let's start with Reflections.

Reflection sheets

(see page 115)

Pick a time period of interest. Perhaps you have a daily routine, and you'd like to make your learning cycles daily ones. Perhaps weekly is more natural for your work, or perhaps you have short projects that vary in length. Whatever the case, we encourage you to start with a time horizon between a day and one or perhaps two weeks.

Start by writing down what you plan to accomplish in the first Plan section. This is roughly akin to calling your shot before you make it in billiards, and it gives you a benchmark against which to compare your results.

As you go through the action part of your cycle (a day, a week, or a short project), write down what you did under the Act section. Don't include every detail, but get the major items. Continue by documenting the results of your actions in the Observe section, and include other pertinent happenings you observed.

Now comes the serious and obviously harder work: answering the questions in the Reflect section. You may not want to answer them all, but look for those that seem to lead you towards insight.

Bill has found a few heuristics that seem to help this go better. First, exercise temporal and especially spatial separation. That is, find a quiet spot *away* from your normal work world to engage in this reflection. Bill has often found it handy to stop somewhere between home and work to do this, either before or after the normal workday.

Second, write observations down as they happen; it's too easy to forget key details after even a few hours. One of the great effects of a written journal is that it gives all recorded events, both recent and long past, equal prominence. Memory tends to exaggerate the importance of the more recent.

Third, don't commit to showing this to anyone else. To learn, you need to be as honest as you can with yourself. If you know you're going to show it to a friend, colleague, or (especially) manager, you may be tempted to engage in a bit of personal public relations at the expense of learning.

Of course, you can still show selected passages to others. Indeed towards the end of this chapter we highlight research that shows the benefits of this. However, the choice should be under your control.

Fourth, combine this closed-loop action learning cycle with fresh ideas from outside. That may be from reading, or it could come from listening to others. Bill has found that even unrelated books can spark breakthrough insights when combined with an intense action learning effort under the guidance of these learning logs.

Finally, before the new action period starts, plan and document what you intend to do in the second Plan section. Then enter it in the first Plan section of a new Reflections form.

Time logs

(See page 119)

While it sounds like a time log you may have been encouraged to use in the past, the Timelog form is organised differently. If you follow the instructions in the spreadsheet and customise the form properly, you'll end up with a daily form on which to track how you allocate emphasis to activities and what causes you trouble (what you most need to improve at).

The form picks a random time each hour at which to log your activity. That reduces inadvertent bias you might get, and it means you only have eight items to record in an eight-hour workday.

Once you've logged the activity, allocate it to one of the project codes you've created when you customised the form. At the end of the day, you can calculate the percentage of time you've spent that day on each project. Over a week or month, you should find that you invest your time in ways that reflect your goals. If you're spending much of your time doing things that rank low in your list of goals, that's an indicator to explore your approach to work more deeply.

You should also allocate each sample time's activity to one of six categories:

- -Client-focused, delivering
- -Client-focused, preparing
- -Client-focused, thinking
- -Company focused
- -Self-focused
- -Goofing off (We said you shouldn't promise to show this to your manager).

By calculating and watching how you allocated your time to these different categories, you may learn something about how to be more effective. Note that it's not necessarily bad to catch yourself goofing off occasionally, and it is good to be honest with yourself about it.

Finally, check whether you were cruising, struggling, or stuck at each of the sampled times. At the end of the day, note what you were doing when you were struggling or stuck. If you notice the same types of events cropping up, you may have identified an opportunity to change the way you work or to seek additional focused learning.

Informed Insight: The Structure of the Logs

So far we have told you about the benefits of logs, and given you an idea of what the ones we use look like. This section explains the background to their structure. In particular, why we have included particular sections and posed certain questions.

The distinction between 'action' and 'observation'

You don't know what data might be relevant to your reflection until you start reflecting. So the structure of the log encourages you to collect as wide a range of data as feasible before the reflection process starts. The trouble is that this could end up with a mass of data so large, you can't see the wood for the trees. So the structure of the logs helps you collect enough of the right kind of data.

We find it useful to distinguish between your acts and observations that relate to those acts.

With words like 'act' there is a temptation to consider only things that actually happened, when in fact what didn't happen might be just as relevant. You might focus on 'you' in the act itself rather than consider the possible consequences of that act, or things that may have influenced those consequences. If you are a person who tends to focus on a literal sequence of events ('I did this, so I look here for the result'), separating 'act' from 'observation' encourages you to look out into the wider environment. If you are a person who tends to focus on the more physical side of things, the separating 'act' from 'observation' reminds you that you need to consider some of the less tangible issues such as your feelings.

Learning through patterns and puzzles

You'll notice that our section of the logs dealing with reflection didn't ask general questions like 'well what do you think?' or 'what did you learn?'. We guided and structured your thinking process. We posed specific questions and a carefully chosen range of them.

The purpose of the logs is to help you learn. We are trying to avoid you confusing 'learning' with 'error correction'. Error correction is usually concerned with responding to symptoms rather than seeking to comprehend underlying causes. Responding to the symptoms can lead to inappropriate action. For instance, Bob was recently working with an organisation whose clients were receiving what was generally perceived as inexpert service from its staff. The response had been to put staff through extensive training programs. The trouble was matters got worse not better. On closer inspection it was clear that management had responded to the symptom, rather than understanding the deeper issues that went to the heart of how the organisation operated. The reality was that workloads were high, and skilled staff felt frustrated that they could not use their skills adequately with their clients. So they resigned. New staff were hired, who initially didn't have the skills to do the job and so provided a poor service. Once they were trained, they felt frustrated that they could not apply those skills, so they left. And so the noose progressively tightened around the organisation.

Many learning theorists believe that learning (rather than error correction) happens in two ways: patterning – seeking out similar events in our experience and modifying that knowledge to fit the current situation; and puzzling – resolving conflicting or contradictory or confusing messages.

That is why you will find in many 'action learning' text books the following set of 'reflection' questions:[1]

-What happened?
-How is it similar or different from other experiences?
-Why is any difference significant?
-How can you explain the difference?
-How can you use that understanding?

If you take another look at our reflection questions, you'll notice that we have expanded on this basic structure, to explore both patterns and puzzles. In fact, in practice, Bob in particular plays around a lot with this part of the reflection sheet; adding and subtracting questions depending the circumstances, but always focussing on patterns and puzzles. Feel free to do that too – and reflect on it too.

Structured conversations

The log's structure establishes a conversation with yourself.

Wutzdorff and Hutchings (1988) identify four elements that should be included in any learning log to develop meaning:

-Questions raised
-Personal insights
-Challenges
-Environmental factors.

But what kind of conversation is appropriate? There are three possibilities.

-A conversation with yourself
-A conversation with another person such as a mentor
-A conversation with a group.

Siebert and Daudelin (1999) undertook an experiment to explore whether there was a difference between reflection in an unfacilitated group setting, a mentor (pair) setting and individual setting. They found that the most learning took place in the mentor setting, the least in the unfacilitated group setting and individual reflection somewhere in between the two. However, all reported more learning than those in a control group not subjected to any 'reflection' questions. Our own conclusion from this work is that a mentor can really impose a structure for the learning process, individuals can pick and choose a bit – dodge the difficult questions. Unfacilitated group discussions can go all over the place, and the 'control' group had essentially no guidance at all. Incidentally that is also why we recommend documenting your response. It is a form of self facilitation that makes it very obvious which questions you have avoiding answering, maybe for a good reason, but maybe not.

Finally, structured reflection can help you move on towards the next stage – planning your next set of actions. Setting some goals. For this we return to Bill's set of logs.

Goals and ELTform : Using the Secondary Forms

While the Reflections and Timelog forms seem central, they won't help unless you can evaluate them in light of some standard. One clear standard is your purpose, your goals in life. The Goals form is designed to capture your goals. We encourage you to fill out a few of those and keep some blank forms handy; you may discover you have (or develop) other goals as you go.

In many ways, ELTform is *the* central form, the Elements of your personal Learning Theory. Goals are usually long-term in nature, and Reflections and Timelog are short-term. ELTform is created out of the synergy of those. As you begin to understand something important about yourself, document it on a clean ELTform. In good action learning style, seek ways to disconfirm what you've written down to increase the rigour of your claims. As you progress, your set of ELTforms becomes a very personal user's manual, describing how you've learned to be more effective in the world in the ways you've chosen to go.

Psychologists Dietrich Dörner and Harald Schaub (1994) have studied why people make mistakes in the work they do. They often see six common errors:

- -a failure to elaborate consistent (or any) goals
- -a failure to collect the appropriate information and creating hypotheses
- -predicting future patterns incorrectly from past patterns
- -disregarding side-effects and long-term effects in planning
- -failing to monitor the effects of one's actions, and
- -failing to reflect on one's effectiveness.

The learning logs as structured here go a long way towards addressing their concerns. They focus on goal elaboration, collecting data, looking at side effects, monitoring results of actions, and reflecting on effectiveness.

Finishing off the Package

To make these four major forms into a useful book that can serve as your organiser, try the Todo to document what you chose to do today.

Use Project_sheet to organise activities at a higher level of aggregation over a longer time horizon. Organise your work into projects, and write the name of each project at the top of one of the mini-tables. Write specific tasks and their due dates in the appropriate tables. Use these tables to help fill out Todo forms, and check off tasks as they're done.

It's handy to have blank paper handy to carry out analyses on the observations you've made. For example, you may want a place to carry out a statistical analysis of a series of your Timelog forms, or you may want to analyse the answers you've given to a particular question in a series of Reflections forms. The Analysis form provides a convenient spot.

In Practice

In practice – Bill's experience

Bob created the Reflections sheet first, based on Shankar Sankaran's original idea. Bill came across the Reflection sheet and decided to try it in an experimental, on-line learning set. As luck would have it, his was the first issue to be addressed by the learning set, so he began paying close attention to his actions, recording them on the sheet, and typing what seemed like pertinent data into email.

After a day or two, Jack Whitehead of the University of Bath wrote back that he couldn't evaluate any of this without knowing what Bill's goals were. Out of that very reasonable request came the creation of the Goals sheet. With the two forms, Bill was able to make good progress in addressing his immediate issue.

At some point, Bill's manager asked him to try a time log. After some initial frustration ('Was he giving me a useful tip, or was he really trying to say he thinks I'm not very efficient?') Bill began recording how he spent his time.

The initial effort involved recording when he started and stopped each task. That took so much time in his interrupt-driven environment that the act of recording both changed what he did and kept him from making effective progress. He experimented with other varieties and solicited inputs from others. Out of that, he developed a time log that combined several useful attributes:

-It didn't require much time from a busy day, and it didn't interfere with work getting done.

-It organised data in useful ways, almost as it was being collected.

-It enabled an easy comparison of the use of time with a person's goals.
-It helped identify types of tasks that cried out for improvement.

He kept using these forms and added others as he found gaps in what he was learning. By the time he was finished, he had developed a corollary to Socrates' claim that an unexamined life isn't worth living: 'An examined life is an exhausted life' (but indeed very worthwhile). That has led to the idea of pacing in the use of these learning logs. Bill finds it useful to use them for a while and then to take a temporary holiday from their use to refresh himself for a new cycle of learning.

In practice – Bob's experience

Bob has tended to restrict his attention to the original 'Reflection Sheet'. He has used this sheet in a wide variety of settings for a wide range of purposes.

The most common use has been as a project management tool – interestingly, with the most mixed success. Perhaps the most successful was in a contract that required him to prepare a monthly report to his client. Both he and his client filled out this form separately, exchanged them and then discussed the similarities and differences to gain insights into the somewhat tricky project. Much less successful was an attempt to use it with fellow researchers on two quite long-term projects. In each project, one of the researchers reacted strongly against the form – they just didn't see the point and felt that they were learning nothing from them. They just wrote the answers down on the form and didn't really reflect on what they had written. Over time the forms fell into disuse.

He has also used it to debrief one- or two-day workshops, and it seems the critical issue here is to allow time for participants to discuss their learning and observations.

A class of senior managers on a professional training course proved particularly interesting. About half of the 30 managers became very frustrated with the form and got relatively little out of it. The remainder had two reactions. One was that it made them stop for ten minutes or so and consciously 'think' rather than 'do'. Just this act gave them opportunities to develop insights, irrespective of the particular questions in the form. The second reaction was from those who focused on a particular issue (or collegial relationship) that troubled them. These seemed to benefit most. Indeed, one manager circulated the form to colleagues engaged in a particular issue, and they discovered two important things – they had very different perspectives on the issue, but had been operating on the assumption that everyone shared the same perspective. They realised that the problem was not the 'issue' itself, but how they were handling the issue.

How to Make the Best of the Learning Logs and How to Avoid Making Them a Worthless Chore

Looking back at this chapter, and the last section on our own experiences with the learning logs, you may well be starting to develop some views on their usefulness to you. You may be thinking that all these forms make the whole idea of learning logs seem rather bureaucratic and daunting. On the other hand, it is clear that we – and others – have used versions of these logs with considerable success.

It's true that some people feel they really benefit from these logs, whilst others find them quite difficult and painful. Some find them useful at certain times and at other times not useful at all.

Over the past couple of years we have been exploring why this might be so, and what helps and hinders the use of these logs. We have sought feedback from the many people who have used them, plus read what the research says about reflection. We've concluded that there are three overarching factors that affect their success: you, your task and your environment.

You

Let's consider you first. Is there something about the way you think or operate that means that learning logs are easy for you?

There is a vast literature on personal styles of working and thinking. However, for the purposes of this chapter it is probably enough to acknowledge that some people find the kind of structured 'reflection' described here easier than others. Some of you will reflect almost intuitively as you work and find the structure constraining. Others find a blank sheet of paper intimidating, and welcome the idea of responding to a set of questions.

Some find the act of writing quite frustrating. You might feel the documenting process slows you down – which of course (as we said earlier) could be a good thing. For instance, although Bob devised the 'reflection' sheet, he finds writing it down very hard work, and some parts of it more difficult than others (especially the 'act' which he finds really boring since he has already done it). However, ask Bob to talk his way through the list (getting someone else to write it down) and there's little stopping him.

Others of you might like the *idea* of a structured reflection process, but will need to play around with it until it suits you. You might well prefer to stick to the structure we have given you, but may be more interested in starting the task at say the 'action' stage rather than the 'plan' stage.

Your task

We've concluded that the task you are reflecting on matters a great deal. Reflection tools seem to work better with particular kinds of tasks – and learning logs are no exception.

For instance, the organisational theorist Mihaly Csikszentmihalyi (2001) describes a range of emotional responses to tasks. They relate to the degree of challenge in the task and the degree of skill that you need to undertake the task.

High challenge, high skill = flow
High challenge, moderate skill = arousal
High challenge, low skill = anxiety
Moderate challenge, moderate skill = control
Moderate challenge, low skill = worry
Low challenge, high skill = relaxation
Low challenge, moderate skill = boredom
Low challenge, low skill = apathy

He observes that learning takes place predominantly when we are in a state of 'arousal'. In other words the task is challenging, but not completely beyond your current capabilities.

This closely matches Siebert and Daudelin's (1999) observation that reflection seems to be most profound when the task is:

- challenging – tough but not too tough
- a bit of a puzzle with real purpose for resolving it
- slightly fuzzy.

We conclude that the best time to use these logs is under these conditions. In other conditions, they may actually promote administrative compliance – just going through the motions. If you go through the motions then it is likely you will learn little – and thus find the logs a chore. Once you find them a chore, you may choose not to use them when they can actually be very helpful. That's probably why Bill alternates between periods of use and periods of non-use of the forms.

Your environment

John Edwards (2001) has studied the Australian organisational scene for many years. His view is that most Australian workplaces regard reflection and learning as:

- a luxury which 'gets in the way of work'
- something to be done in your own time and not the firm's
- not relevant because the firm is in perpetual chaos.

Furthermore in Australian organisations:

- -people aren't permitted to admit ignorance
- -people are pressurised into providing quick fixes
- -people are not confident about being reflective
- -there is no place for formalised learning processes (as distinct from technical training)
- -reflection tends to be individualised and occur off the work site
- -the business must keep running at all costs.

Consider now Siebert and Daudelin's (1999) claim about what promotes reflection and learning in organisations:

- -Autonomy and freedom to move within the task
- -Feedback from others about the task
- -Access to other people
- -Support from other people
- -Stimulation from other people
- -Pressure to deliver.
- -Clear focus.

So what?

If these observations are true – and they certainly coincide with our own experiences – then the best time to use these logs is when there a project of some importance over which you have some degree of authority, which has some degree of urgency and is puzzling enough to push you intellectually, and which also interests others with whom you can talk.

In Closing

Learning logs are just tools. They are means to ends, not ends in themselves. If they start becoming ends in themselves, then the point has been lost. This chapter has, hopefully, allowed you to consider whether you wish to use this tool and hinted at some of the ways in which the tool may be useful to you. It's also provided you with some thoughts about when the tool might be the right tool in the wrong circumstances, or completely the wrong tool. However, one of the delights about promoting this tool is that people are forever finding new ways of using the tool itself or the ideas that underpin it. Indeed, that's how we developed it in the first place.

Over to you. And please let us know how it goes.

Notes

1. We are indebted to Bob Dick for these insights, although he warns us that he wouldn't bet his salary on them.

Bibliography

Csikszentmihalyi, M (2001) 'Happiness in the Third Millennium'. Paper presented at the Ninth International Conference on Thinking, Auckland, New Zealand

Dörner, D & Schaub, H (1994) 'Errors in planning and decision making and the nature of human information processing' in *Applied Psychology: An International review.* Special issue on Human Error. pp433–453

Drucker, P (1999) 'Managing oneself' in *Harvard Business Review.* Mar-Apr pp65–74

Edwards, J (2001) 'The Things We Steal From Children'. Paper presented at the Ninth International Conference on Thinking, Auckland, New Zealand

Seibert, KW & Daudelin, MW (1999) *The Role of Reflection in Managerial Learning Connecticut.* London: Quorum Westport

Wutzdorf, A & Hutchins, P (1988) *Knowing and Doing: Learning through experience.* New Directions for Teaching and Learning Series No 35. San Francisco: Jossey Bass.

Appendix

The Forms

Elements of a Learning Theory: Goals, Values and Aspirations

Period: from to

What do I want to achieve?

Why is it important to me?

What am I willing to give up to attain this?

Reflection Sheet

Period: from to

Plan
What was planned to be done during this period (transferred from previous report)?

Act
What parts of the plan were done during this period?
1.
2.
3.
What was done in addition to the plan?
1.
2.
3.

Observe
What happened as a result of these actions?
What other relevant things happened (these could be environmental)?
How did you feel; how did you react?

Reflect

During the period covered by this report note down and reflect on:

1.The most interesting issue...

2. What worked well (eg. significant achievements)...

3. What did not work well...

4. The most puzzling or confusing issue...

5. The most unexpected issue...

6. Any risks and threats to the project...

7. Any opportunities for the project...

8. Any implications for the principles and purpose underpinning the project...

9. Differences between the plan and the action...

10. What was noticed but not addressed? Why? Would addressing that have improved the outcome?

11. Any other comments or observations...

Plan

In the light of each of the above comments, what should be done during the next phase of the project?
(Note: This gets 'pasted' into the Plan section of the next period.)

1.

2.

3.

Elements of a Learning Theory

Period: from to

What am I learning about the relation between my goals and values and my actions?

Upon what basis do I make this claim?

How can I seek to disconfirm this hypothesis?

What did I learn from attempting disconfirmation?

Is this learning consistent with my goals and values?

If so, how can I reinforce the learnings?

If not, what should I consider changing?

Time Log

Snapshot Time	Activity Description	Project Code	Category (check 1) Client-focused, delivering	Client-focused, preparing	Client-focused, thinking	Company focused	Self-focused	Goofing Off	State (check 1) Cruising	Struggling	Stuck
8:28											
9:10											
10:40											
11:02											
12:38											
13:33											
14:35											
15:37											
16:17											
17:04											
	Count										
	Percentage										

Project Codes:		# of Entries	% of Time
T1	Task 1		
T1	Task 2		
T3	Task 3		
O	Other		

Summary:

Bill Harris
Everett, Washington, USA

Personal-Professional Development Through Critical Incidents in Action Research

David Tripp
with
Jeannie
Wilson

Critical Incidents in Action Research

Why use critical incidents in action research?

It can be taken as axiomatic to action research that to achieve good outcomes we have to understand our existing practice in order to identify what to improve. To do that we have to systematically examine our normal ways of practising and problematise what we're doing and its implications. The production of critical incidents from entries in self-reported observation journals is an effective way of generating such understandings.

There are a number of different kinds of critical incident because what makes an incident critical is entirely a matter of perception. I therefore categorise critical incidents according to how they are generated (see Appendix), but rather than discuss their, in this chapter I report an actual case that can serve as an example of one way to develop and use a critical incident in action research.

Although the value of a case can be limited by its context, the principles and processes illustrated here are generic, and can be applied to any facilitation of a workplace-based action research approach to professional development and performance improvement.

Exactly how professional development and performance improvement are related is not my concern here, but it is relevant to note that I will show how this kind of critical incident analysis contributes to four different areas of professional practice:

- Use of profession-specific knowledge.
- Theorising practice.
- Improving outcomes.
- Developing personal-professional understanding.

A teaching situation

Although it's a 'typical example' of this kind of analysis, it is most important to note that the context was unusual for this kind of work because Jeannie was taking my unit on action research for professional development, and this case is constructed from some of our correspondence about an assignment in which she was required to develop a starting point for her next action cycle from a critical incident. Rather than simply 'facilitating', I had to ensure that Jeannie performed a pre-specified kind of analysis to a certain level in a set time.

This caused some difficulties, for example, as the editor of an early draft, Pam Swepson (my thanks to Pam for her comments on the draft), wondered why I chose to use a 'transmission' strategy with Jeannie rather than a 'dialogue' strategy, because the former 'seemed to contradict the advice given to Jeannie about her teaching'. The following points about the background may help to clarify this.

First, part of facilitation is indeed transmission – and when I think it helpful, I transmit! Here, Jeannie was paying the university for me to teach her both an improvement process and about teaching, and I think much of my transmission was necessary: Jeannie had very little experience of critical incident analysis or knowledge of educational theory at that point, and an excellent way of facilitating learning about them is to demonstrate their practical value. Situating students' learning in their workplace experiences is an effective way of teaching and learning about practice and the values that inform it, but I would approach facilitating experienced professionals to make significant changes to their established practices quite differently.

Second, although perhaps I did transmit more of my ideas than would be appropriate in most situations, there appears to be more than there was because here I've mainly told the transmission part of our much bigger story: we had phone calls, a meeting at the university, assignments, feedback and an email correspondence over 16 weeks, and I could not also tell that story. Moreover, Jeannie's personal observation journal, my analysis, and our subsequent correspondence, were all written in confidence to each other, not for publication, and in editing them for this context and audience, we think I have made things appear more coherent and teacherly than perhaps they were.

I've thought for some time that there's another paper here about facilitation at a distance: email is a poor substitute for some aspects of the kind of conversation that one has face-to-face, and I'd like to explore how that affects facilitation, in particular how it tends to be one person making several points which the other answers all together. But that's yet another story. No doubt others will tell those stories better than I ever could.

The issue of authorship

I am most grateful to Jeannie for making this account possible, but who benefits, from what work, in what ways, and how much, are always complex issues in collaborative work, and in this case what is fair is that much more fraught by the kinds of asymmetries produced by the student/teacher relationship. On the one hand, this chapter could not have been written without Jeannie's contribution – on the other, her contribution was assignment work that I designed, supervised and edited. How then should we formally recognise authorship of this interdependent whole?

In spite of it being such an important issue in most facilitated action research, there are as yet no generally accepted ethical guidelines for resolving it (Tripp 2000). We discussed four possibilities; we could:

-anonymise Jeannie

-name Jeannie in a footnote

-name David, with Jeannie sharing in the title
-name David and Jeannie as co-authors.

All had advantages and drawbacks: the first had some value as it's ostensibly problems in Jeannie's practice that we expose here; the second had no merit as it literally marginalised Jeannie without protecting her; and the fourth did not recognise the differences in contribution. Although still somewhat arbitrary, we therefore felt that the third, in conjunction with this brief discussion of the problem, was fairest. It also enabled me to clearly distinguish between us – myself as author and Jeannie as subject.

Jeannie's Critical Incident Report

Background

At the time of this incident, Jeannie was working in the Corporate Banking sector and teaching SRE on a voluntary basis in schools. As she wrote in her journal, both she and the children enjoy these lessons: 'I always include the activities that the students enjoy the most in my lessons, and each week when I walk into the room I get an enthusiastic greeting, so I know that the majority of students enjoy seeing me.'

One of the reasons that I chose this incident is because it is a good example of a particular event that is but one instance of an on-going trend. Jeannie had already written in her journal about her concerns over Evan's problem behaviour, but had done so in general terms, and one use of critical incidents is to have a specific incident to analyse in a detailed diagnostic fashion in order to better understand the general pattern. The following is an edited version of her first draft.

Extract from Jeannie's observation journal

As I conducted this Year 4 lesson I could see the furrow on Evan's brow as he focused on my lesson about the importance of resolving problems with other people peacefully. I had introduced heroes including Whina Cooper and Sir Edward Dunlop, and Biblical heroes including Queen Esther and St Paul.

I then asked my students to work in pairs, using the stories of these people to develop a strategy that they would use to resolve problems with each other peacefully. They were to illustrate their ideas by drawing a picture, or writing their own story, poem or play.

Whilst Evan had concentrated on what was being taught, he did not participate at all in this activity, but managed to disrupt his partner and the pair working opposite him. Nothing I said encouraged them to settle down and start the activity. By the end of the class the only thing that these two pairs had achieved was to write their names on the sheet of paper I had provided.

I felt disappointed with their lack of effort, but I believed that they would learn their lesson when I publicly distributed the stars that I use for positive reinforcement to encourage students who work conscientiously.

Analysis

I reflected upon whether this incident arose because of my teaching style. Perhaps my lesson plan was not flexible enough. Whilst I have a solid theological foundation and I am an accredited as an SRE Teacher, I am not a fully qualified teacher. In order to build my confidence I prepare for each class as if I were preparing for a lead role in a Broadway production, by rehearsing what I want to say and memorising the sequence of topics that I want to cover. Also, being conscious of avoiding an overload of theological and moral issues, I am careful to balance the content of each lesson in order to meet what I feel are the students' needs.

Time is another problem. I only have half an hour each week in which to cover the recommended SRE lesson plan. Whilst the curriculum is a useful guide for managing each lesson, sometimes I feel that there is insufficient time allowed to cover the theoretical content and to complete the activities, especially with younger children, so I don't allow students to deviate much from the points I wish to make.

Returning to Evan, I can see him churning over the things that I teach and I am sure that he has a million questions that he wants to ask but never does. Could the reason be that he's not given the opportunity? I do not exactly ask the children if they have any questions, I just assume that they will ask if they do. On further reflection I realise that it's always the same children who do ask the questions. Perhaps these students feel more comfortable about asking. Perhaps they are also encouraged at home to freely question what they do not understand more than Evan. Perhaps Evan feels too intimidated by the teacher-student relationship. Maybe I am afraid to open myself up to the firing line of 30 inquisitive minds. Perhaps I am not as sensitive as I think I am in meeting the needs of students like Evan. Do I know what their needs really are?

Reflecting upon this incident makes me suspect that I am not satisfying Evan's needs by not directly inviting him to voice his opinions and ask any questions. If Evan has doubts about what he has learnt it's no wonder that I cannot encourage him to participate in activities that he may feel have no value to him. Furthermore, he would disrupt the surrounding students (so he would not be alone in producing no work).

All this means that my teaching style needs to change. My lesson plan must include time for students to ask questions about things important to them.

Jeannie's Action Cycle

Plan

My critical friend helped me to realise that I should not be so worried about getting 'it' right. I am not in a Broadway show. If I run out of time and do not complete my lesson plan then I shouldn't worry. It is the quality of learning that takes place that is important, not the quantity. My focus should be more on trying to identify and satisfy each of my students' needs and curiosity, and less on ensuring I do cover what I had planned for each half-hour lesson.

Therefore I will:

- -periodically ask the students if they have any questions during each lesson
- -invite them to discuss issues that I may not have realised were important to them
- -allow time to delve into the issues that a student may have at the time
- -try to involve the rest of the class (if I feel it is appropriate) so I do not lose their attention while I am dealing with one student.

Some anticipated outcomes will be:

- -That this change in technique could result in my lesson plan being tossed out the window.
- -There is an improvement in the number of different children who participate in the class discussions.
- -There is an increased level of enthusiasm with which the students complete the set activities, especially if I am successful in engaging Evan in discussion.

Description of implementation

My action plan was implemented during a lesson about Jesus' triumphant entrance into Jerusalem. To ground this biblical passage with a life-situation I encouraged the students to think about why the spectators would have been so excited about seeing Jesus, and to think about when they were excited about seeing someone very special to them.

Near the end of this segment I asked the class: 'Do you have any questions?' I was thrilled to see Evan's hand go straight up, but I was shocked with what he wanted to know. He asked: 'What is the Second Coming?' I had no idea where that came from other than from discussions with friends or family. 'Well the first time Jesus came to Earth is known as the First Coming and we read all about his activities in the Bible,' I said, waving my Good News Bible in the air. 'Christians believe that he will come again and this is what is known as the Second Coming, but we don't know when to expect that and we have been waiting for 2000 years so far.'

Evan responded to this by saying that he doesn't expect it ever will happen if it hasn't happened already, and besides, he didn't think that what was written in the Bible was true.

I couldn't pass up this opportunity to explore these issues further with the class, so I plunged the students into a discussion about unexpected events and why some people did believe that what was written in the Bible is true.

Before resuming with my lesson plan I returned to Evan to ask if he had any further questions. He seemed content with our discussion and because of the way he enthusiastically engaged in the set activity, I believe his curiosity had been satisfied for the time being.

Reflection

I certainly felt pleased with the way I managed to handle this deviation to my lesson plan. I would never have been able to catch a glimpse of what was being churned around in Evan's mind if I hadn't asked if anyone had any questions. SRE teachers are aware that the majority of children in their classes do not come from a religious background, but whilst it is their choice to join the class, an assumption should not be made that they will believe in what is being taught. In the future I will encourage the students to voice any disagreement with what I have taught in the hope that I will help them to develop their critical thinking; and, with careful management, I would hope that this strategy would also help to develop a healthy respect for other people's opinions.

David's Feedback on Jeannie's Critical Incident

This was obviously a very useful and piece of work in which you took all the expected action inquiry steps, and thereby achieved a successful practical outcome. But there was (as always!) also scope for improving your critical incident analysis.

Critique several aspects first

There are usually several significant issues in any one incident, and it's a good idea to identify more than one of these. I've suggested that one way to render an incident 'critical' is to ask: 'What is this incident critical of?' (Tripp 1996). That question does lie behind your critique of not allowing time for questions, and you could use it to identify other things to consider. Having done that, you can then choose what's most important to improve through your action cycles.

For instance, you mention not getting to know any of the children at all well (because you only see them for half an hour a week), and we could ask what that is critical of (translation: let me make some more trouble for you!). It could be taken as critical of your not doing enough about getting to know them well enough to teach them most effectively. It's important, for instance, to know whether this boy's behaviour is any different in your class to other teachers'. In general, nothing will change until you have formed a 'working relationship' with the child, but it's difficult for you to plan ways of improving that until you know whether you're trying to deal with a well-established and chronic habit, or special treatment meted out to you, because it'll affect how you go about it.

Another point that the incident could be seen to be critical of is your faith and reliance on stars (which is implicit in what you write, but not consciously dealt with). I think it would be good to consider the value and ideology of that method of keeping control and the children on task. From your description I very much doubt that not receiving a star would affect Evan's behaviour much at all, because he's already publicly displaying the kind of behaviour that will ensure he doesn't get one. I also think that those who are pleased to receive a star are not working for it primarily, but for you and their interest in the work. And are you happy to be using an 'other esteem' and what could be a shaming process anyway? If so, in what ways is it a 'good' process? If not, what's led you to (a) be using it, and (b) fail to critique it thus far?

Develop your analysis further

Turning now to the issue that you did deal with, it may help to summarise it first.

Asking: why? (as you did in steps 2 and 3) is a good start to developing a critical incident; your answers enabled you to see what to do in step 4;

	Step	**Result**
1	Identify an event that was critical for you.	Evan did not do the activity, and also prevented three other students from doing it.
2	Analyse the incident to diagnose why this happened.	Evan was upset because he wasn t getting answers to questions he had about what you were teaching.
3	Reflect on your practices to recognise your role in the problem.	You weren t giving Evan sufficient opportunity to ask his questions.
4	Plan a changed strategy to improve the situation	You could provide specific opportunities for questions from the children.
5	Implement and monitor the plan to improve your usual strategy.	Success! Evan took the opportunity given, asked a question that was bothering him, and then participated well in the activity.

the action you then took was very effective in terms of improving your practice because you produced a more successful teaching strategy.

Although improved practical strategies are an essential and very valuable outcome, the idea of critical incidents is also to develop yourself professionally in other equally important ways, particularly using professional knowledge to theorise your practice, and also to increase your personal-professional understanding. At present, your analysis is too much of a general reflection to achieve either of those aims.

Theorising the relation between Evan's behaviour and your delivery

You decided that the incident was critical of the fact that you did not allow the children's interests and needs to deflect you from your well-rehearsed plan, and that Evan's disruptive behaviour was one result. Then, with a little help from your critical friend, you brainstormed the best changes to make to improve things. That was great in practical terms, but in addition to designing technically competent action, a professional practitioner has the ability to draw on theory to explain their actions – a professional knows *why* as well as *how* (Tripp 1993).

For example, professional knowledge suggests that sticking too rigidly to a plan not only prevents the children from getting answers to questions that are important to them, it also prevents learning an important life-long learning process – establishing their own learning agenda (Boomer 1982). That specific point can be linked to a more general view: for such reasons, good teaching is a responsive process, more of a dialogue than a transmission, and it has to be consciously and deliberately constructed as such.

The theorisation of action in the general sense of developing knowledge about practice (in contrast to developing practical skills) is also central to professional practice, and to make such connections to other aspects of your practice is to generalise, which is a theorising process.

Returning to the narrower focus of your concern, you considered changing Evan's behaviour in essentially emotional terms (Evan as frustrated questioner), and you could have drawn on conflict resolution theory to provide a more professional explanation of that – ie. that children who are not allowed to express their needs or opinions cannot have them acknowledged or validated by their significant others; that causes strong emotions which severely inhibit learning and tend to lead to dysfunctional behaviours which can easily become established ways of being. Allowing such a cycle is not good professional practice because it is not in the best interests of the child.

It's also important to examine an observation from another theoretical perspective, and a rationale from cognitive psychology would look very similar – that is, that it's difficult to concentrate on any one thing when you've got lots of other things to think about, especially if the things are complex or emotionally laden.

Both of these theories endorse your new strategy, and would thereby give you a strong professional rationale for the change; they also inform what you could do, and strengthen your action with Evan by providing beneficial outcomes for everyone.

Explore your new strategy in relation to your philosophy

Another aspect of theorising practice is to see how a planned change fits with our philosophy. You might hold, for instance, that education is primarily about growth, and learning things is only one aspect of that. General professional knowledge tells us that growth is stimulated by appropriate challenges, and that implies that it's better to teach children how to understand and deal with a problem than it is to remove it. As it stands, your chosen strategy prioritises learning things, however, and doesn't allow for the fact that we have to learn put aside pressing thoughts in order to concentrate on what has to be done now (or else all Monday would be spent de-briefing the week-end!).

Incorporating that apparently contradictory view could further improve your planned strategy by leading you to formulate a second strategy to support the first – that is, that one of the ways to help children to grow in that respect, is to open the issue with them so that they can take some responsibility for dealing with it themselves.

You would need to check the rationale for that: in cognitive terms it would make learning more active for them, and in terms of their growth it would be good for the children to learn to ask their questions openly.

Taken together with the other professional knowledge we drew on earlier, we have now established a sound professional rationale and secure basis for making changes that are most likely to improve your teaching and learning practices. Perhaps it's also worth noting how a 'theoretical' analysis leads to very practical outcomes, proving the fact that *there's nothing so practical as a good theory.*

One other point in concluding this section: you correctly based your plan on your understanding of the situation, and it worked first time! But what if it had failed or caused other problems? In all action research we verify an analysis experimentally by changing what we do and observing the effects, but we need to be reasonably sure that our plan will work. It's a matter of professional judgement just how far to check out our understanding of the situation and any hypotheses behind a plan before implementing it of course, and because it was such a well-tried strategy, I think you were right to move straight into implementation without further verification. So although my further analysis is useful in other ways, it was not a necessary precursor to action in this case.

Personal-professional practice

Critical incident analysis can also develop *personal-professional* practice, namely those aspects of practice that have to do with our understanding of ourselves as professionals. That is a deeper concern than working practical strategies because it involves relating who we are to what we do. I have already touched on this in places (such as in relating your strategy to your philosophy), but not in terms of critiquing your existing practice, and I can make some more trouble for you there. When I looked back at your original analysis, I noticed that you thought that Evan had questions to ask. That came from your interpretation of your observation of his behaviour. That's a very useful hypothesis, but it would have been useful to get more information on it, the best source of which was the child himself. The fact that you didn't ask him pointed to a contradiction between your values and those embedded in your existing practices.

Why not ask the child what's happening with him? You get more information, and another significant benefit is that it involves him in dealing with the problem. Involving everyone concerned is an important first step in dealing with any problem, because if the child (ie. the person most concerned) isn't involved, they can take no active part in, or responsibility for, improving things. And if your solution is something that you do to him, not something he's chosen to do, how can you make him take some responsibility for any failure, or praise him for any improvements?

Working with the child on a behaviour problem is much better than just trying to manipulate the environment so that the child has no choice but to desist the problem behaviour. In terms of growth the latter is exactly the reverse of what we should be doing because it's what makes minor difficulties into major behaviour problems later. Anyway, how can we know how to manipulate the environment effectively if we don't know what the child is thinking, feeling and trying to achieve?

Classroom behaviour is a shared problem, so the teacher's role is to help the child to accept what's a problem for a teacher as their problem also, and the first step in that process is to raise the problem with the child, finding out what's happening with them. But it's only the first step: we all have great difficulty in accepting that if what we're doing is a problem to others it's also our problem; and children certainly don't see their behaviour as shared problems without skilled and appropriate help.

The contradiction here is that you value children as intelligent, thinking, feeling, beings with strong wills and many capabilities, so why treat Evan like a billiard ball here? The answer is that it's an endemic practice in teaching: I've found that nearly all the teachers I've worked with over the past decade have been trying to modify children's behaviours without either using the child as a source of information or involving them as an active participant in the process. Why is that? The problem lies in our experience: first, in terms of our personal histories, it feels normal because that is how we were treated; second, in terms of our current situation, we see the experienced teachers we are learning from treating children in that way, so we tend to reproduce those teaching practices (note that it wasn't a problem for your critical friend).

I cannot take that any further for you, but I think that you can see how such a consideration moves away from asking what strategy will work to asking who we are that we favour a particular strategy. Such questions increase your understanding of who you are as a person who is a professional teacher, and helps you to avoid contradictions inherent in unexamined practices. That is the kind of personal-professional development so well facilitated by critical incident analysis.

Conclusion: On David's Facilitation

When facilitating critical incident analysis, it's obviously important to maintain a balance between validation and critique. A comment such as the following validated a purely practice aspect of Jeannie's work:

> DT You suggested that you were over-preparing your lessons, but there's nothing wrong in preparing everything down to the last word if, as you say, you need to have done that to feel confident about taking the lesson. In fact, your rehearsing of your new strategy was probably key to its success.

A facilitator also has to ensure that they receive feedback as well as giving it, and Jeannie commented at length on all the issues raised. One of her comments must be included here as it was the basis of a critical incident about my facilitation skills:

> JW Your last page of comments about manipulating the classroom environment and treating the children like billiard balls concerned me. This is the last thing I would want to be accused of, and I am worried that you thought this behaviour was reflected in my report. I don't believe I do stereotype the children: instead I try to understand what makes each child tick so that I know what sort of activities would more effectively help them to learn and how I can be more sensitive to their needs.
>
> DT Absolutely, I know that's what you try to do at all times, but it is a fact that to use any process which attempts to effect a change in anyone's behaviour without involving them in defining the problem and planning and implementing the change, is to ignore the thinking and feeling aspects of their humanity. I raised it only because I knew your intention was the exact opposite, and you appeared to be unaware of the contradiction between your 'espoused theory' and your 'theory in use' (Argyris & Schon 1974). Such contradictions occur in our practice when we don't problematise strategies we've adopted from others.

Using a critical incident to further personal-professional development is a very delicate process, and because it critiques our view of ourselves it may be hurtful. My use of the billiard ball metaphor was inappropriate, not because it was not apt, but because it was too hard-hitting a way of pointing out to Jeannie that she was doing something of which she did not approve.

I was lucky that Jeannie took it so well, and an apology should have been forthcoming, but because I was in transmission mode (tutor to student who seemed to have missed the point), I didn't pick this up, which is ironic in that I didn't notice that I didn't approve of the way I dealt with Jeannie's not noticing herself doing something of which she did not approve! Clearly this is a shortcoming my own personal-professional practice I need to work on: perhaps I have greater difficulty in accepting that *if what we're doing is a problem to others it's also our problem* than I thought; certainly this incident is critical of my inability to read and respond to both the content of a student's explanation, and the feelings underlying it. Why do I have this difficulty? What can I do to overcome it and so improve my facilitation skills? I'm working on that, and it will be yet another story, which just goes to show the on-goingness of personal-professional development.

Bibliography

Argyris, C & Schon, D (1974) *Theory in Practice.* San Francisco: Jossey Bass

Boomer, G (1982) *Negotiating the Curriculum.* Sydney: Ashton

Tripp, D (1993) *Critical Incidents in Teaching: The development of professional judgement.* London, New York: Routledge

Tripp, D (1996) *The Scope Program.* Perth: Murdoch University Centre for Learning Change and Development

Tripp, D (2000) 'Participation in research and evaluation' – paper presented at the Collaborative Action Research Network Conference, Rugby, UK.

'Hey Look At This': Photography As Participatory Action Research

Anne Noble
& Deborah
Jones

> To see something like this come alive in words and pictures is just beautiful. And for your family to see it too... 'Hey look at this,' my kids said, as we all began to look at the pictures. They thought it was great and they kept coming up with ideas too.
>
> (Bill Herbert, Cleaner[1])

Starting Points

We begin our story with a clear stand that photography – the 'engine of visualization' (Maynard 1997) – can make a powerful contribution to participatory action research. It provides a technology that literally enables researchers and their audiences to see the world in new ways, to make the invisible, visible – to say 'hey look at this' (Bill Herbert, Cleaner). Photography is a technology through which it is possible to think and to imagine, to create new kinds of interpretive knowledge (Park 2001).

We show how powerful this interpretive process can be by telling the story of one participatory action research project. The project, based in Wellington, New Zealand, brought together a photography teacher and students, community arts workers, community workers and a local cleaners' union, including officials and the cleaners themselves. The most tangible product of this project was a photographic exhibition, *For the Love of the People: Photographs and stories from the work and lives of seven contract cleaners* (For the Love of the People 1999).

In reflecting on this case, we also wanted to inquire into the relationships of photography to participatory research, and to show how photography opens up new possibilities for inquiry. The 'action turn' in research itself pushes the boundary of our thinking about what constitutes knowledge and its legitimation as 'research'. We also use our reflection on this case study to develop the argument that photography itself can create its own kinds of knowledges, going beyond its use as merely 'illustrating' or 'documenting' research processes.

Multiple levels of reflection and action make up this chapter:

- Anne drew on the project as an action learning process for herself, creating a model of collaborative practice to reflect on and evaluate. As we will show you, Anne's research design was originally driven by ideas about photography, and her readings and reflection during the process gradually wove in the perspectives of action research. In particular, she made connections with the concepts of participatory action research (PAR) (Friere 1979; Hall 1982; Reason 1994). This collaborative chapter is part of Anne's reflection process, and builds on many conversations between us during the time the project was in process.

-For Deborah this collaborative reflection and writing project is an opportunity to develop her passion for creative forms of research methodology, and for using modes of knowledge from the humanities to inquire into organisational life. Her involvement is as a collaborator in reflecting on the research process, and as a co-writer.

-The core inquiry process is the photographic project set up to generate and publish knowledge about the work and lives of a group of contract cleaners. We describe this process in some detail below.

-After the photographic project was completed, Anne and a union worker interviewed the cleaners about their experience of the process.

-In addition, the project had a pedagogical purpose for the students concerned, who were learning about photography and in particular about the processes of documentary photography. For this chapter we downplay the pedagogical aspects.[2]

Our main focus in this chapter is on the relationship between photography and participatory research. For readers who are interested in the details of how the process worked as participatory action research, we have included these in section 3. For those who are more interested in our key argument, section 3 can be left out.

The Process

The inquiry

For the Love of the People began as a social documentary project for a final year photography paper at Massey University. The Projecta Foundation – a philanthropic foundation that supports projects for social change with an interest in photography – brought together the School of Design with a community arts group, Hutt Valley Community Arts (HVCA). HVCA had been approached by a group of cleaners and a trade union (the Service and Food Workers Union – SFWU), who wanted to explore how photography might speak to a wide audience about the life and work of contract cleaners.

The objectives of the project were to:

-honour the contribution to society by cleaners

-challenge the lack of awareness and negative public perceptions about the work of cleaning

-make visible the problems facing contract workers, in particular their concerns as members of a large group disenfranchised by the Employment Contracts Act (ECA).[3]

Four students worked with seven contract cleaners for four months. Together the group made images of home and of work, of participation in community life and of dedication to improving conditions for fellow workers.

This was seen as a project in visual communication. While the communication objectives were stated clearly from the start, the specific outcomes were not pre-determined. The design and outcomes were emergent through the collaboration between participants. The project succeeded because the agendas of each group of participants were congruent, and because the relationships between groups were handled well. Unplanned-for outcomes included a very satisfying exhibition, a publication, and television and press coverage of the union's political message.

In hindsight, the objectives can be re-stated as research questions:

- What are the contributions that cleaners make to society?
- What are the key aspects and positive features of their work?
- What are the problems they face in their work, especially in their situation as contract workers?

There were two main phases to the project:

- Creating the photography: project design and photographic projects. This was the original pedagogical project, and mostly involved the photographers and the cleaners. This was the project as originally designed.
- Creating an exhibition and publications from the photography. This developed after the first phase was completed, and all the participants wanted to go on to make the images more widely available to the public. This involved the whole research team.

After these phases were completed, the project was evaluated by Anne in consultation with the union.

Design origins

The design was created initially from the perspective of photography, rather than of research. The decision to use a participatory design model had its origins in post-modern analysis of documentary photography. A major contribution of the post-modern critique of photography has been to draw attention to the unequal relationships that are hidden or ignored in the practice of photography. The meaning of the photographs is constructed by the makers and the viewers and the subjects are rendered powerless and silent (Rosler 1989). Post-modern analysis of photography also exposes the lack of objectivity in the genre of documentary photography; how the meaning and context of supposedly 'truthful' photographs was constructed by those who made them and the people who viewed them. Park (2001) points out that much participatory inquiry also supposes a kind of objective knowledge, which, if anything, is given even greater assumed absolute truth-value by its participatory status. By contrast, this project is based on the idea that knowledge – collaborative or otherwise – is inevitably partial. Consciously interpretive ways of creating knowledge are 'synthetic and integrative, rather than analytic and reductive' (Park 2001 p83). Interpretive knowers re-describe or re-present the object of knowing, allowing the 'new and unexpected' to arise from the interpretive process. (ibid)

The challenge presented for contemporary documentary photography is to devise methods and strategies that give primacy and power to the voices of the subjects. *For the Love of the People* is a project of documentary photography that has its practice rooted in a commitment to empowering the subjects of the photographs through facilitating their participation in the telling of their stories, the editing of the photographs and the design of the context in which the images are seen. The creation of meaning is a collaborative endeavour.

The participants

It is clear from what we have already told you that the project involved a wide range of research participants, with complex multiple relationships to one another. We use Yoland Wadsworths's elegant four-part formulation to distinguish some key features of these relationships. She distinguishes 'four conceptual groups' of those involved in a research project:

-The researcher or researchers
-Those the research is for (to help meet their interests, solve their problems, etc). She calls this the 'critical reference group'.
-The researched.
-Those who may need to be convinced by the research. (Wadsworth 1997 p10).

As Wadsworth points out, the 'critical reference group' may not be a 'group' as such, and 'within it there may be different interests represented, different viewpoints, different ideas, attitudes and values'. She goes on to argue that: 'the thing to sort out is what are the shared interests, views, ideas, etc., driving her research, and which is it intended to serve?'(ibid)

Here we set out the key groups:

-The researcher or researchers
—a group of seven contract cleaners
—the Service and Food Workers' Union

—Hutt Valley Community Arts
—the Wellington School of Design, Massey University (four student photographers took part, led by Massey University lecturer Anne Noble)
—a group of seven contract cleaners
—the Service and Food Workers' Union.
-Those the research is for (to help meet their interests, solve their problems, etc)
—a group of seven contract cleaners
—the Service and Food Workers' Union
-The researched:
—a group of seven contract cleaners.
-Those who may need to be convinced by the research:
—a group of seven contract cleaners (in terms of their self-image)
—other cleaners and low-paid workers
—employers of cleaners
—politicians
—'the public' in term of the perception of cleaners and their work
—the families and communities of the cleaners.

Clearly the critical reference group is the contract cleaners themselves. These represent a marginalised group of workers: as mainly Samoan and Maori workers they are ethnically marginalised;[4] they work in an invisible and stigmatised occupation with low pay, poor conditions and little security; they are contract workers. Their jobs depended on a contract between their employer and a client company for the provision of a service. The Employment Contracts Act provided no protection for contract workers if their employer loses the contract to provide a service. To change this was one of the key objectives of the contract workers' campaign.

Fig 12.1: Paula Atatagi, at a Commercial Cleaners' Picket, May 1999

(Photographer: Lynette Shum)

The cleaners as critical reference group

In the process of the project, the cleaners were involved at every phase. Their concerns informed an initial brief prepared for the students by the participants. In designing the exhibition and publications, a community worker came into the process, and her input was vital supporting cleaners' participation by talking with them, raising cultural issues (ie. the relationship between Maori and Samoan), and negotiating the place of images on walls in relationship to each other. The project was able to provide financial support for cleaners, to cover the cost of attending meetings. Copies of the collaborative photographic essays produced by students in book form were presented to each cleaner as a record of their lives, along with a video documenting their participation in the photographic process.

The photography completed, the participant groups met regularly to design a photographic exhibition. Text to contextualise readings of the photographs was designed collaboratively, based on interviews with cleaners. Much negotiation took place. The cleaners kept the focus on the stories that were key to their participation in the project. Funding was found to publish a brochure containing the cleaners' stories and images from the exhibition, as well as a poster publicising the union's campaign to raise the profile of the rights of contract workers.

Traditional social documentary photography might have portrayed these workers as poor victims, oppressed by the capitalist system. Instead, in response to the brief, the photographic essays produced by the students showed people who were proud of their contribution to the community, enjoyed and valued their work, were committed to their families, their wider community and fellow union members. The exhibition worked as a community development project by re-presenting strong positive images of Maori and Pacific island people to themselves their families and communities, as well as to the uninformed public who had been the intended audience.

Fig 12.2: Mafoe Eric at Home with her Family (L) and Leading a Service and Food Workers' Union Picket (R)

(Photographer: Victoria Birkinshaw)

The process as Participatory Action Research (PAR)

In this section of our chapter we reflect on our understandings of the project as PAR. We set out each of the stages of the process in more detail, showing how it was done, and we give examples to show how the researchers interacted collaboratively with the cleaners as the critical reference group.

In our introduction we have described the project in terms of two main phases and an evaluation. Below we give more details of what was done at each stage, highlighting key issues that had to be resolved.

Phase One: Creating the Photography

Stage One : Project design

The participants here were the cleaners and officials of their trade union, the Service and Food Workers Union (SFUW), The Hutt Valley Community Arts group (HVCA) and the Massey University School of Design, represented by Anne. What made this first collaboration work was the existing, and well-articulated, commitment of the School of Design to an Archive of Contemporary Culture, and its excellent fit with HVCA's community development objectives. First HCVA and Anne established a primary objective shared by both: an inquiry into how to employ photography to empower a normally voiceless group to tell their stories in images and words. Anne and HVCA mapped out the stages of the project, including both the pedagogical purpose and a later exhibition.

At this stage the university was committed only to producing photographic essays that might form the basis of a later exhibition to be organised by Anne, HVCA, cleaners and union. The students would be involved as a component of their course, practicing collaborative documentary practice. When the course finished they would be invited to participate in the development of the exhibition, but this wasn't part of course requirements. HVCA and the university were jointly funded to develop the project by the Projecta Foundation. This first relationship provided the context for connecting with the cleaners and SFUW for help in creating a photographic exhibition about the life and work of seven contract cleaners.

The next development was a first meeting with some of the cleaners, the union, HVCA and Anne. Anne showed images of previous work and talked about photographs and how they communicate, giving examples of stories being told visually. The various agendas were tabled. The union was clear it wanted to profile the cleaners' plight, to politicise, promote and publicise. The cleaners wanted to share their stories, to unionise other workers and to get their message across on behalf of other workers. The group agreed to go ahead. The importance of the educational objectives was acknowledged, and the cleaners were delighted to participate with young people. Anne could commit students' participation to creating the photos, and they agreed to proceed to that point, and then would reflect on what had happened and would design the final stage of the project.

The second meeting included all cleaners participating, the union, HVCA and Anne. The aims of the project were agreed. The ownership of images and consent to the process were discussed, with agreement to a two phase consent process on the part of the cleaners who were the subjects of the photographs: consent prior to starting; and retrospective consent at the end of the project to archive the images, with embargoes and restrictions on access and use.

Stage Two: The photographic projects

The students, Anne and the cleaners were most directly involved at this stage. The students chose to participate in this project to fulfil course requirements – they did have other choices – and were then briefed by Anne and then at a meeting with cleaners, union, HVCA and Anne, with further discussion of basic goals for each group. They agreed to meet monthly in spite of the difficulty for the cleaners, who work at night. The cleaners were surprised at first by the amount of time involved. They had thought the student involvement would be a couple of visits by photographers to workplaces, with access facilitated by the university. As it turned out, the photographers worked alongside seven contract cleaners for four months, at home as well as work, and in community life. The relationships between students and cleaners were valued and the process worked well.

Phase Two: Creating an exhibition and publications

After a review of images and of the process of the project by everyone involved, nearly everyone decided to continue. The photographers worked without academic credit, and Anne continued in order to develop a model of collaborative practice to reflect on and evaluate. At this phase in the project the cleaners' and union's original intent to use the exhibition for political protest became more dominant. They decided to open the exhibition on Labour Day, coinciding with the launch of the union campaign to improve conditions for contract workers. A decision was made to publish a brochure in association with the exhibition, as well as a poster publicising the SFWU campaign. Four further meetings of all the groups were held, and the project was joined by a community worker. At various times during the year meetings of all the participant groups looked at photographs and talked, imagined and planned the exhibition and associated publications.

Photography Student John McCormack, with Cleaner Olive Harding at a Meeting of All Participants at the HVCA Far Site Gallery to Discuss the Exhibition Layout (L).
SFWU Campaign Poster. (R).

(Photographer: John McCormack)

Text to contextualise readings of the photographs was designed collaboratively. A union worker interviewed the cleaners and the transcripts were edited during readings at the meetings. Much negotiation took place. The union argued for more polemic. The student photographers stressed the need to discern those images that by their strength and relationship to other images made a point that did not need re-stating in words. In this process the position of the cleaners as the critical reference group was reinforced. The cleaners drove what they wanted the exhibition to show/say, keeping the focus on the stories that were key to their participation in the project. It emerged at one meeting, for instance, that stories that demonstrated the success of standing together as a group against the companies were of paramount importance for the cleaners as making a stand for their fellow workers or their fellow Samoans. It was through a development of this conversation at a later date that the title for the exhibition emerged – '... for the love of the people'. Other themes were noted: the value of their work; pride in doing a good job; cleaning as a contribution; the importance of their work as cleaners in the whole scheme of their lives and for their families. At later editing stages the cleaners insisted that certain stories, which had been edited out by Anne and the photographers, should be reinstated, and this was done.

Photographs and Text Edited Collaboratively for the Exhibition Brochure

Bill Herbert

I'm a registered priest. I'm a parish leader for Te Rongopai Parish in Upper Hutt. I do social work a lot for the community. People are so demanding, particularly in the church.

I referee rugby league, the senior reserves to the social grades, on Saturday and Sunday. I'm also the kaumatua at the kura kaupapa. I am also the caretaker there. I do hospital visits twenty four hours of the day. Tomorrow I'm going to do a land blessing for the Union Health Centre in Newtown.

I live one day at a time Sweet Jesus. I love work now because Abe (the supervisor) has been put off. Denise (his wife and also a supervisor) is still there. Abe was very abusive. It was the Union that did it. John (the Union secretary) got us all to write a letter each, and out of eighteen workers eleven wrote letters against him. P & O asked Abe to resign.

We are now getting paid for the hours we work. If there's a problem we can go up to the boss without being abused - "you f... arse hole." We're all happy. We all talk to each other, we have fun.

I went to get some sugar for the guys and Andrew McDonald (the area manager) says, "I'm going to come up there and start firing people and I'm not going to worry about the Union." He was shaking. I just responded by saying "That's a lot of wind blowing."

It's no good having the qualifications if you haven't got a heart. Denise always says to us, "I did a paper for this - I did a paper for that" and I said to her, "You should do a paper for your heart."

I live one day at a time Sweet Jesus

Paula Atatagi

they cut your hours and increase the workload

(Photographer: David Read)

The group workshopped ideas for the exhibition layout with the images laid out on the floor on a large roll of newsprint, collecting and clarifying ideas. At an important meeting to discuss the exhibition, structure was worked out and complex cultural issues negotiated as decisions were made about the kind of opening for the exhibition, the use of cultural decorations, and the final order of images. The group arranged a day to hang the exhibition collectively.

There were moments when the interests of all groups represented came into conflict. While for Massey University the outcomes were mostly positive, in being associated with an exhibition that received much positive publicity on television and in the newspapers, and positive feedback from within the community. However, the University also got caught up in some of the unforeseen difficulties associated with such a complex participatory project. In a case of the right arm not knowing what the left arm was doing, the same week that the exhibition opened, the University's cleaning contract with a particular firm expired and many of the contract cleaners lost their jobs. The irony of this was spotted by a local community newspaper which ran the headline: *University sponsors photos then dumps cleaners.* Not only did this result in some negative publicity for the University, but it incurred the wrath of the very union with which we were trying to collaborate.

Further conflict occurred over the issue of co-ownership of the images. Until the images were lodged with the Archive of Contemporary Culture they were still technically the property of Massey University and not available for public use. The union, however, saw a more immediate use for the images in the lead-up to the 1999 General Election in New Zealand and without consultation published them on the front page of the pre-election issue of the union's newspaper alongside a message urging union members to vote the then government out of office. This placed the university in a potentially awkward position as owner of the images.

Issues of ownership and copyright were complex to resolve and might have been helped by clearer contractual agreements at the start of the project. However, given the experimental nature of the process, at the outset no one was prepared to predict the exact nature of the outcomes. It might be seen as an aspect of participatory design practice that where no one individual or organisation drives the process, some of the outcomes will be unpredictable, while others will be not entirely to the satisfaction of all concerned. Another aspect is that objectives will be formed and modified in the process of developing the work. It would be potentially limiting to set all the boundaries at the beginning.

Perhaps most importantly, because of the attention paid to participatory process, the project remained in development. The exhibition was continually being reconceptualised and was always emergent.

Evaluation

A final evaluation phase was built into the project from the start. Interviews were conducted by students, Anne and the union during and after the project to establish the degree and quality of ownership of the project.

Observations based on these interviews included these key issues related to PAR:

1. The participatory design model enabled participants to speak for themselves. The cleaners felt that their ability to define their own lives and issues of concern, to empower their families, and speak on behalf of their wider community through the images and their stories, was of greatest significance.
2. The traditional power relationships in the practice of documentary photography were overturned. The opening of the exhibition created sufficient interest to attract national television and the local newspapers. Whereas the subjects of photographs are often silent in a gallery context, the voices of this previously

invisible group were broadcast loudly and clearly. The cleaners' initial objective of wanting their concerns to be heard was met.

3. Authorship was shared and quality was not compromised. With the sharing of creative decisions no one person could lay sole claim to be photographer, author, editor or curator. Contrary to expectations, when authorship was no longer privileged, the collaborative work produced was of a consistently high quality.

4. Process and experience assumed primary importance for all concerned. The participants valued the process even more than the outcomes. The physical outcomes of the project – the exhibition, brochure, posters, photographic essays, image resource and oral histories – were the visible but not the only significant outcomes. For the photography students the first-hand experience of the contribution photography could make to community development was of greatest significance.

Photography in Participatory Action Research

This project began as an adventure in developing community based collaborative photographic practice. There are implications therefore in (at least) two different domains:

- The possibilities that PAR can create for explorations in subjects such as photography as well as in more conventionally defined 'research'; and
- The question of what art and design thinking can bring to discussions of action research? What new kinds of research might evolve? What overlaps are there?

It is not unusual for photographs to be used as part of the data in research projects, whether the photographs are taken by the research 'subjects' or by 'researchers'. There has been a range of previous work in the social sciences which has incorporated photography or video. In some of this work the photographs are taken by the 'outside' researchers, in other cases by the research 'subjects' as part of a kind of visual diary: in both cases, photographs are treated as a form of data. More recently photography has been incorporated along with other forms of creative expression into collaborative research projects (Brinton Lykes & The Association of Maya Ixil Women 2001). But photographic images are not generally acceptable presented as the outputs of research. What has not been acceptable in research domains is the proposition that a selection of photographic images is not just data, but interpretive work in itself.

The 'action turn' in research is based on the idea that the involvement of communities in the production of research is critical to what research institutions should now be engaged in. This movement out to communities opens up for questioning and exploration our traditional ideas of what 'research' looks like and how we communicate our 'findings' more widely. Photography serves this exploration powerfully.

In relation to PAR, Friere argues:

> For me the concrete reality consists not only of concrete facts and physical things, but also includes the ways in which the people involved with these facts perceive them. Thus in the last analysis, for me, the concrete reality is the connection between subjectivity and objectivity, never objectivity isolated from subjectivity.
>
> (Friere 1982 p30)

Images and the contexts in which they are shown are generated not through one person's mind but through the joint action / reflection of individuals, groups and communities. Photography thus enables the creation of new knowledge, which is 'synthetic and integrative, rather than analytic and reductive' (Park 2001 p83).

This is obviously a more general point about the aesthetic dimensions of research, and it has broad implications for the ways that we create research knowledges. These extend not just through the visual and performing arts, but loop back to engage with debates about creative ways of presenting written research texts. There has some recent discussion in organisational research, for instance, of the importance of the aesthetic dimension (Strati 1992, 1999, 2000). In this work the aesthetic is argued to be a valid way of knowing organisational realities, along with other, more conventional, rational and analytic modes of academic knowledge. However even here the 'artistic object' is taken to be organisational life, and the researcher becomes a kind of art critic, comparable to someone who comments on films or paintings. In distinction from this approach, we argue that it is also valid to see the researcher as an artist. In the case of photography this kind of researcher is able to think and imagine research through a 'visual engine'. Such research is itself visual, and does not require the accompaniment of words to make it 'real research'.

Acknowledgments

Thanks to the following individuals and organisations for their contributions of skill, time and knowledge which have contributed to this paper: Pauline Harper (HVCA), Annie Newman, Lee Tan, and John Ryall, of the Service and Food Workers' Union, Claire Robinson, Muriel Tunoho (Hutt Union Health Service) and the photographers – Lynette Shum, David Read, Victoria Birkinshaw and John McCormack. Special thanks to the cleaners: Hinetemoa Kahu, Mafoe Eric, Bill Herbert, Paula Atatagi, Lalopua Sanele, Olive Harding and Hagavave Kato Amosa for sharing their lives and for their dedication to making a difference.

Notes

1. We use the actual names of the research 'subjects'/collaborators. This use of actual names emphasises their participatory status and the intention of the researchers to honour and make visible the lives and works of cleaners. Their identities were clearly 'exhibited' in the exhibition that presented the photographic research, and their names were also attached to their words on exhibition text panels. The participants all gave consent for the use of their names in the exhibition and also in this published work.
2. See Noble & Robinson, 2000 for an account of the pedagogical aspects.
3. The ECA was later scrapped (in 2000) when a new government took power.
4. Taking the population as a whole Maori are 14.5%; Pacific Island people 4.8%; and those of Asian origin 5.5% in relations to the Pakeha majority of European descent (Ministry of Women's Affairs 1998).

Bibliography

Brinton Lykes & The Association of Maya Ixil Women (2001) 'Creative arts and photography in participatory action research in Guatemala' in Reason, P & Bradbury, H (eds) *Handbook of Action Research: Participative inquiry and practice*. pp363–371. London: Sage

For the Love of the People (1999) *For The Love of The People: Photographs and stories from the work and lives of seven contract cleaners.* Exhibition Brochure. Wellington: Far Site Gallery

Friere, P (1982) 'Creating Alternative Research Methods: Learning to do it by doing it' in Hall, B, Gillette, A & Tandon, R (eds) *Creating Knowledge: A monopoly?* pp29–37. International Council for Adult Education, Toronto

Hall, B (1979) 'Breaking the Monopoly of Knowledge: Research methods, participation and development' in Hall, B, Gillette, A & Tandon, R (eds) *Creating Knowledge :A monopoly?* (pp57–67) International Council for Adult Education, Toronto

Heron, J & Reason, P (2001) 'The practice of co-operative inquiry: Research "with" rather than "on" people' in Reason, P & Bradbury, H (eds) *Handbook of Action Research: Participative inquiry and practice.* pp179–187. London: Sage

Maynard, P (1997) *The Engine of Visualisation : Thinking through photography.* Ithaca: Cornell University Press

Ministry of Women's Affairs (1999) *Women.* ('New Zealand Now' series 1998) Wellington: Statistics New Zealand – Ministry of Women's Affairs

Noble, A & Robinson, C (2000) 'For the Love of the People: Participatory design in a community context' in Scrivener, Ball & Woodcock (eds) *Collaborative Design.* pp81–93. London: Springer-Verlag

Park, P (2001) 'Knowledge and participatory research' in Reason, P & Bradbury, H (eds) *Handbook of Action Research: Participative inquiry and practice.* pp81–90. London: Sage

Reason, P (1994) 'Three Approaches to Participative Inquiry' in Denzin, NK & Lincoln, YS (eds) *Handbook of Qualitative Research.* pp324–339. London: Sage

Rosler, M (1989) 'In, around, and afterthoughts (on documentary photography)' in *The Context of Meaning; Critical histories of photography.* pp302–340. Cambridge Massachusetts: MIT Press

Strati, A (1992) 'Aesthetic understanding or organizational life' in *Academy of Management Review.* 17 (3), pp568–581

Strati, A (1999) *Organisation and Aesthetics.* London: Sage

Strati, A (2000) 'Putting people in the picture: Art and aesthetics in photography and in understanding organizational life' in *Organization Studies.* 21 (10), pp53–69

Wadsworth, Y (1997) *Do-it-yourself Social Research.* 2nd edition. Sydney : Allen & Unwin

Victor J Friedman & Israel Sykes

Introduction

The purpose of this chapter is to illustrate how 'reflecting on reflection-in-action' can serve as a method for conducting action science research. The concept 'reflection-in-action' was coined by Donald Schon (1983, 1987) to describe how professionals think while performing their practice. Action science is a form of action research distinguished by its focus on the building and testing of theories in social practice (Argyris et al 1985; Friedman 2000; Schon 1983). Both reflection-in-action and action science are concerned with the 'indeterminate zones of practice' characterised by uniqueness, uncertainty, instability, and value conflict (Friedman 2000; Schon 1987 p11). This chapter begins with a discussion of reflection-in-action and how it differs from 'reflection *on* practice'. It then illustrates the use of 'reflecting on reflection-in-action' for learning from success by uncovering the 'theories in practice' (Argyris & Schon 1974) of an exceptionally successful social service organisation.

What is 'Reflecting-in-Action'?

Schon's research (1983, 1987) challenged the prevailing notion of 'technical rationality', which views professional practice as the possession and application of scientifically based knowledge and techniques for matching appropriate solutions to well-defined problems. Through a careful study of exemplary professional practitioners at work, Schon (1983) concluded that the core competency of professional practice is 'reflection-in-action'. Reflection-in-action is so deeply embedded in a practitioner's reasoning and behaviour that it is usually attributed to personal and untransferable 'artistry'. Schon (1983, 1987) attempted to make the underlying structure of reflection-in-action explicit in order to make this artistry more understandable and learnable.

The conditions for reflection-in action are created when the practitioner's smooth and almost automatic 'knowing-in-action' fails to produce the intended results. Knowing-in-action refers to a kind of tacit knowledge (Polanyi 1967) that enables people to perform everyday tasks – from tying one's shoes to driving a car – with little or no conscious thought. The skilled practitioner experiences these moments of blockage or failure as a 'puzzle' in which there is something unique, unclear, or not fully understood in the situation. Skilled reflection-in-action requires the ability to engage the experience of uncertainty, or 'not knowing', in order to let new meanings emerge.

When reflecting-in-action, skilled practitioners question the assumptional structure of 'knowing-in-action' (Schon 1987 p28) and 'reframe' the problem from the 'materials' of the situation (Schon 1983 p131). Reframing may involve perceiving the situation differently, and/ or questioning underlying assumptions, desired outcomes, and values.

Reframing also leads to alternative action strategies for achieving intended consequences and to 'on-the-spot experiments' (Schon 1983 p141; 1987 p28) to test the new framing. Experiments may involve taking action in the problem context, or simply articulating the reframing so that others can react to it, and carefully observing the situation's 'back-talk' in order to determine whether the action has opened space for moving forward.

The skilled practitioner knows how to both impose the frame on a situation while at the same time being sensitive to where it does not fit. Thus, when an experiment does not lead to the intended outcome, it generates a new puzzle and on-going reflection-in-action. This cyclical, iterative process of 'appreciation, action, and reappreciation' (Schon 1983 p132) continues until the problem is considered solved or the practitioner disengages from the context.

Although Schon (1983) studied exemplary professionals in order to explicate this kind of thinking, reflection-in-action is not a rare skill. Rather it is a more highly developed and refined performance of the 'artistry of everyday life' (Schon 1987 p32). Professional practice involves learning of 'new ways of using the *kinds* (italics in the original) of competences (sic) we already possess' (Schon 1987 p32). These competencies are bounded within a 'community of practitioners' who deal with similar kinds of problems or situations and share a common body of knowledge, values, norms, and institutional structures (Schon p33).

Reflection in vs reflection on

The appearance of *The Reflective Practitioner* (Schon 1983) stimulated a tremendous amount of interest and discussion among practitioners and researchers in fields such as education, social work, psychology, management and planning. Today there is even an academic journal, entitled *Reflective Practice* devoted entirely to the 'enhancement of practice through reflection' (Ghaye 2000 p5). However, this intense activity has obscured some critical distinctions between reflection 'on' and reflection 'in' practice (Seibert & Daudelin; Sykes & Goldman 2000).

Schon describes the distinction between 'reflection on' and 'reflection in' in the following terms:

We may reflect *on* (italics in original) action, thinking back on what we have done in order to discover how our knowing-in-action may have contributed to an unexpected outcome. We may do so after the fact... or we may pause in the midst of an action... In either case, our reflection has no direct connection to present action. Alternatively, we may reflect in the midst of an action without interrupting it... during which we can still make a difference to the situation at hand – our thinking serves to reshape what we are doing while we are doing it. I shall say, in cases like this, that we reflect-*in*-action (italics in original). (Schon 1987 p26)

The concept of reflection *on* practice (eg. Bleakley 2000; Watson & Wilcox 2000) conveys a sense of stepping back from the practice context and thinking retrospectively about a professional experience. It involves conscious thought about the situation, one's own actions, feelings, and/or thinking. Reflection-in-action, on the other hand, represents a kind of thinking characterised not by stepping back from the action context but rather by stepping into it. It is neither retrospective nor fully conscious thought, but occurs so automatically that skilled practitioners are at pains to articulate how they actually produce it (Schon 1987 p31). Reflection-in-action is focused on a specific practice context and never ends with insight alone, but rather involves action to transform or 'make something' of the context (Overmeer 1998; Schon 1987 p31).

Schon has described the potential benefits of the informal interplay of 'reflection on' and 'reflection in' action:

> But our reflection on our past reflection-in-action may indirectly shape our future action... As I think back on my experience... I may consolidate my understanding of the problem or invent a better or more general solution to it. If I do, my present reflection on my earlier reflection-in-action begins a dialogue of thinking and doing through which I become... more skillful... these several levels and kinds of reflection play important roles in the acquisition of artistry.
> (Schon 1987 p31)

Although both kinds of reflection are important, they are different and distinguishable. For our purposes here, what seems most significant is that reflection *on* action, can be used as a methodology for systematically studying reflection-in-action.

The rest of this chapter will attempt to demonstrate, by way of a case study, that rigorous reflection *on* reflection-*in*-action constitutes an important method of action research or action science (Argyris, Putnam, & Smith 1985; Friedman 2000; Schon 1983 p319). Action science attempts to create communities of inquiry within communities of practice by integrating social research *into* social practice. It focuses on building and testing theories of practice in situations characterised by uniqueness, uncertainty, instability, and/or conflict. The goal of action science inquiry is to help practitioners, both individually and collectively, discover the tacit choices they have made about their perceptions of reality, their assumptions, their goals, and their strategies for achieving them. By making theories of practice explicit and subject to choice, action science research generates learning from both failure and success.

'Reflection on reflection in' as a method of action research

Sykes and Goldman (2000) used 'reflection on reflection-in-action' as an explicit research method in their study of 'Kesher', an Israeli non-profit organisation that provides information, consultation and support to parents of children with special needs. 'Kesher', which means 'connection' in Hebrew, is noteworthy for its unusual ability to forge partnerships between parents, professionals, and agencies that find themselves at an impasse in their efforts to solve a specific problem. Typically such situations are characterised by escalating cycles of conflict, frustration, and alienation, but Kesher has developed an approach that helps both parents and professionals to cope more effectively and make progress towards optimal solutions (Rosenfeld, Schon & Sykes 1996).

In order to learn from Kesher's success in this complex task, Israel Sykes, a researcher from the Brookdale Institute, and Maya Goldman, the founder and director of Kesher, embarked on an extended dialogue on Goldman's practice (Sykes & Goldman 2000). As the dialogue unfolded it came to resemble the mapping of an underwater site. At first they observed what was happening above the surface, but could only guess as to what was happening underwater. Maya described events that occurred during the work of the Kesher team, without being able to explain why they had chosen to act in a certain way in a given situation. Through repeated 'dives' at different 'sites', the inquirers immersed themselves in Maya's stories and began identifying and mapping various areas of practice and the relationships among them. Eventually they put these pieces together into a relatively comprehensive and coherent theory of Kesher's practice (Sykes & Goldman 2000).

The rest of this chapter will highlight the research process that Sykes and Goldman (2000) described, through which they were able to formulate this theory. This process is described as consisting of the following processes:

-immersion/reconstruction
-differentiation/conceptualisation
-crystallisation/validation.

Although there tends to be a temporal order to these processes, they sometimes occur simultaneously or cycle back on each.

Immersion/Reconstruction

'Immersion' into specific stories of practice is a form of data collection involving joint and intentional inquiry through which the researcher enters into the practitioner's world. It generally began when Maya identified a significant practice 'event,' such as the following story:

Shula contacted 'Kesher' by telephone and wanted to know how we could help her prevent her son from being placed in special education. She said that it was hard for her talk about it on the phone, but when we invited her to come to the office, she said that she couldn't because she worked full time and had to care for her children after work. We suggested that we come to her workplace during a break and she agreed to our suggestion.

When we met, she began to talk about her son, Danny. It was clear that she was describing a child with mental retardation. It was also clear that her unwillingness to place him in special education was based on experience that one had to listen to very carefully in order to understand. Shula told about the syndrome that had caused retardation in her older daughters, both of whom were placed in special education settings. When she was pregnant with Danny, the doctors had told her that boys did not develop this syndrome, so she decided to keep the pregnancy. Then he too began to develop signs of retardation. Now she refused to send him to a special education framework, saying 'this child is not going to get the stigma of retardation!'

Even though the beginning of school was only a week away and Danny was not yet registered in any educational framework, I focused on understanding where the mother and the family were coming from. I avoided suggesting any solutions or alternative frameworks. The moment the discussion turned to the emotional side – and the focus was on words such as 'how sad' and 'difficult' and on identification with her disappointment with the fact that it had happened to her son as well – the mother told the story of her life and the lives of her children. It was easy to understand her very negative associations with special education system and why she was so opposed to placing her son there.

Only after the mother understood that I understood, did I begin to speak about how I see things or how they look from the outside. I began to ask about the child, his development, his appearance, and how he feels in a regular class when he can't fit in or develop. We began to speak about the price Danny pays and slowly the conversation turned to ways that might enable her to find a place that suits Danny, together with consideration of the pain the family is undergoing.

The dialogue developed into a discussion about the advantages and disadvantages of the regular educational system, which is better for the family but might leave the child behind, as opposed to a school for retarded children, which was a very charged issue for the parents. The absolute 'no' that was expressed at the beginning became a 'maybe, depending upon the school…'

Israel's initial response to events such as these was to dive deeper into the experience with probing, open-ended questions about the background of the relationship (between the client and the system, among organisations, and among the staffs of different organisations), the objective details of the event (what was done, what was said, and by whom), and the subjective details of the event (what did the Kesher staff think and feel during the event).

Using his own intuition and associations, Israel also formulated and tested various hypotheses regarding Maya's experience. This inquiry process was not only designed to help Israel reconstruct a coherent picture of a complex situation, but also to help Maya revisit her experience and bring to the surface aspects of her reflection-in-action of which she had only been dimly aware. Immersion created a shared psychological space in which Maya's actual experiences merged with the experience that Israel constructed for himself on the basis of her description.

As a picture of the complex reality emerged, Israel asked the following kinds of questions in order to reconstruct Maya's framing of the problem: How exactly did you initially understand the problem? What solution did you want to reach? What steps did you foresee on the way to a solution? What difficulties did you anticipate, and how did you prepare for them? This line of inquiry led to the discovery that, rather than focusing on the substantive issue, Maya framed the initial problem as the need to develop a trusting relationship with the mother. Based on her experience, she came to this encounter with the belief that without such a relationship there would be no way of achieving an optimal solution.

Israel's inquiry revealed that to Maya, 'trust' meant that the parent feels certain that the professional understands, wants to help, is capable of helping, and will not cause any harm. Although the need for trust may seem obvious, it is often overlooked when substantive issues frame client-professional encounters from the outset. Maya, however, *imposed* this framing on the situation, and this frame focused her attention on certain aspects of the situation while helping her to make sense of her ongoing encounter with the parent.

Maya's framing led to certain actions. Israel and Maya examined these interventions and her 'on-the-spot experiments' with questions such as: why had she acted thus, and not otherwise? What lay behind her decision to respond in a certain way in one relationship, and in a different way in another? To what did she pay special attention during and after the intervention? What did she examine? What evidence did she seek to measure progress following the intervention? What feedback instigated change in the direction of action?

For example, Maya's initial framing led her to refrain from asking too many information-gathering questions and from providing information or recommendations early in the encounter. Rather she encouraged the mother to tell *her* story and responded by appreciating both the mother's presentation of the problem and identifying with her emotions. As the broader, more complex picture emerged, Maya was able to reframe the substantive problem from 'should Danny be sent to special education?' to 'how do we best meet both Danny's needs and the needs of the family?'

In what sense could Maya's actions be seen as experiments? Maya's theory about Kesher's clients helped her make sense of the encounter with Shula and guided her moves, but she could not be certain that her framing was not distorting the situation or blinding her to key aspects. Therefore, she attended closely to the mother's reactions to her series of interventions. When she perceived that the mother 'understood that I understood', she took this as an indication that her trust-building moves had worked and that her initial framing had been appropriate.

At that point, Maya began asking a series of specific questions about Danny, how he feels in a regular school, and the 'price he pays' for being in a regular school. These questions reflected a shift from trust-building to a focus on the substantive problem. Having clarified and acknowledged the family's needs, Maya focused on understanding Danny's needs. These steps represented experiments because they were designed to test:

- Maya's understanding of Danny's needs compared with those of the mother
- the mother's willingness to reconsider her initial perspective on her child's needs, and
- Maya's more general hypothesis that the mother will be more open and less defensive if she feels understood and respected by the practitioner.

Maya's questions were crafted to gradually raise threatening issues while carefully observing the mother's reactions at each step. The mother's change from 'no' to 'maybe' indicated to Maya that the reframing experiment had succeeded in changing the situation and opening space for movement towards a solution.

Differentiation/Conceptualisation

Collaborative inquiry into Maya's reasoning and actions across a number of different practice stories revealed that there were clear patterns to her ways of framing and acting in situations like this one. As these patterns of reasoning and behaviour were made explicit, distinctions were made in the initially undifferentiated, complex practice experience. For example, the handling of referrals was roughly differentiated into two principal dimensions: the development of a relationship of trust with the parents and relevant others, and learning about the problem and designing an optimal solution. The development of trust was then differentiated as a four-stage process involving:

- setting preliminary conditions for a relationship
- seeing the situation through the client's eyes
- responding with relevant information and the professional's own perspective, and
- formulating a shared perspective while taking differences into account.

Finally, each of these stages was then further differentiated to yield a detailed theory-of-action that included a description of the stage, the assumptions underlying professional actions at that stage, appropriate and desirable outcomes at that stage, and the action strategies for achieving those outcomes.

This process of differentiating Maya's raw experience led to the naming and defining of concepts that were central to Kesher's work. For example, Maya's meaning of 'trust' described above became the basis for a formal definition. The outcome of the process of trust-building was defined as creating a 'shared perspective', which did not necessarily mean agreement but did require a stance of 'the two of us (client and professional) facing the problem together'. In addition, inquiry revealed that Kesher set very high standards for finding solutions to the substantive problem. Maya and Israel came to call this 'the journey towards an optimal solution' and specifically defined the criteria that defined such a solution.

As the research process developed, the researchers encountered a variety of events that could not be accounted for in the two-dimensional model of Kesher's practice. The attempt to cope with these 'missing variables' led to the mapping out of additional area of practice involving decision-making. In the context of the relationship with the client, the Kesher team often found itself facing decisions about the boundaries of the relationship, the degree of responsibility the professional accepts, the place and time of interaction, and the type of help to the client. These decisions often involved key dilemmas, which Maya and Israel explored and conceptualised as 'decision axes'. For each decision axis, represented as a continuum between two opposing strategies, the researchers identified criteria and decision rules for guiding action.

Crystallisation/Validation

Once Maya and Israel had brought these rules and concepts to the surface, they still needed to analyse them, understand the limits of their validity, and make them comprehensible. The understandings arrived at through face-to-face dialogue were crystallised as Israel wrote them down, Maya read and commented on them, and so forth. These components of Kesher's theory in practice were ordered and systematised and gaps were identified and filled in.

The process of going from Maya's raw experience of action to stories to theory-building exacted a price. Actual practice is an extremely complex and dynamic process, so any attempt to make knowledge-in-action and reflection-in-action explicit can only be an approximation. Furthermore, although Maya was the founder and guiding spirit of Kesher, there was no guarantee that her theory of action could be generalised to the entire organisation. Therefore, it was important to validate the emerging theory. One way of testing the theory was to present it to the Kesher staff, who identified those components they believed accurately represented their thinking and action. Those aspects of the theory that were problematic or unclear were revised according to the staff's comments.

Generalisability

Although this theory of practice was developed on the basis of a single organisation that provided a particular kind of service to a specific target population, it can be generalised to the work of individuals and organisations with similar services and clients. Because action science assumes that each situation is unique in some way, generalisability means something different than in normal science:

To see this site as that one is not to subsume the first under a familiar category or rule. It is, rather, to see the unfamiliar, unique situation as both similar to and different from the familiar one, without at first being able to say similar or different with respect to what (Schon 1983 p138).

In other words, action science theories become explicit parts of a practitioner's 'repertoire' that can be used as templates for reflecting on a different problem (Schon 1983 p138). The key is not only to see the similarities but especially the differences. For example, Victor Friedman has been conducting an action science intervention with a program that helps schools meet the needs of 'at risk' students. In order to illustrate reflection on reflecting-in-action, he distributed copies of Sykes and Goldman (2000) to his clients. To Friedman's surprise, they were mostly interested in the substantive aspects of the theory of practice, which addressed many of their own key uncertainties and dilemmas. This discovery set the stage for inquiry into what is similar, what is different, and how the theory can be tested in their practice.

Conclusion

The interaction between Israel and Maya was not clinical supervision, therapy, nor a journey of self-discovery. Rather it was an attempt to utilise a rigorous process of 'reflection on reflecting-in-action' to generate theory and actionable knowledge from an exemplar of successful social practice. Prior to this research, Maya's effectiveness was well known, but her knowing-in-action remained tacit and unavailable to those not in direct contact with her. Learning from exemplary practitioners is not new, but using the structure of 'reflection on reflection-in-action' as an analytical tool can greatly improve its richness, quality, and actionability. This kind of research focuses not only on the features of a particular case and the actions taken, but also attempts to represent the path of inquiry that led from an initial framing to the eventual outcome (Schon 1983 p317). It delves deeply into the processes whereby a practitioner engages a variety of practice situations, and explores and makes explicit the practitioner's assumptions, values, framing, reasoning, and experimentation. Reflection on reflection-in-action thus can be a tool not only for illuminating a practitioner's artistry in a particular practice area, but also for providing maps for practitioners in similar areas who wish to inquire into and improve their own practice.

Fig 13.1:The Process of Reflecting on Reflecting-in-Action

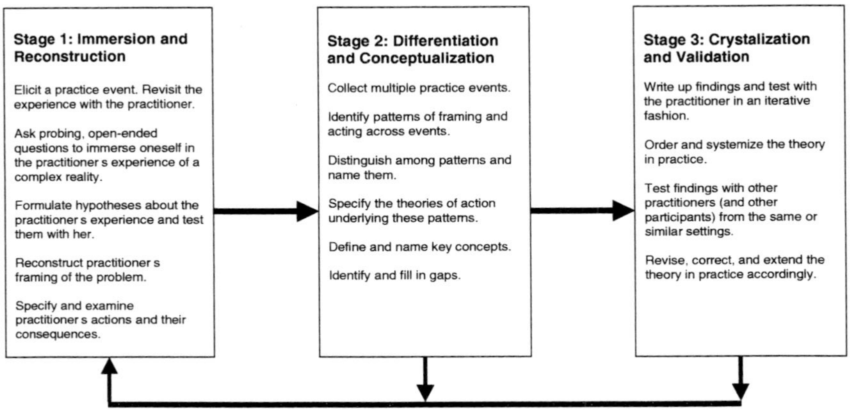

Stage 1: Immersion and Reconstruction

Elicit a practice event. Revisit the experience with the practitioner.

Ask probing, open-ended questions to immerse oneself in the practitioner s experience of a complex reality.

Formulate hypotheses about the practitioner s experience and test them with her.

Reconstruct practitioner s framing of the problem.

Specify and examine practitioner s actions and their consequences.

Stage 2: Differentiation and Conceptualization

Collect multiple practice events.

Identify patterns of framing and acting across events.

Distinguish among patterns and name them.

Specify the theories of action underlying these patterns.

Define and name key concepts.

Identify and fill in gaps.

Stage 3: Crystalization and Validation

Write up findings and test with the practitioner in an iterative fashion.

Order and systemize the theory in practice.

Test findings with other practitioners (and other participants) from the same or similar settings.

Revise, correct, and extend the theory in practice accordingly.

Notes

1. Kesher began operations in Jerusalem in 1988 as a project of the Jerusalem Council for Children and Youth and today functions nation-wide under the auspices of the Izzie Shapira House in Raanana.

Bibliography

Argyris, C, Putnam, R & Smith, D (1985) *Action Science: Concepts, methods, and skills for research and intervention.* San Francisco: Jossey-Bass

Argyris, C & Schon, DA (1974*) Theories in Practice: Increasing professional effectiveness.* San Francisco: Jossey-Bass

Bleakley, A (2000) 'Writing with invisible ink: narrative, confessionalism, and reflective practice' in *Reflective Practice.* 1(1) pp11–24

Friedman, V (2000) 'Action science: creating communities of inquiry in communities of practice' in Bradbury, H & Reason, P (eds) *The Handbook of Action Research.* Thousand Oaks: Sage pp159–170

Schon, DA (1987) *Education the Reflective Practitioner.* San Francisco: Jossey-Bass

Ghaye, T (2000) 'Into the reflective mode: Bridging the stagnant moat' in *Reflective Practice.* 1(1) pp5–10

Overmeer, W (1998) 'Reflecting on what?' – paper presented at an online conference on 'The Reflective Practitioner' (in memory of Don Schon) held on Actlist 1–29 March

Polanyi, M (1967) *The Tacit Dimension.* New York: Doubleday

Rosenfeld, J, Schon, D & Sykes, I (1995) 'Out from under: lessons from projects for inaptly served children and families' – research report M-41-96, Brookdale Institute, Jerusalem, Israel

Schon, DA (1983) *The Reflective Practitioner.* New York: Basic Books

Schon, DA (1987) *Education the Reflective Practitioner.* San Francisco: Jossey-Bass

Seibert, K & Daudelin, M *The Role of Reflection in Managerial Learning: Theory, research and practice.*

Sykes, I & Goldman M (2000) 'Learning from success: producing actionable knowledge by reflecting on the practice of a successful project ('Kesher')' – research report RR-370-00, Brookdale Institute, Jerusalem, Israel

Watson, J & Wilcox, S (2000) 'Reading for understanding: Methods of reflecting on practice' in *Reflective Practice.* 1(1) pp57–68.

Getting Started and Gaining Entry: A Personal Experience Conducting Action Research in a Singapore Healthcare Context

Stephanie Chee

This chapter describes the various difficulties faced in gaining access to and approval for my fieldwork for my action research in a private hospital in Singapore and how I managed to overcome these difficulties. The activities presented include, firstly, establishing research involvement among informants and collaborators and, secondly, seeking research approvals from the various organisational authorities. This account could be very useful to action researchers who face similar situations in their own organisations. By keeping a reflective journal I was able overcome many hurdles that came my way.

Gaining Entry

To establish involvement among the research participants and collaborators, I gave serious considerations to the following factors:

- -Building effective personal and working relationship.
- -Negotiating roles for researchers and stakeholders.
- -Determining the level of participation.

To seek research approvals among the various authorities, I had to increase my acumen and sensitivity towards the channels of communication, individuals' idiosyncrasies and the issues of opportunities and timeliness.

Establishing Research Involvement

Relationship building

Since the inception of the Gleneagles education department in 1989 (where I started my research), there had always been a close collaboration between the nursing division and the education department, and between the nurses of the maternity units and me. Since I was the only nurse educator assigned to take charge of the staff development function for the five maternity units of Gleneagles Hospital, I had vested interests in ensuring that the professional development offered was both relevant and useful for them.

Fuelled by the continuing debate concerning excellence in clinical nursing practice and value added services in healthcare delivery, the head nurses and ward sisters of maternity units became increasingly concerned with the quality of practice of their nurses. Changes that were happening in the Singapore healthcare environment served as a catalyst for nurses and midwives to re-examine their practice and their roles in clinical settings. The staff of the maternity units was aware of the need to improve their practises.

I felt that a reference group from a group of colleagues could help me to be more effective in using action research. It was also important to work with this group to identify the details related to the central question addressed in this fieldwork, ie. 'How can action research complement nursing educational practice to enhance nursing practice?'

Establishing research involvement from the nurses was one of my main concerns right from the beginning of the study. As the primary researcher facilitating the study, I had to be mindful of the many considerations that had to be thought through if this group of head nurses and ward sisters, ten in total, was going to function collaboratively. The collaborative element in action research required commitment and energy from the people involved in the study. It was challenging but time-consuming.

I was cognisant of the pre-planning requirement in action research in which I would need to identify who were my research stakeholders (Fig 14.1). I needed to set up personal and working relationships with these people. My direct stakeholders were comprised of the head nurses, ward sisters (ie. assistants to head nurses) and nurses from the five maternity units. The other direct stakeholders included the director of nursing and the assistant director of nursing who gave the approvals to the study. The indirect stakeholders included the senior manager of education, general manager and managing director. The process of rapport building took into consideration the following critical factors: the importance of building relationships, to build a climate for change, to negotiate roles and responsibilities, and to agree on mechanisms for participation (Dick 1995).

Fig 14.1: Direct and indirect research stakeholders at Gleneagles Hospital

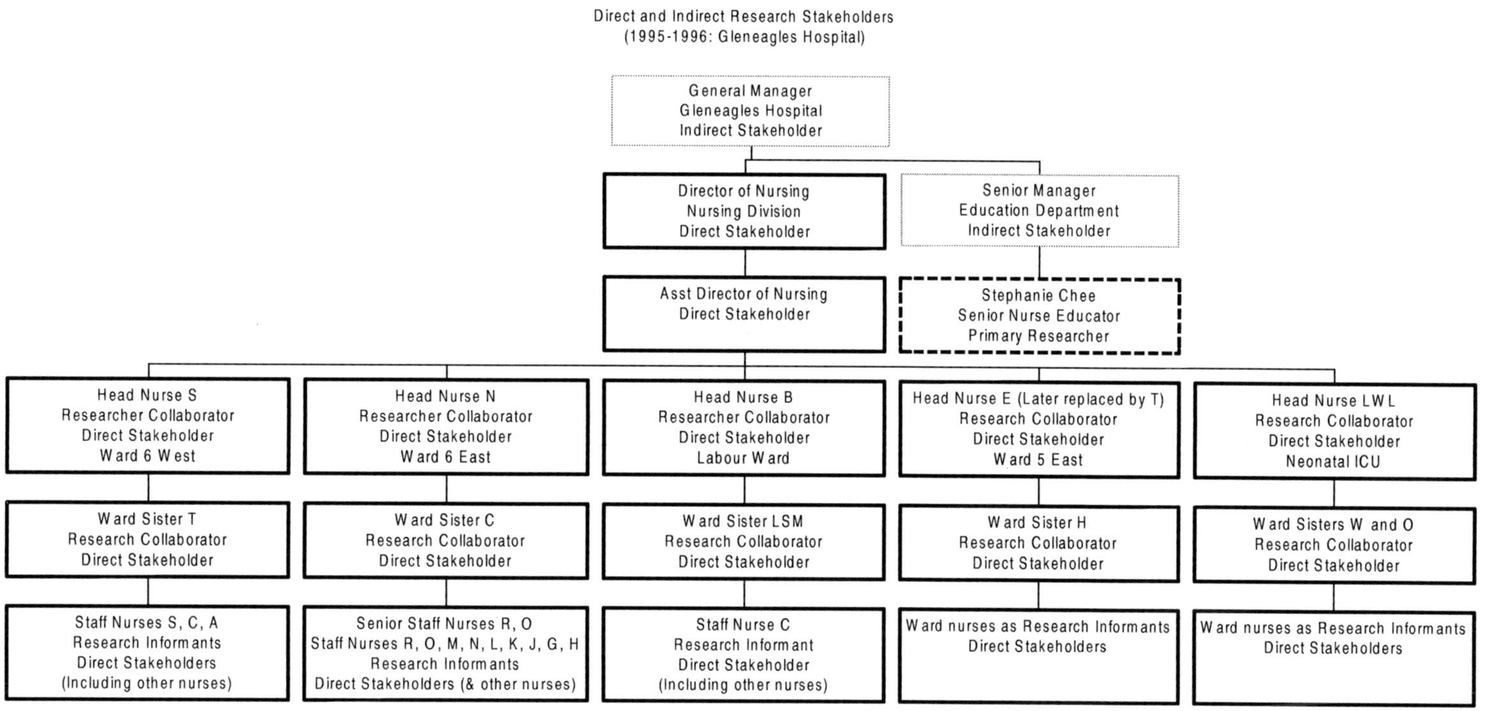

In my attempt to build relationships, I needed to increase the level of trust between the nurses and myself. Although I have been a familiar figure to most of them since 1986, I did not want to take our relationships for granted. I made my intentions explicit and explained that I had their interests at heart. In my day-to-day practice I put into good use the principles of human communication skills (DeVito 1994). I preferred relationships that were open and flexible. There was a need to create and sustain the quality of personal relationship with the stakeholders at the outset. This was evident from my personal journal entries:

> I was able to get to know the new orientee better, the head nurses talked to me and interacted with me more and told me about their problems and needs... They are comfortable with me and vice versa.
>
> (19 January 1995)
>
> ...I waited until all the nurses had left the meeting room... I talked to her [head nurse] about her plans. She divulged to me ... her mother who is 70... and is in Malacca [Malaysia]... she misses her family... She felt that... has not been supportive of the nurses and not sensitive to changes that are affecting the nurses. Also, she shared with me the doctors' remarks...
>
> (20 January 1995)
>
> ...I was so delighted to hear from her [a senior nursing officer, equivalent to a head nurse] about how satisfied she was with my assistance. I quote: 'You have done so much for us... You [have] continued to do so much for our maternity units.'
>
> *(23 January 1995)*

Establishing rapport with the director of nursing was equally important. Excerpts of my journal revealed evidence of my good working relationship with the director of nursing. She commented:

> ...because of your continuity and efforts... the maternity units are what they are now, with good quality assurance performance indicators.
>
> *(26 January 1995)*

Having affirmed the trust level between the key stakeholders and myself I progressed to the next stage of involvement, ie. identifying the desired outcomes of the overall process of change. It was a conscious effort to work towards nurses' involvement in the research.

Identifying the desired outcomes of change

In an attempt to seek support and approval from the stakeholders, identifying the desired outcomes of change formed an important part of the approach. These stakeholders comprised the head nurses, ward sisters, the assistant director of nursing for the maternity unit and the director of the nursing division. These individuals were the key decision-makers for implementing change.

The desired outcomes of change were discussed among these stakeholders. They hoped to see that all their nurses were competent clinically. Also, that their work performance was desirable and their practice standards were consistent. They felt that it was essential to devise an effective clinical assessment checklist to understand and improve the clinical competencies of the nurses. The following extracts of my journal entries, dated 23 January 1995, illustrated my transactions with the key people and their comments:

> ...it is a good management control system for understanding and monitoring staff clinical performance...
>
> (by head nurse, E)
>
> ...it is a good management control system...
>
> (by assistant director of nursing, C)
>
> ...to announce to the nurses (the plans to improve clinical competencies) during the next in-service session in February 1995...
>
> (by ward sister, C)

The support from the head nurses, ward sisters and nurses was forthcoming. They understood the end results to be achieved. The areas on the development of the skills assessment checklist and clinical competencies of nurses will be discussed in subsequent sections. Another important consideration in establishing research involvement was on the issue of role negotiation.

Role negotiation

My role in this study was influenced by the relationships formed and the goals identified. There were many decisions, which needed attention.

Firstly, I needed to negotiate with the head nurses and ward sisters for the appropriate people to participate at different stages of the study. I anticipated that those people who had direct involvement in the study were the head nurses, ward sisters, and nurses. The director of nursing, assistant director of nursing, the head of education department, general manager and managing director would have only indirect involvement in this study.

Secondly, in terms of the level of involvement in action and research contributions, I anticipated that the contribution towards taking action by the stakeholders would take priority over the research knowledge contribution. I expected that the knowledge contribution to research outcomes would come from my own and from my research collaborators' analyses and interpretations of data collected.

Thirdly, in terms of attending research meetings, I anticipated that nurses would have to attend meetings during their working time. Also, meetings must not be too frequent and time consuming, otherwise, that would disrupt their normal work schedule. I decided that meetings would be held once a month on the average. In terms of clerical support for the purposes of internal communication, co-ordination and data recording, I would expect myself to do most of the work.

Fourthly, all suggestions and feedback from stakeholders would have to be considered. Verbal consent was obtained from all stakeholders who participated in this study. Those who participated in this study but did not wish to sign the written consents could choose to do so.

The above issues related to the role negotiation were ascertained and agreed upon before any stakeholder committed herself in the study. Having emphasised the need for role clarification and negotiation, the next important consideration in research involvement was the level of participation by stakeholders.

The level of participation

The level of participation for individual stakeholder fluctuated from a continuum of non-involvement to full responsibility. Dick (1995) describes the various levels of participation, in ascending order, as follows:

-non-involvement
-indirect consultation through representatives
-direct consultation
-process consultation
-co-research
-full client responsibility.

In the early part of this study conducted at Gleneagles Hospital, the level of participation by the stakeholders stopped at the level of process consultation. I was unable to involve them totally in the research process and data interpretations for several reasons.

The first reason had to do with the way the research question was formulated: 'How can action research complement nursing educational practice to enhance nursing practice.' It did not have a direct link to the job descriptions of the head nurses, ward sisters and nurses. The existing job descriptions of the head nurses, ward sisters and nurses did not emphasise the need for them to participate in clinical teaching and/or research.

Secondly, nurses' participation in research was not expected by the organisation. On the contrary, expectations such as quality service delivery and productivity management were valued greatly by the organisation.

Thirdly, the action research approach required in this research design was totally alien to the group. At the same time, I was not very confident in its application. I was a novice to action research at this early stage of my study.

Finally, the meeting time for planning, discussion and reflection was short, both during and between meetings. Action research meetings were held once a month on the average. Under all these circumstances, high levels of participation were not achieved.

This low level of participation had to do with the way the research intent, process and outcomes involved the stakeholders' self interests. Although the level of participation was anticipated to be low, I consciously made several attempts to provide as much direct participation as possible and to as many nurses as possible. Those who were less directly involved were given many opportunities to give and get information.

Having established a common understanding among the nurses for research involvement, I began to focus my attention on securing further support and formal approvals from the stakeholders and ethics committee for my research intentions.

Establishing further approvals

I was aware of the need to seek and secure maximum support from other representatives at the organisational and ethics committee levels before concrete research plans were laid. Approvals from these representatives could have negative or positive influence over my research outcomes. The representatives included:

- the same group of head nurses and ward sisters (10 of them) – representing the maternity Unit-Based Quality Assurance committee (UBQA committee) in terms of quality assurance in midwifery practice
- the head of Quality Assurance department – representing the organisation with regard to clinical and service quality issues
- the head of medical affairs – representing the hospital research ethics committee
- the head of my nursing education department – representing the education department with regard to clinical nursing educational issues
- the directors of nursing – representing the nursing division in terms of research relevance to nursing practice
- the general managers – representing the organisation in terms of organisation relevance
- the managing director – representing the organisation in terms of organisation relevance

-the Human Research Ethics Committee – representing the University of South Australia in terms of research ethical issues.

Directly or indirectly, I worked with and around the above approval bodies (Fig 14.2). The subsequent descriptions highlighted the way in which I sought approvals from these representatives.

Fig.14.2: Lines of Authority in Relation to Research Approvals

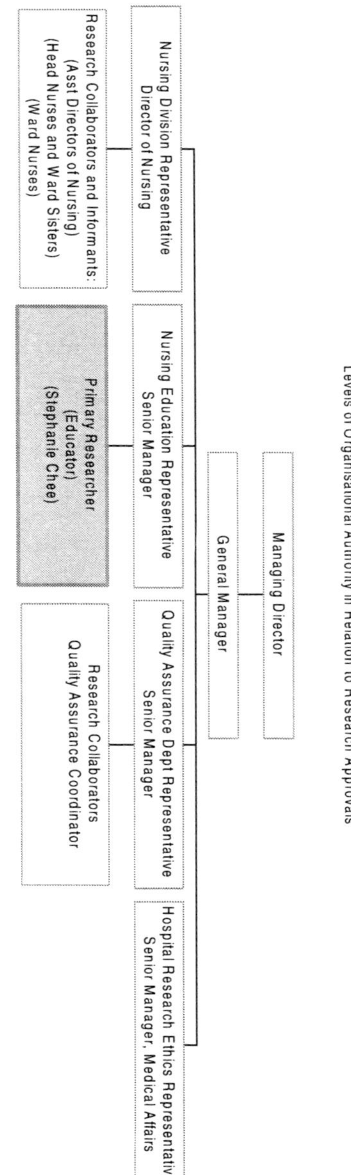

Approval from the Unit-Based Quality Assurance (UBQA) committee

A report for submission to the UBQA committee was prepared on 6 March 1995. The members of the UBQA committee comprised 10 members who were head nurses and ward sisters of the five maternity units. The report contained these headings:

-Purpose of Auditing Nurses' Clinical Competencies
-The Structure of Audit
-The Audit Process and Feedback
-The Outcome of the Audit
-Training Activities to follow.

The contents presented in the memorandum were self-explanatory in terms of rationale, actions and evaluation. At the end of the UBQA committee meeting on 7 March 1995, the team concurred that the skills assessment checklist could be instrumental in improving the nurse's competencies. All agreed that it should form part of the UBQA activities.

Approval from the Quality Assurance Department representative

The primary function of the quality assurance department was to facilitate and initiate quality related activities for the hospital and the nursing division. As my area of research suggested some areas of quality audits of the nurses' competencies, the chief executive officer felt that it was more appropriate for the hospital Quality Assurance Department to follow up with my research proposal. However, my intention was more towards assessing and developing the nurses' competencies than auditing the nurses' competencies. Verbal approval from the representative of the Quality Assurance Department was obtained on 9 March 1995.

Approval from hospital research ethics representative

One of the tasks of the head of the medical affairs department was to oversee issues related to hospital research and ethics. He approved my research project without hesitation. His approval was based on the fact that my research did not involve any invasive procedures.

Approval from the nursing education representative

Initially, there was slight hesitation from the nursing education representative for me to carry out the competency assessments of the maternity nurses.

Extracts from my journal entry dated 26 January 1995 are as follows:

> ...[Reason given by the representative] put it on hold as... at the moment there is no quality assurance monitoring... Let the quality assurance people initiate it... [I was] asked to concentrate on the orientees and my obstetric nurses...

> The support from this education representative was evident from my journal entry dated 9 March 1995:
>
> ...with her [the education department representative's] advice, a memo [to the director of nursing] was drafted... to seek [the latter's] approval for my research work...

On 12 March 1995, the above memo was amended and approved, taking in further suggestions from the education representative.

Approvals from the directors of nursing

My applications for research approvals went through three directors of nursing between June 1994 and 10 August 1995. The first instance of research application was approved by the acting director of nursing in June 1994 with no reservation. In September 1994, a new director of nursing was appointed. With the appointment of the new director of nursing, I did not want to take for granted that the approval from her predecessor still remained.

This new director of nursing was a total stranger to me. I waited till March 1995 before I approached her for my research approval. On 12 February 1995, I gathered from my department head that this director of nursing queried the education department over some costing issues. It appeared that she was unhappy about the situation. I felt that the timing to inform her about my research intention was inappropriate.

This delay in research approval did not deter me from my on-going effort to assess the nurses at the maternity units. Assessing nurses and learners was part and parcel of my educational role in the clinical areas. Meanwhile, I made an effort to continuously test the appropriateness of the skills assessment checklist by assessing nurses.

After some discussion with the head of my education department on 9 March 1995, a memorandum was sent to the director of nursing dated 12 March 1995 to seek her approval for my research studies. She met me in her office on 20 March 1995 to talk about my research proposal. She advised me to make certain amendments. Having made the amendments, I sent her the revised version of the clinical assessment checklist on 21 March 1995 with a covering memorandum. It read:

> Thank you for seeing me on 20 March 1995 and advising me with regard to the above area of action and research which I plan to carry out. This is the amended copy of the clinical assessment checklist for your perusal and approval. I truly appreciate your support and look forward to your final approval.
>
> I did not receive any response from her for several months. Her delay in response caused me much anxiety. With this delay, I was unable to involve the head nurses

and ward sisters at a high level of participation and involvement in my action research. Gaining entry into the client's system had been a challenge for me. It had to be negotiated appropriately and in a timely manner.

I waited almost three months before I eventually made up my mind to speak with the director of nursing to enquire about the outcome of my research approval. On 6 June 1995, I met her outside her office. I reiterated to her my research intention and that I needed an official approval from her. I followed immediately the next day (7 June 1995) with a memorandum to confirm her verbal approval. I wrote:

> I am glad to hear from you yesterday that you have no objection towards my action research. This research aims to explore the effects of using action research methodology to improve the clinical competencies of maternity nurses.
>
> In order to plan, act and reflect upon actions within the research framework, I am required to work collaboratively with certain key people from the maternity units...
>
> The Chief Executive Officer... has granted me the approval to conduct this action research...
>
> I will seek your opinions and decisions whenever necessary... I look forward to your formal approval as soon as possible. Thank you in anticipation of your support.
>
> cc Chief Executive Officer...

My persistence in seeking research approvals eventually paid off. To my pleasant surprise, I received a formal research approval from the director of nursing on the same day. She wrote:

> I think your research project... can be very beneficial for the nursing department. As such, I have no objection...
>
> You had my verbal approval quite some time ago, sorry for keeping you waiting for the official go ahead signal...

On reflection, I felt that these actions were effective in overcoming the difficulties and had speeded up the approval process:
-my earlier verbal informal communication with the director of nursing on 6 June 1995

- -the follow up communication through memorandum on 7 June 1995 to confirm her approval
- -having the memorandum (dated 7 June 1995) sent 'through' the head of my education department added weight to the communication
- -a duplicate copy of the memorandum (dated 7 June 1995) to the chief executive officer particularly influenced the quick response.

Not long afterwards, the above director of nursing left her position for another assignment.

With the arrival of another director of nursing on board, the whole process of research approval started once again. This application was the third and also my last round of research application. On 10 August 1995, I received a letter from this director of nursing. She wrote:

> I refer to your request to conduct a research on action research in nursing education in Gleneagles Hospital. As we agree that your research will not involve obtaining patient data, I have no objections to your proceeding with your project...

My action research fieldwork at Gleneagles Hospital was discontinued in March 1996 as I was posted to another hospital within the Parkway Healthcare Group. It had been an interesting and challenging but stressful experience in going through the motions of seeking formal research applications under these hierarchical and bureaucratic circumstances. In addition, the constant flux of top management personnel had caused much delay to my final research approval, and created much inconvenience during the start-up phase of my research fieldwork at Gleneagles Hospital.

Approvals from general managers

I did not encounter difficulties in seeking approvals from the several general managers who came and went at different times during the course of my research studies.

I did not proceed with the fieldwork because of the delay in the response from the director of nursing, as described above. However, the first general manager did not stay in his position for long. He had to take on another assignment within the Parkway Group Healthcare. As a result, the second general manager came on board in August 1995. Again, I went through the motions of applying for an official research approval from him.

The second general manager resigned less than six months with the organisation. At the time of his resignation in January 1996, my immediate superior informed me that I was to be posted to another hospital within the Parkway Group Healthcare by the end of February 1996. Therefore, I did not bother to write to the third general manager who came on board in January 1996. However, I mentioned to this third general manager about my doctoral research. He told me verbally that his predecessor's agreement would remain unchanged. That was a relief to me.

On reflection, if only there was an official nursing research work group or committee, it could have eased my research undertaking.

Approval from the managing director

As early as 7 June 1994, I received an approval from the managing director for me to conduct my action research. Part of the reply letter stated the following:

> I refer to your memorandum dated 6 June 1994; I have no objections and hope your findings from your research could be put to good use by our nursing division...

Another formal approval from my managing director, to conduct the assessment of the nurses' competencies from the maternity units as part of my action research, was obtained on 7 March 1995. A memorandum, dated 8 March 1995, from the managing director to the head of the Quality Assurance Department, indicated his support for my work.

I updated my managing director of my PhD progress through my personal monthly correspondence with him. Most of the time, these monthly correspondences were written in the form of a one-page letter. Through this private correspondence, he was kept informed of my hurdles, actions, progress, outcomes and feelings about my research work.

Conclusions

The path towards the pursuit of research approvals posed real challenges for me as an action researcher. The above discussions implicitly highlighted the conservative, hierarchical and complex nursing healthcare setting in which I was operating, and demonstrated the amount of change I experienced, and therefore the need for a flexible research methodology like action research. It also showed the non-research-oriented environment in which I worked. The organisation had not provided a simple and efficient structure for employees who wished to seek research approvals and to execute research activities.

Although the formalities involved in the research approvals retarded my research progress it gave me the opportunities to practise meaningful journaling, to analyse the many happenings, and to drill in me the cyclical nature of action research processes. The rigorous and systematic observation and reflection in the action research process enabled me to improve my personal ability to replan for further actions.

Bibliography

DeVito, JA (1994) *Human Communication: The basic course.* Sixth edition. New York: HarperCollins College Publishers

Dick, B (1995) 'Session 6: Stakeholders and participation' in *Action Research and Evaluation On Line.* Lismore: Southern Cross University.

Part 4

Applications

Part 4

Applications

Shankar Sankaran

The proof is in the pudding, as they say. Both action research and action learning emphasise practice and this section of the book is about their practical implementation. While many books have been written about practical applications of action learning and action research in the West very little has been published about their applications in other parts of the world. One of the aims of this book was to document such cases from the Asia-Pacific region. This section of the book contains examples of people in the Asia-Pacific applying action learning and action research as well as experiences of people from the West engaged in applying them in the Asia Pacific region (Rimanoczy). In Part 1 of this book Marquardt talked about his experiences in applying action learning across cultures.

Both action learning and action research have been applied across a variety of applications and situations showing their versatility – education (Bruce-Ferguson, Bingfang, Hughes, Boyd and Tripp and Jones in Part 3), management development (Sankaran, and Lange in Part 2), commercial business (Goh), manufacturing and engineering (Kwok and Sankaran), healthcare (Wilson-Evered and Hartel and Chee in Part 3). A common thread that runs through most of these cases is the application of action learning and action research to introduce change in organisations and communities.

These case studies show that local adaptation is required which Marquardt has also pointed out in Part 1. Rimanoczy's experience in Thailand is an example of how action learning was adopted to suit Thai culture. The 'acculturisation' of action research and learning is an interesting feature of Bruce-Ferguson's attempt to include Maori traditions into action research and Bing Fang's attempts to apply it in Chinese culture.

The cases also show how action research is an emergent phenomenon as explained by Dick in Part 1. Both Kwok and Sankaran and Sng have shown how their concept of action research evolved to suit their situation. Hughes and Chee in Part 2 have shown how action research can start off in a small way in one part of an organisation – in the 'cracks' of an otherwise 'hierarchical' organisation. Sankaran and Sng and Kwok have explained how they believed that a new approach to introduce change was necessary in a traditionally hierarchical organisation. They took the courage, as senior managers, to introduce action learning by making it 'politically' palatable to their own organisations to implement change that resulted in significant business improvement. Another common aspect evident in the cases is how action research and action learning have been used to work within the 'politics' of the 'power' structure of an organisation. (Chee in Part 3, Hughes, Sankaran, Kwok and Bruce-Ferguson).

Action research can be applied in areas that have traditionally used 'positivist' approaches to research. Boyd's chapter is an attempt by someone brought up in the 'scientific' tradition to explore whether the research he has done previously included elements of action research by analysing four cases.

The participative nature of action research, emphasised by Dick in Part 1, is a common thread in many of the cases (Wilson-Evered and Hartel, Kwok, Bruce-Ferguson, Sankaran and Sng) showing that people are more willing to accept change if they are involved in implementing it.

The use of 'open systems' approaches to action research illustrated by Davies in Part 2 was helpful in setting the scene to introduce action learning and action research in some cases. Goh, Chee in Part 2, Kwok and Sankaran and Sng have used 'search conferences' that use an 'open systems' approach to trigger off action learning. These cases also show that action learning and action research can form part of a 'holistic' approach to apply 'systems thinking' to address complex problems. Hughes also talks about the holistic and systematic approach of action inquiry.

Most of the cases also show how the researchers underwent a 'personal transformation' through their involvement in these cases. As Zuber-Skerritt has pointed out in Chapter 1, each one of these action learners and action researchers became 'personal scientists' who were able to actively construct their own theories about the situations in which they found themselves.

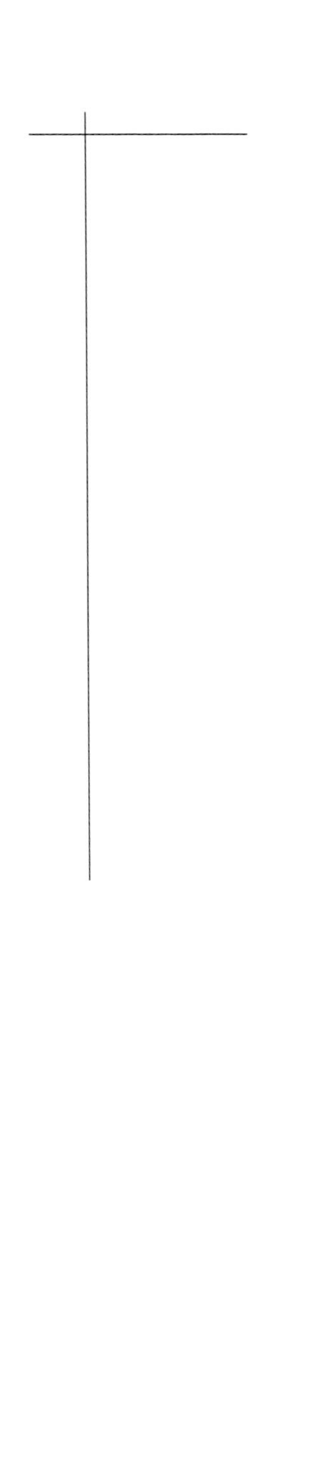

Changing Practices in Organisations: A Case Study of Action Research in a New Zealand Polytechnic

Pip Bruce-Ferguson

Introduction

How often do we, as managers or grass-roots staff, bemoan changes and developments in our organisation, wishing we had the power to affect their progress? How often do we hold back from action, believing that we are powerless to intervene effectively? This study describes my decision to take action in the face of developments that I felt were irreversible within my institution, but the effects of which were negatively impacting on the staff with whom I work.

My position within the organisation is that of a staff developer and also, latterly, of a research leader. At the time I commenced my intervention my prime responsibility was, along with my fellow team members, to support new staff entering the organisation by providing teaching skills and coaching ongoing development, and to support staff with longer experience as they continued their development. Staff in New Zealand polytechnics are required to undertake up to 12 weeks of 'tutor training' within their first three years of appointment, a point that is critical to my intervention. My unit is commonly perceived as a supportive place, outside of new staff's departments and also outside of the Human Resources section, so we are often used as a sounding board for staff fears and concerns, especially as these affect their teaching.

New Zealand polytechnics gained the right to offer degrees under an Education Amendment Act in 1990. Prior to this, degrees had been offered almost exclusively in universities, with the polytechnics being seen as the providers of 'vocational and technical' education. Such education did not require polytechnic staff to engage with research, although some 'research and development' activity has always been a feature of the organisation. However once our polytechnic chose to offer degrees, then engagement in research became mandatory (NZQA 1993 p12).

Our first degree was accredited in 1992, and others quickly followed over the next three years. I began to hear a chorus of concern from staff who, it seemed to me, feared engagement in research that they perceived as requiring quite different skills from those they had developed as classroom teachers. As a conscientious staff developer, I worried about the stress that our research requirement was placing on these staff, particularly alongside the need for them to boost their credentials. Staff in polytechnics in the past tended to be appointed on the basis of trade and professional backgrounds, not necessarily academic credentials. Teaching on a degree forced them to gain at least first degrees, if not Masters degrees. So they faced study on top of teaching, and were required to show also how they were engaged in research. The stress levels were considerable. I decided to take action.

I need at this point to declare some assumptions that underpinned my intervention, and explain their basis. The first assumption is that good staff, using the principles of reflective practice, are already engaged in a form of self-research, a point supported by Gilbert (1994) and Woodhouse (1997). We teach a course called 'Reflective Practitioner' in our tutor training programme, so the concept was familiar to staff. Furthermore, in undertaking my own tutor training elsewhere, I had picked up a course in action research, in which I had further observed the compatibilities between reflective practice and classroom-based research.

The second assumption was that given the stress staff experienced already, any attempt to work with them in research needed to be not only user-friendly but time-efficient, and that it should clearly benefit the organisation, not be something done for purely legalistic purposes. I assumed that staff would have scant energy to invest in research; I also assumed that classroom-based research would benefit the wider polytechnic. I had worked in the organisation for seven years by the time my intervention commenced, and felt I understood its culture fairly well. I believed that what needed to happen, both for the staff and for the institution, was the development of a recognition that classroom-based research is an appropriate and legitimate form of 'research engagement', which would meet the legal requirements while simultaneously improving classroom experiences for both staff and students. At the time I commenced my action, the only formally acknowledged research that was occurring was in the Business Studies and Science departments, both of which used traditional research methodologies which I feared could dominate what 'counted' as research in our organisation if no action was taken to broaden acceptance of alternative approaches. Such traditional approaches might then become hegemonic within the organisation (Gramsci 1971), dominating our research culture and becoming 'the way we do things around here' (Hill 1993).

My third assumption, and an important one given New Zealand's attempts to operate biculturally, was that action research would be compatible with Maori[1] ways of operating. Maori processes tend to place a high value on group action and consensus, and I could see that action research might be familiar for Maori staff needing to undertake research. This assumption was correct as far as it went, but fell short of ideal (Bishop 1996a), as I shall discuss shortly.

My fourth assumption was that to intervene effectively, I needed to take a broad approach to facilitating change, operating not only at grass roots level but also within the formal power structures of the polytechnic. (I use the words carefully; managers in organisations will know that the formal power structures may well be subverted through non-violent non-co-operation by workers.) I had not sought to participate in the formal power structures of the organisation prior to this, although I had always taken an active and interested part in 'think tanks' and the like. I did not have articulated assumptions about how power operates in organisations – my decision to take a broad approach was largely intuitive and empirical. My investigation of theories about how power operates emerged as I progressed. Having outlined the main assumptions that underpinned my action and the reasons why I believe I had developed these assumptions, I shall now describe the intervention itself.

The Intervention

My action involved developing an action research course that could be included as an optional module in a compulsory employment requirement, part of the twelve-week tutor training programme referred to earlier. I needed to design a course; have it accepted through our course credentialing processes; and for historical reasons irrelevant here, arrange for a co-tutor approved by Auckland Technical Institute to assist with the first presentation of the course. Details of how this course was structured and the historical background are available in my doctoral thesis (Bruce Ferguson 1999). It was a 70-hour (equivalent) course and required staff to identify their own research question that they could investigate in their own practice situation within the time frame for the course, which was spread over about a six-month period.

This placement was very strategic. It was designed to build on the reflective practice that staff already used, thus ensuring familiarity. It was designed to meet their employment contract requirement to engage in the tutor training programme, therefore not imposing an additional burden on them in terms of time.[2] It was designed to introduce classroom-based research into our research culture, and to ensure that teacher knowledge 'counted' as valid research in the organisation. It was also designed to help staff to see how they could obtain publishable research reports based on their own classroom practice, which could meet the organisational and legal requirements for staff teaching on degree programmes.

The course has been offered every year since 1993, the year in which the first occurrence was possible. Numbers have been small – never exceeding 12 people – but this is similar to numbers on other optional courses we offer. A benefit, in terms of both research and wider organisational culture development that emerges from courses offered by our unit, is that staff mingle with others from different departments. Therefore, in my course, arborists are able to observe the questions and research processes used by lawyers; nurses to observe those of cooks, etc. I believe that this interdepartmental mingling – uncommon in the wider institution outside of my unit's courses – contributes substantially to a feeling of appreciation of the work and different methods used in the various departments. I believe this helps to build a cohesive culture in which mutual respect is developed within the organisation.

Effectiveness of the Intervention

What lessons did I draw from this attempt to influence my organisational culture? How effective did I, and my action researchers, perceive it to be? What would I do differently if I had the opportunity again? These are important questions. In general, the action researchers found the process familiar, as I had assumed they would. A couple of the many comments made when I interviewed participants a year after they completed the course included the following:

- 'There were lots of processes that came out of the particular action research project that I was doing, that I had always been doing – for me, the process of action research is an everyday thing' (a Maori Studies researcher).
- A Business Studies tutor said, 'I've got a better understanding of concepts. I think the course probably brought together many skills that were lying there, but I think it actually brought them together'.

Nobody found the process unfamiliar, although another Business Studies tutor did explain that he found it 'initially very loose. It wasn't till I actually realised what it was about that I realised it wasn't. It in fact helped me process things very easily and to deal with things'. My first assumption, then, that staff would relatively easily move from use of reflective practice to its practical outworking using the action research approach, was justified.

Not so the second. I had attempted to include the course in an existing and compulsory programme in order to assist staff who were already facing considerable time stresses. But, as with much research, the tasks they chose to pursue took longer than they thought. This is not surprising. When I critiqued thirteen studies on research culture development for my thesis, in seven of them time was mentioned as the major problem, and in my interviews with the action researchers three quarters of them cited time as problematic (Bruce Ferguson 1999 p253). Ramesh Shah, one of the identified 'case study' students cited in my thesis, was an experienced researcher in traditional methods. He said: 'This was supposed to be a small, two-week project, for my own reflection. Action Research turned out to be a very time consuming, but rewarding, interesting and worthwhile project' (ibid p243).

However the second aspect of the assumption (that we needed to resist the implementation of traditional research methods as the main standard of 'the way we do [research] around here' was justified. In 1999, in an internal document, the statement was made that Research at the Institution is expected to:

-assist staff employed by the Institution to maintain currency in their field of knowledge, or
-contribute, either directly or indirectly, to the identification and improvement of best practice in teaching and learning at the Institution; or
-be applied to stakeholder activity (student, staff and the wider community).[3]

Clearly, classroom-based research, including action research, is officially being encouraged in this statement. Therefore, my assumption that the organisation could benefit from including classroom-based research as a valid approach has been supported.

The third assumption I made was that action research would prove to be a familiar and compatible process for Maori staff. My previous experience with Maori staff and community members in the Waikato had prompted the observation that in both education-related and social exchanges there was a high emphasis placed on collaboration and discussion. Previous study (work for my Masters thesis, Ferguson 1991) had reinforced this belief and also made me aware of the extent to which Maori have suffered from being researched *on* rather than researched *with*. The research questions and processes have tended to be pakeha (non-Maori), and the benefits have often enhanced the academic reputations of pakeha rather than producing practical outcomes for Maori. Durie (1992) reinforced this observation. Hence, my assumption that action research, depending as it does on collaboration and active involvement of interested parties, could be a beneficial research process for Maori. To a degree, this assumption was right, as the familiarity of the process to at least one Maori Studies researcher has been cited in this paper already.

However, my reading for the thesis alerted me to the fact that many Maori have moved beyond action research into 'kaupapa Maori' research methods. These are methods that rely on distinctively Maori ways of doing things (Bishop 1996a & 1996b; Vercoe 1997). I risked promoting a research approach that was familiar and hopefully non-exploitative, but less than ideal for many Maori. I think this is an important point, and not just for research culture development. In any organisation employing or servicing the needs of ethnic groups that are different from the numerically and politically dominant group, it is easy to ignore the extent to which hegemonic processes and practices disenfranchise those from different ethnic backgrounds. I discussed a couple of the ways that I was aware of this happening for Maori, in my thesis, such as the timing and ways we held meetings (Bruce Ferguson 1999 p147ff). Doubtless there are many other ways that I still don't recognise. I have tried to compensate for this inadvertent repression by both myself and my institution by becoming actively involved in two formal attempts to redress the balance – membership of working parties aiming to promote awareness of the legitimacy of assessment in Te Reo (the Maori language) and also a working party to promote Maori protocols and principles in research, discussed shortly.

The fourth assumption I had made was that my intervention needed to be broad-based. I felt, on the basis of past experience, that work at purely grass-roots level would be less effective than if I participated also in the formal power structures of the polytechnic. I think this approach has been justifiable as far as it goes; nevertheless I describe below how my understanding of the operation of power was broadened through my study of the work of Michel Foucault.

Reflections on the Theory of Power, and How Individuals Can Exercise Power

I was introduced to Foucault's work by my chief supervisor, Professor Sue Middleton. Middleton has written extensively on uses of Foucauldian methods in organisations (Middleton 1995, 1996, 1998) and was able to guide me into an exploration and appreciation of the ways in which power operates in organisations.

According to Foucault, power circulates, 'It is never localized here or there, never in anybody's hands, never appropriated as a commodity or a piece of wealth. Power is employed and exercised through a net-like organisation… in other words, individuals are the vehicles of power, not its points of application (Foucault 1980 p98).

If you adopt a perspective of power as being dynamic, rather than one that sees power as a property to be held and withheld, you can gain the recognition that you *have* individual power to exercise. This is certainly what happened in my case. Foucault refers to power operating through 'micropractices', subtle ways through which discourses work to approve, and disapprove of, what may be said and done in institutions (see discussion in Danaher, Schirato & Webb 2000).

Recognising the ways that this principle operates in my organisation, I deemed it essential to gain access to the formal power structure that was shaping the development of our research culture. Accordingly, I gained nomination and appointment as staff representative on the newly-formed Research Committee. In this role I was able to argue for the inclusion of definitions of research that validated classroom teaching as an appropriate field of study (a lengthy discussion of this appears in Bruce-Ferguson, 1999 p140ff). It was important to have teacher research recognised in the definitions that prevailed for, as Lather (1991 p125) puts it, 'to put into categories is an act of power' and I wanted teachers to exercise their power. The effectiveness of this intervention at a time when the organisation's research culture was still nascent, is shown in the retention of classroom-research-friendly definitions remaining to the current day.

Subsequent work also drawing on Foucault's principles involved me in membership of a 'Working Group on Protocols and Principles for Research with Maori', which has culminated in joint research presentations with Hera White, HOD Maori Studies (White and Bruce Ferguson 2000a, 2000b). In this work, we recognised the Foucauldian notion that power and knowledge are inextricably intertwined, and sought to influence policy development in the organisation. As Ransom (1997 p23) explains the concept:

> If power and knowledge are intertwined, it follows that one way to understand power – potentially to destabilize it or change its focus – is to take a firm hold on the knowledge that is right there at the centre of its operations.

Ransom (1997 p25) talks of 'the structural flaws and unexpected crevices within a particular power-knowledge dynamic' that exist. Our working group operated in just such a crevice as it helped to create policy in this area. Under Hera's chairing, a group of polytechnic staff (mainly Maori; only myself and one other person were non-Maori) succeeded in having our policy passed by the Academic Board. This policy was intended to ensure that the developing research processes in our organisation empowered Maori rather than repeating past research flaws.

Conclusion

Foucault's work deserves a far more thorough explanation than has been possible in this brief chapter. Its possibilities for people working in large organisations are considerable. It can help people see how they might challenge the dominant orthodoxies of their organisation and, coupled with an action research approach, work to bring about change and improvement. I commend both Foucault's theory of power, and action research's transformative potential, to managers wishing to understand and influence the development of their own organisations. (Note: The Waikato Polytechnic changed its name to Waikato Institute of Technology – Wintec for short – on 1 October 2001).

Notes

1. New Zealand's indigenous people, with whom we have a Treaty that guarantees equal partnership.
2. This aspect proved somewhat unsuccessful, as I shall explain when discussing the limitations of this case study.
3. The Development of Research at the Institution: The Report of the Research Working Party to the Board of Deans, 1 April 1999.

Bibliography

Bishop, R (1996a) *Collaborative Research Stories: Whakawhanaungatanga.* Palmerston North: The Dunmore Press

Bishop, R (1996b) *Keynote Address: Addressing issues of self-determination and legitimation in Kaupapa Maori research.* Presented at the New Zealand Association for Research in Education Conference, Palmerston North 1995, Wellington: New Zealand Council for Educational Research

Bruce-Ferguson, P (1999) *Developing a Research Culture in a Polytechnic: An action research case study.* Thesis submitted in fulfilment of the requirements of the Degree of Doctor of Philosophy, Hamilton: The University of Waikato (available online: http://www.wintec.ac.nz/research/resources.htm)

Danaher, G, Schirato, T & Webb, J (2000) *Understanding Foucault.* St Leonards: Allen & Unwin

Durie, A (1992) *Whaia Te Ara Tika: Research methodologies and Maori* (abridged). Paper presented at the Seminar on Maori Research, Palmerston North: Massey University

Ferguson, P. (1991) *Liberation Theology and its Relevance to the Kiwi Christian.* Unpublished M Soc Sci thesis. Hamilton: The University of Waikato

Foucault, M (1980) 'Truth and Power' in Gordon, C (ed) *Power/Knowledge: Selected interviews and other writings 1972–1977.* Brighton: Harvester

Gilbert, J (1994) 'The construction and reconstruction of the concept of the Reflective Practitioner in the discourses of teacher professional development' in *International Journal of Science Education.* 16 (No. 5) pp511–522

Gramsci, A (1971) *Selections from the Prison Notebook* Hoare, Q & Nowell Smith, G (ed/trans) London: Lawrence and Wishart

Hill, R (1993) *Establishing and Sustaining a Research Culture – A Working Paper.* Hamilton: Department of Business Studies, The Waikato Polytechnic

Lather, P (1991) *Getting Smart.* New York: Routledge

Middleton, S (1995) 'Doing Feminist Educational Theory: A post-modernist perspective' in *Gender and Education.* 7 (1) pp87–100

Middleton, S (1996) *Canes, Berets and Gangsta Rap: Disciplining sexuality in school 1920*–1995. Paper presented at the Rethinking the Lives of Women Educators Poststructuralist and Materialist Feminist Approaches, New York

Middleton, S (1998) *Disciplining Sexuality.* New York: Teachers College Press

New Zealand Qualifications Authority (1993) *The Approval and Accreditation of Degrees and Related Qualifications.* Wellington: NZQA

Ransom, J (1997) *Foucault's Discipline* Durham. London: Duke University Press

Vercoe, A (1997) 'He Taru Tawhiti: Some effects of colonization in Maori Research' in *Waikato Journal of Education.* 3, pp41–54

White, H & Bruce-Ferguson, P (2000a) *Developing Appropriate Bicultural Research Protocols in a Tertiary Education Institution.* Workshop presented at the World Congress on Action Research, Action Learning and Process Management, University of Ballarat, 10–13 September

White, H & Bruce-Ferguson, P (2000b) *Developing a Policy for Conducting Research with Implications for Maori.* Workshop presented for New Zealand Association for Research in Education Conference, University of Waikato, Hamilton, 30 Nov–3 Dec

Woodhouse, D (1997) *Auditing Research, and the Research/Teaching Nexus.* Paper presented at the Research and the New Tomorrow Conference, UNITEC Institute of Technology, Auckland.

Bridging English as a Foreign Language (EFL) Teaching and Learning in High Schools in China: An Action Inquiry Approach

Ge Bingfang

Introduction

In this Chapter I will explore the application of action inquiry approaches (AI) – action research (AR), action learning (AL) and reflective practice (RP) in the context of teaching English as a Foreign Language (EFL) in China. It describes how the author – a high school EFL teacher and researcher in China – explored action research approaches actively with action researchers around the world by using electronic discussion lists to apply these approaches to his concerns related to EFL teaching in China. The chapter then describes a project undertaken by the author to deal with the anxieties of teachers and students associated with EFL learning and teaching.

The Action Inquiry Approach

In the EFL context, as in others, learning is affected by various factors. Williams and Burden (1997 pp203–8) put forth 10 basic propositions that they consider to be crucial for language teachers, among which are:

- -Learners learn better if they feel in control of what they are learning.
- -Learning is closely linked to how people feel about themselves.
- -Learning takes places in a social context through interaction with other people.
- -What teachers do in the classroom will reflect their own beliefs and attitudes.
- -There is a significant role for the teacher as a mediator in the language.
- -Learning tasks represent an interface between teachers and learners.
- -Learning is influenced by the situation in which it occurs.

To handle these smoothly and effectively, Action Research (AR) might be an effective means, even if it may not be the only one. Action research has its academic roots in sociology, social psychology, psychology, organisational studies and education (Dash 1997). There are several definitions of Action Research. According to Dick (2000):

> Action research consists of a family of methodologies which pursue outcomes of both action (change) and research (understanding). It uses a process which alternates between action and systematic reflection, or achieves theory-practice integration by some other means.

Wadsworth (1998) presented Figure 16.1 to show the cyclic nature of the AR process:

Fig 16.1: Cyclical Reaserch Process

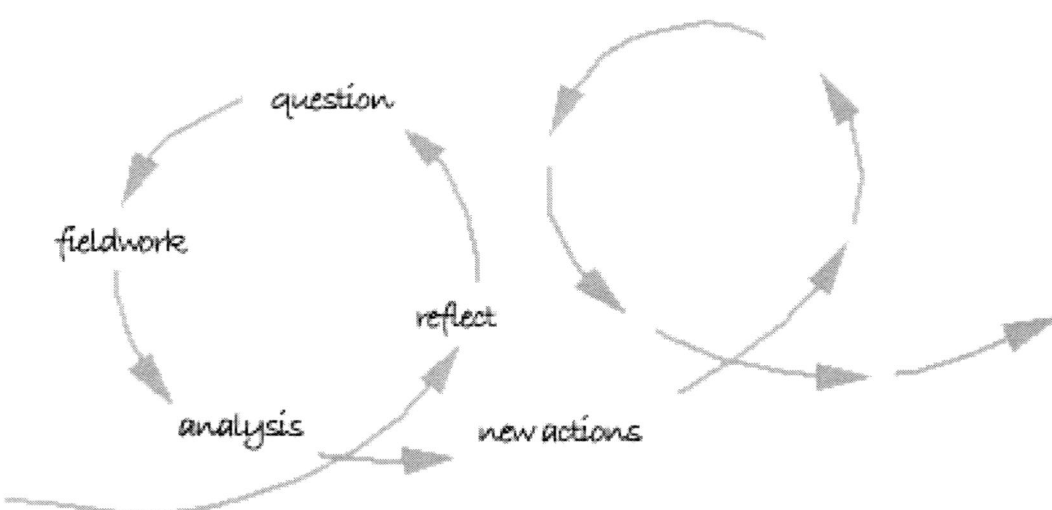

There are different varieties of AR, though, such as Action Learning, Action Reflection Learning and Participatory Rural/Rapid Appraisal. In a paper on the history of AR, after summarizing the differences among the three varieties of AR, technical action research, mutual-collaboration action research and participatory action research, Masters (1995) cited the following by Grundy (1982 p363):

It is not in the methodologies that the three modes of action research differ, but rather in the underlying assumptions and worldviews of the participants that cause the variations in the application of the methodology.

It is clear that people believe that the methodologies are roughly the same with different varieties of action research. More often than not, the person using AR may not worry about which variety is being used; it is the practicality and appropriateness that matter.

Action Research is understood by many as action *and* research. I believe that action and research take place at the very same moment. If you view it as action, then it is action. If you reflect on it, then it is research. But there is more to it. In an email on the AREOL9 (Action Research and Evaluation On-Line Course, sponsored by Bob Dick of Southern Cross University, Australia, No. 9) discussion list, I wrote ([AREOL-G02-L:121] AR/TEFL/Change. March 4, 1999):

> I view reflection as the *key tone* in AR. But we need information on which to base our reflection: data. I believe we've been thinking all the while. What really matters is that the *data basis* is always changing, which affects our decision making, which brings about changes to our action, and which in turn changes the undesired for the desired, the bad for the good, and the good for the better.

It is my view that reflection, which is generally believed by Action Researchers to be the prerequisite for the expected change of both action and understanding, is based on actions taken, being taken and/or to be taken. Being reflective means more than merely being speculative; it means starting with reality and beginning to overcome that reality by reasserting the importance of learning (Newman 1998). We research while we reflect, as well as while we act. According to Sankaran (1997), when we reflect, we should always view it as a new start.

And that's why I tend to view AR as an approach to change and understanding. Action is the starting point as well as the destination of our research.

So I should like to define the *AI Approach* as (see figure 16.2):a planned set of cyclical multi-member research methodology based on actions, which give rise to question-based systematic reflective thinking and understanding, which in turn give way to further actions expected to bring about change for the desired. To some extent, it is a combination of different varieties of Action Research viewed as a research approach.

Fig 16.2: The Action Inquiry Approach

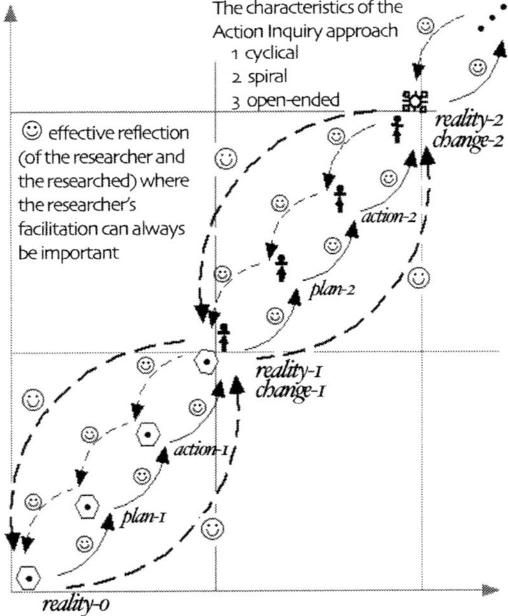

This said, the AI Approach is based on action and is more than action alone: it includes practice. Action in an AI context is more than practice: it requires people to think about what to do all the time, to look back, to look ahead and to look at the present in relation to the past and the future. It is change based on effective reflective thinking and planning. Just as AR is viewed as being multidisciplinary, so too it is multi-interpretative. So while we say that the AI Approach is scientific, we have to add it is *also philosophical.*

Nowadays more and more importance is being attached to the curriculum subject of EFL to senior high school students in China. So it has seen the rapid development of the teaching and learning of EFL as an important compulsory course in the curriculum. The introduction of the AI Approach might be able to bridge the parties engaged in the process of EFL learning and teaching.

Action Research in China

Action research in China is mainly adopted in educational settings. It began in the early 1990s. (Wu Zongjie 1995, Wu Xin 1996). These authors stressed the importance of action research in curriculum renewal and teacher development.

To my knowledge, in China AR is mostly dealt with within the scope of teacher education. It lays emphasis only on the part of the teacher mainly as an approach of doing teaching research and teacher development.

Confucianism has been influencing every aspect of Chinese society. One of its ideologies is that the student should be obedient to whatever the teacher says. Although things have been changing, obedience is still evident in many places. So AR can be important in building up equal relationships between the teachers and the students in that they are all participants in the same research.

Yet, how to build up equality is really a critical issue. Here openness is important. Only on an equal basis can openness be achieved. While we try to change the teacher-centered process of language learning, which dominated China several years ago, we might feel it much better to try out the student-centered methodologies. Yes, better student-centered than teacher-centered, regarding the whole process. But why not be co-operative?

Also, in EFL teaching in China, as in other educational activities, more often than not, teachers would probably say that they have no time to spare for educational research. On the one hand, they often find themselves busy with their routine work: classes in China are usually big (average 40–50), and teachers have to give 10–15 classes per week. On the other hand, they find it difficult to do research work, often for the lack of theories and/or methodologies. Although they have had a semester for each of the three subjects of educational psychology, pedagogy and ELT methodology at college or university, most still find it hard to do educational research. Under such circumstances, teaching and research are isolated from each other, even if teachers may want to bring them together. And AR may serve to bridge the gap.

I used the word 'bridging' because I want to remind the practitioners of the aim of AR: to achieve *change* on the part of the students as well as the teachers themselves based on mutual understanding and cooperation. Just as we work out plans for our own teaching and research, so do we for the students to learn better, to change for the desired, and to observe the changes together with them. It's ideal that change happens to both parties at the same time.

The AI Approach stresses the equality between the engaged parties 'in action'. But in TESL/TEFL, I think it is up to the teachers to arrange for the action research to go on efficiently by effective facilitation.

Bridging EFL Learning and Teaching in Senior High Schools in China: A Case Study in Brief

Project: Moderating the students' and teachers' anxieties in EFL learning and teaching

After we did a research on the senior high school students' extrinsic motivation in EFL learning, I decided to do one on the anxieties of both the teachers and students in EFL teaching and learning.

In studying language-learning anxiety, more quantitative research than qualitative research can be observed. Most of the quantitative research is based on the Foreign Language Classroom Anxiety Scale (FLCAS) designed by Horwitz and Young (1991). They make an investigation, work out the statistics, and then do a summary, trying to find out the relationship and interrelationship between the different variables. Such studies help clarify some underlying obscurities and thus build up the foundations on which to make the teaching more pertinent and efficient.

Brown (1994 p255), when talking about teaching oral communication skills, recognizes 'the anxiety generated over the risks of blurting things out that are wrong, stupid, or incomprehensible' as 'one of the main obstacles learners have to overcome in learning to speak', and in fact, in the whole EFL/ESL learning process, we think. Anxiety is 'highly situation specific'. For example, some information is heavily culturally bounded. If the EFL learner could read every word but couldn't possibly make sense of the discourse, anxiety will probably come up with some of them. 'Cultural lead-in is particularly important in high school EFL learning and teaching because in most places in China it is the beginning period (junior) and the transitional period from beginning to intermediate (senior) of the whole EFL learning process' (Ge 1998 p37), which will surely help the learner build up enough schemata and in turn reduce their learning anxiety.

That considered, this time we have been using the AI Approach. We view ourselves as what Schön (1983) termed as the 'reflective practitioners'. It covers the following phases.

Phase One: Deciding on the roles

My colleague and I, having decided on the research themes, set down to the first plan, about the project as a whole. We began with questions like:

-Are there some anxieties in EFL learning and teaching?
-What roles will the researchers take?
-Who will be our referees?
-Who will be the participants?

We decided that we would take up multi-roles – to act as facilitators, counsellors, practitioners, researchers and participants. All the teachers to be engaged were to act as participants and researchers. And all the students to be engaged were to be participants, with their group 'leaders' acting partly as co-facilitators.

Phase Two: Deciding on the themes and approaches

In this phase, first of all, as it is a theme that has been explored by so many experts in various disciplines, we decided to look through the literature available. Second, we tried to define what we meant by anxieties. As we intended to learn more about the problem on the part of the students so as to get some background information, we worked out a questionnaire to get some quantitative data from more than 150 students almost equally distributed in the three senior grades of our school. All these questions were concerned with the students' anxieties in the EFL learning process. As we tended to keep track of the students so that the research would go on for about three years as planned, we selected the then Senior Grade One students as our 'stakeholders'. So the Senior One teachers were to be our 'client teachers'. All the collected data connected with the other grades as well as with the Senior One students were seen merely as background information.

At the very beginning, we decided to do this research project using Action Research. The problem was that, as Pam Swepson points out under the headline of 'Which science, which action research?', there are different varieties of Action research. It is difficult to decide:

> Part of the problem of understanding science or understanding action research is that there are so many models of what they are. It is less easy to adopt a model of action research, but I suggest one where these 'metaprocesses' are in practice. It pursues action and research outcomes at the same time. It pursues a cyclic path to allow for at least one stage of critical reflection on the outcomes and the

> process. This stage of critical reflection searches for both confirming and disconfirming evidence. Action research tends, but is not necessarily, participative and dealing with qualitative data. (after Bob Dick, 1993)
>
> (Pam Swepson, 1994)

So, after some consideration, we decided on the principle of appropriateness: use whatever is appropriate within the family of action research. But we did decide on the chief methods: Action Research, Action Learning as well as Participatory Action Research. The project is to take on transparency to our student and teacher 'stakeholders'. We were to divide the class of students into six groups, each one constituting eight to 10 members, with a leader in each. It would be a qualitative research. The five teachers (three senior one teachers of English, my colleague and I) formed one learning set ourselves while at the same time each was assigned to supervise one or two of the student groups when needed. The seven learning sets were required to meet at least once every two or three weeks. But each member should fill in the given sheet of paper more often. As it was a non-profit project, all the members were more or less free to enter or quit the sets. What's more, both the teachers and the students were very busy.

Phase Three: Deciding on the plans and predicting possible difficulties

The aim of the project, of course, was to achieve change, namely, to moderate the anxieties, both on the part of the teachers and the students. Because of the large number of students, whether or not we could achieve satisfactory results depended largely on how effective the participation of the 'stakeholders' would be.

The possible difficulties anticipated were:

- -The diversity of (1) the anxieties of each stakeholder and (2) the attitude towards (or the belief in) the possible change.
- -The extent to which they would cooperate in the course of the project, especially when being interviewed.
- -The degree to which the student facilitators could possibly live up to their roles.
- -The attitude towards the time and effort to be taken.
- -The keeping of Action Learning logs.
- -The modification and adjustment of the plans.
- -The evaluation of reflective thinking and its effectiveness.
- -The cycling of each 'round': a new start leads to a new and better result.
- -Teacher immersion.

Phase Four: Implementation

1. Initiating the project

What was special with this project was that our qualitative research started with a quantitative analysis. Many would frown at such a practice. But I hold it correct to use whatever is viewed by the research as necessary. For example, common sense tells us that a person with the medium level of anxiety (in the psychological sense) can achieve the best possible results. This is tested by my questionnaire.

2. Organising the learning sets

Each learning set has eight to 10 students. It was voluntarily formed following the suggestions of the teacher facilitators: Consider the level of anxieties and then go together. As time goes on we planned to change the groups dividing them according to what sort of anxieties they have. Some of them did not join any set. That was fine. We asked them to help the leaders take notes during discussions if they felt like doing so, and could enter one set or another whenever interested. Or else, they could just turn a deaf ear and a blind eye to what was happening around them.

3. Choosing the leader

See if he/she can be a good co-facilitator to us.

4. Talking to them about the project: what is happening and what will happen

We told the students what problems they had, if any. And above all, that anxiety is neither bad nor good in itself: It has no derogatory sense at all. A medium level of anxiety is the best point. Eggs will never be hatched without a moderate temperature – neither too high nor too low! The key point to them was, and still is, to bring into consideration what sort of anxieties they were having and meanwhile to do reflective thinking. We also made it clear that it was only effective reflection that would work. It was important for them to note down whatever they thought about the problem every two or three days and we encouraged them to keep an 'everyday diary'. The openness has been, however, a problem, especially when doing the interviews.

For most of the points here we also made them clear to the teacher participants.

5. Interviewing

During the interviews, what we felt important was that we should start them talking, especially about what they felt about the research, how to take notes and what to reflect. But when the core part came, quite a few felt uneasy to tell us the anxieties, especially at the beginning. One of them even quit because she 'hated' being asked such questions. Many, however, grew more and more cooperative, which was more than what we expected. So participation has been effective.

When we 'interviewed' the teacher participants, we simply chatted, which was good. Problems also occurred regarding the time limit, shortage of techniques of the facilitators and frequent 'ineffective' reflection. As teachers' anxieties more or less lie in the students' academic achievements and the evaluation of how their lessons are conducted by the students, the school authority or the governmental departments, they are usually more difficult to remove. But it seemed effective: this did help their students a lot.

6. Collecting data

As I stated, different from 'normal' formulae of action research, at the very beginning I collected quantitative data. But they were only for reference. We have based our evaluation on the qualitative data. We have been using the *Action Learning (AL) Guide* designed by Sankaran (1999) for 'diaries' and Williams' *Action Research Learning Log* (1997) for writing the summary over a certain period of time. And we also ask the teacher participants to keep the guide and the log, as well as memos occasionally. So every week we collect the Action Learning notes from the student facilitators and the teachers, and regularly supervise the participants on the possible problems they have been experiencing.

7. The interpretation of data

In group work (group thinking), some students just kept silent. But they did not leave their set(s), which I interpret as their still having interest in the set(s). I think those silent students, although they unnecessarily agreed with everything others said, did experience change. In action, they were 'trying out' what the majority of the group agreed on after their discussion, as is evident in their Action Learning Diaries/Guide. So in group work/thinking, silence in itself does not mean participation, nor does it mean non-participation.

Now, this project is still going on. Among the Senior One students, many have found that reflective thinking helped them to think effectively. They looked before they leapt; they did enjoy the rainbow after a summer rain, whether they had been caught in the rain or not! Those who had been too anxious and those who never did all of the day's work seemed to be exerting influence over one another.

On the part of the teachers, helping the students reflect on their action learning process really helped them understand their students better. No quantitative research could match this.

So, both parties have been experiencing some sort of change or other. More have come to realise that creative thinking is based on effective reflective thinking. If a child falls into a big jar of water and cannot get out, everyone on the scene will try to get him out. We would undoubtedly think of taking him out. But what if you could not? How can you bridge your thinking (want to save the child) with the expected result (save the child)? Effective reflective thinking! By collecting related data and thinking reflectively, through the AI Approach, we would probably find another solution to this problem in emergency: Why not try to break the jar?

Thus bridging EFL learning and teaching through the AI Approach is more of a conceptual problem than a technical one.

Bibliography

Brown, HD (1994) *Teaching by Principles: An interactive approach to language pedagogy.* Upper Saddle River: Prentice Hall Regents

Dash, DP (1997) *Problems of Action Research: As I see it.* Working Paper No. 14. Lincoln: Lincoln School of Management (available online: http://www.lincoln.ac.uk/lsm/schoolpages/Research ResearchHomePage.htm)

Dick, B (2000) *Action Research International Author Guidelines.* (available online: http://www.scu.edu.au/schools/gcm/ar/ari/ari-auth.html) (20001017)

Dick, B (1999) *The Change Process and Action Research.* Session 2 of Action Research and Evaluation Online (AREOL) (available online: http://www.scu.edu.au/schools/gcm/ar/areol/areol-session02.html)

Ge, B (1998) 'High School English Teaching: The cultural lead-in' in *Journal of Huzhou Teachers College* (in Chinese), 20 (3), pp37–40

Masters, J (1995) 'The History of Action Research' in Hughes, I (ed) *Action Research Electronic Reader.* The University of Sydney (available online: http://www.behs.cchs.usyd.edu.au/arow/Reader/ rmasters.htm)

Newman, J (1998) 'On Becoming a Better Teacher' in *Tensions of Teaching: Beyond tips to critical reflection.* Toronto: Canadian Scholars Press & pp183–210. New York: Teachers College Press (available online: http://home.istar.ca/~jnewman/betterteacher.html)

Sankaran, S (1997) *Memo to Myself: A tool to improve reflection during an action research project.* (available online: http://www.scu.edu.au/schools/gcm/ar/arr/arow/rshankar.html)

Sankaran, S (1999) *An Action Research Study of Management Learning: Developing engineering managers of a Japanese multinational company in Singapore.* PhD dissertation. Adelaide: University of South Australia

Schön, DA (1983) *The Reflective Practitioner: How professionals think in action.* New York: Basic Books

Swepson, P (1994) *Action Research: Understanding its philosophy can improve your practice – some comparisons with the philosophy of science.* Paper presented at the Second World Congress on Action Learning, Action Research and Process Management, Bath, UK

Wadsworth, Y (1998) *What is Participatory Action Research?* Action Research International, Paper 2 (available online: http://www.scu.edu.au/schools/gcm/ar/ari/p-ywadsworth98.html)

Williams, B (1997) *Action Research Learning Log.* (email address: bobwill@actrix.gen.nz)

Williams, M & Burden, RL (1997) *Psychology for Language Teachers: A social constructivist approach.* UK: Cambridge University Press

Wu, X (1996) 'Action Research: An important approach to English teachers' professional development' in *Journal of Southwestern Normal University (Philosophy and social sciences edition) 3* (in Chinese)

Wu, X (1998) 'Enhancing high school English teachers' professional development by looking into the classroom' in *English Teaching and Research Note. 2* (in Chinese), pp28–30

Wu, Z (1995) 'Action Research: A new approach to language teacher education' in *Foreign Language Teaching and Research. No 2* (in Chinese), 102, pp48–53.

Action Inquiry for Educational Change

Ian Hughes

Introduction

Action Research On Web (AROW) is a long-term project to introduce action inquiry into a university faculty of health sciences, and to develop the knowledge and skill required to do this. The project runs from a World Wide Web site (http://www.cchs.usyd.edu.au/arow) that offers open access to one-semester courses, learning modules, an electronic journal, tools for action inquiry; support for learning sets and action research project webs.

Action inquiry is a framework for learning, research and change that includes a number of related approaches including action research, action learning, reflective practice, collaborative inquiry and continuous improvement (Tripp 1996). It is distinguished from other approaches to research and learning by its dual objectives, its holistic or systemic approach, and its capacity to work at multiple levels. Action inquiry combines action (purposive activity to change or improve something) with inquiry (in this context, referring to learning, research or both) in a single process. Rather than breaking a problem into separate parts and attending to one variable at a time, it acts on whole complex systems. With systemic thinking comes an ability to operate at multiple levels, and accommodate reflexivity.

The AROW System

AROW is a system for learning and research nested inside a university faculty that is dedicated to teaching and research in 'clinical and related aspects of the health sciences' (Faculty of Health Sciences 2000 p7). The positivist paradigm (Zuber-Skerritt) is dominant in the faculty, including an assumption that the same methods can be applied in natural, biological and social research. The 'clinical' orientation of the faculty carries this assumption into professional practice, including the administration of health services. For reasons that are outside the scope of this chapter, I came to the conclusion that the positivist paradigm has an important place, but is not enough to achieve all of the faculty's aims. I decided to introduce action inquiry as a method of inquiry, a change practice and a subject for learning.

In introducing and establishing action inquiry into a wider system with which it is not fully congruent, I have not engaged in a struggle to organise the totality. I have not attempted to change the faculty or the university as a whole, but in Robert Flood's words, to 'organise within the unorganisable' (Flood 1999 p192). After five years I can see that transformation of learning and research is happening, in small local sites inside a larger organisation that is changing at a slower rate.

I started planning the AROW project in the Faculty of Health Sciences in The University of Sydney in 1994. This was not in response to demand expressed at that time, but to prepare for an anticipated need identified in planning processes. In 1995 I designed a one-semester course in action research as a learning system following a somewhat instrumental approach (Davis et al 1974). In the following year, face-to-face seminars were replaced by email discussion supported by material published on a web site. An electronic reader (Hughes 1996) was added. In 1997 the course was offered as an international professional development program. In 1998 I re-designed the website, with sub-webs added to support action inquiry projects. Online enrolment was enabled in 1999, and an employer-sponsored course was offered to rural health professionals in workplace learning sets. In 2000, Overseas Learning Sets were inaugurated, in Singapore in collaboration with Management Learning and Action Research. In the same year, resources for community action research were added, and an associated psychology research project commenced (Campbell 2000). An electronic journal, Action Research e-Reports (Hughes 2001a), was published on the site in 2001. Study modules in community action research, planning and evaluation, as well as resources for learning sets were added during 2001 and negotiations for collaborative partnerships are continuing. This development (summarised in Figure 17.1) followed principles of action inquiry and organisational learning (Hughes 1997, Senge 2000). AROW has grown and developed as a self-organising system.

Fig 17.1: Arow Time Line.

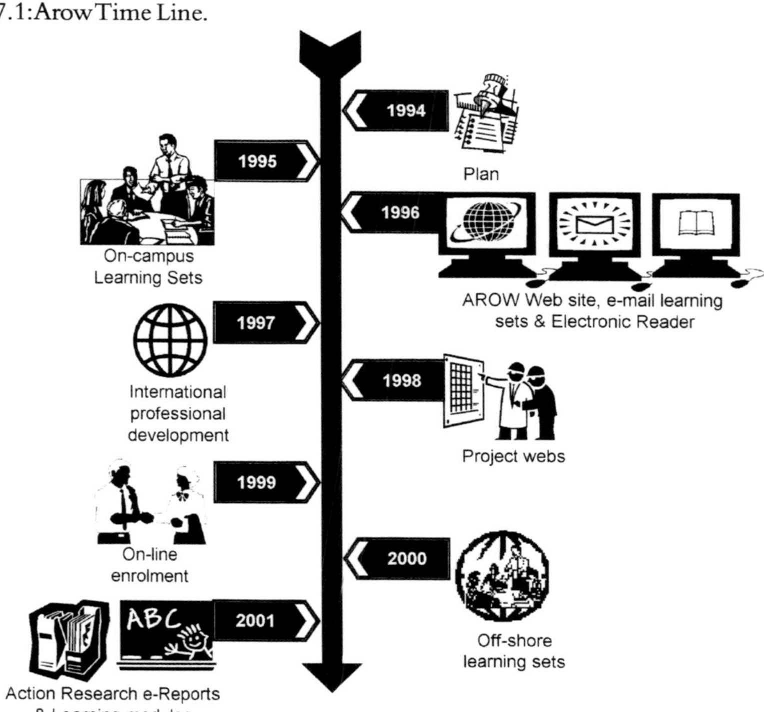

The AROW system includes several elements. The AROW website is the gateway and resource centre. It is supported by several e-mail lists, which are used by members of learning sets. AROW staff includes the Coordinator and a part-time research assistant employed in the Faculty, and learning set advisers employed by collaborative partners. Students join learning sets for one semester, or for an entire Master of Health Science program (two years part-time) or students may take some modules without joining learning sets. Visitors come to AROW for free access to resources, and some contribute feedback, suggestions and ideas.

AROW collaborates with a wide action inquiry network, particularly through Arlist (Dick 2001) and enjoys collaborative relationships with Management Learning and Action Research (MaLAR) in Singapore, Southern Cross Institute for Action Research (SCIAR) in Australia, and Centre de Formation en Recherche Action (CIFRA) and Deutsche Gesellschaft for Technische Zusammenarbeit (GTZ) in Central Africa.

The process of organisational change can be discussed by looking through the four 'windows' that Flood suggests can be used to deepen our systemic appreciation and develop strategies for change. Though I did not use these 'windows' in planning change, I find they are useful for description. The four categories are systems of process, of structure, of meaning and of knowledge-power (Flood 1999).

Process

Processes are the ways things are done, and looking at systems of process involves viewing of the flow of events. Processes have been a major focus of attention in AROW, and it would be easy to devote the whole of this chapter to them. This would result in a partial view, excluding other important considerations.

Action Research, a one-semester course offered since 1995, is designed as a learning system. Each student designs an individual learning project to increase his or her understanding of an aspect of action inquiry, suited to his or her individual learning needs and opportunities. The project may contribute directly to improved professional practice, workplace change or development of new knowledge. Learning is structured by three assignments and four learning cycles. The assignments are: a proposal for a learning project; reflection and discussion in learning sets; and a final paper in electronic format.

Learning is organised into four cycles, corresponding to the phases of action inquiry. Each cycle has phases of planning, acting, observing and reflecting, as summarised in Table 17.1:

Table 17.1: Learning cycles

Week	Cycle/Phase	Learning Project Work
	Cycle 1	
1	Reflect	Reflect on personal learning goals
2	Plan	Draft plan for learning project
3	Act	Circulate draft learning plan to learning set
4	Observe	Read draft plans from learning set members
	Cycle 2	
5	Reflect	Comment on own & set members draft plans
6	Plan	Revised plan for learning project
7	Act	Circulate revised learning plan to learning set
8	Observe	Read revised plans from learning set members
	Cycle3	
9	Reflect	Comment on own & set members learning plans
10	Plan	Plan presentation of work in progress
11	Act	Present work in progress to learning set
12	Observe	Read works in progress
	Cycle 4	
13	Reflect	Comment on work in progress
14	Plan	Plan final report
15	Act	Write and submit final report
16	Observe	Read examiners feedback on final report

(after Hughes 2001b)

Strategies for improvement of process aim to increase reliability and efficiency.Various models for process engineering or quality management are offered in the management literature, most originating form manufacturing processes.They cannot be applied directly and uncritically to learning organisations. Knowledge is not a commodity produced in research laboratories, distributed in books and 'poured into' student's heads by teachers (Zuber-Skerritt, Chapter 1). Students are not passive raw materials to be made into graduates through processes acting on them. Each student constructs his or her own knowledge in his or her own local context.

The learning system as it now operates is an outcome of continuous improvement through process management cycles, which have been a feature of AROW since its inception. For example, I send an e-mail message to each action research student every week during semester. I save these messages, and recycle them in the following year, with editing. Over five years, I have repeatedly improved the weekly emails. I ask each cohort of students to evaluate their learning experience, and use this feedback to improve the next presentation. I review and revise the web site, with new resources added each year. The navigation structure has been revised twice, as the site has grown. Student evaluation now shows less confusion and greater overall satisfaction than five years ago.

As resources have been added to the site, students become more independent as learners, releasing staff time from individual tuition to further improvement of the learning system. However, the core business of AROW cannot be reduced to reliability and efficiency of teaching. Issues of effectiveness, meaning and power must also be addressed.

Structure

According to Flood (1999), structure refers to the patterns of co-ordination, communication and control in a system. The formal hierarchy of AROW is simple. As co-ordinator I am responsible to the Head of School and Academic Board for administrative and academic matters, respectively. The students, staff, collaborating partners and visitors all refer to the Coordinator.

The AROW web site, with associated e-mail lists, is the centre of communication. The home page gives access to course information and on-line enrolment; study guides, communication tools, readings and other learning resources. The site also accommodates a journal (Hughes 2001a) and other resources for action inquiry. The website is not a virtual classroom. We think of a virtual classroom as an online learning environment that 'should not he much different from a real classroom or training room' (Porter 1997 p24). That is, a place in cyberspace where students meet and learn. But AROW participants live and learn in workplaces and suburbs. AROW Students learn in various learning environments. They have access to varied off-line learning resources in their workplaces, homes, cities and suburbs. They use different search techniques, have different interests, and so gain access to different on-line resources. The design of the AROW web site reflects awareness of the range of individual differences among students and their environments.

The heart of learning in the AROW system is the learning set. Many people have adapted Reg Revan's (1982) original idea, so that today there is a range of related approaches called learning circles, learning sets or by other names. AROW learning sets have fewer than ten members who interact by e-mail each week. Offshore learning sets also meet face to face about once each month, and some students participated in employer-sponsored workshops as well as e-mail learning sets. Learning set members share knowledge and resources. Some of this activity is organised in the learning cycle, and some occurs informally during or between learning set meetings. Learning sets introduced into the faculty through AROW have since been adapted to other activities including educational research, doctoral coursework and offshore learning.

AROW is an opportunity for international and cross-disciplinary cooperation. Students have provided mutual support to projects in education in South Africa; youth work in Canada; nursing in Sydney;

theological education in USA; physiotherapy practice in rural NSW; and aged care in Singapore. AROW has supported action inquiry in health care and education. These have been real projects supported and facilitated using computer mediated communication.

Strategies for improvement of structure are usually about improving the bureaucratic structure of an organisation (by making the hierarchy more flat, for example) or developing alternatives to bureaucratic structures, such as collective decision making, participatory structures, open systems or communal systems guided by values and purposes, rather than rules and hierarchy. In the case of AROW I have not attempted to transform the university bureaucracy, but try to build a community of practice in the spaces and cracks, of a traditional university (Senge et al 2000 p377). I have found support and collegial relationships through electronic communication with like-minded people outside my own university, and from that base, began to slowly build a community of interest within my own institution. This strategy left AROW relatively independent within the university bureaucracy.

During 2001, following the institution of offshore learning sets a year earlier, the weak emphasis on rules and formal procedures came up against the administrative requirements of the larger organisation. Administrative procedures had to be adapted to accommodate learning sets operating outside the national boundary. By this time the AROW system was accepted in the faculty, and had demonstrated its value on instrument grounds. Ways were found for the bureaucracy to accommodate this new way of doing things.

The growth and development of AROW can be seen as a change in the larger system of which it is a part. This change was brought about by process of accommodation by the whole to a part, rather than by top-down strategic planning for the organisation as a whole. The meaning and purpose of AROW was not defined at senior levels of the organisation and handed down. Meaning is constructed in the AROW system.

Meaning

AROW is a system for learning; a system that learns; and system with meaning for a larger organisation, of which it is part. A primary purpose of AROW is to facilitate learning about action research and action inquiry by students and people seeking professional development. In this light, I refer to AROW as a learning system, meaning a system for learning. AROW is also a system that learns, Though AROW is not an organisation, but part of one, the term 'learning organisation' can be applied to smaller systems that learn, and are embedded inside organisations (Argyris & Schon 1978; Senge 1990). In Peter Senge's 'Fifth Discipline' model, (Senge 1990; Senge et al 2000) the learning organisation is at a conceptual level above the learning system. A learning system involves learning, and a learning organisation involves meta-learning (learning about learning). In thinking about AROW as action for organisational change, my focus is on AROW as a learning organisation. My strategy is not to try to change the whole faculty or university into a learning organisation, but to grow AROW as a learning organisation inside a School nested in a faculty, forming part of the university. Systemic thinking tells us that a change in one part will have implications for the whole.

An early problem was to devise ways of learning and teaching that were consistent with the principles and practices of action inquiry. Learning sets were adapted to this purpose, and they required dialogue space in which to operate. A decision was taken early, that this would not be in classrooms on campus.

Email is a medium that lends itself to dialogue rather than discussion or debate. Conventional learning in university teaching often presents theories and ideas in the form of a debate, in which two (or more) views are presented in opposition to each other, with one view emerging as superior. Many teachers encourage discussion, in which two (or more) views are presented and defended in a search for agreement on a common view, which may (or may not) contain ideas or elements of various theories. Dialogue is different. Views are presented, and listened to, to that the listener enters into and comes to appreciate the frame of reference of the presenter (Flood 1999). In the practice of dialogue, people pay attention to the words and also to the spaces between the words. This is facilitated by a silent pause after a presenter has spoken, so that meaning can be appreciated and reflected upon (Senge et al 2000 p75). Asynchronous email provides pauses for reflection. Members of an e-mail learning set do not reply immediately, but have time to read, think, reflect and compose a response. In an additional advantage, the sender of a message receives his or her own words back from the list server, and so has an opportunity to read and reflect on what he or she wrote.

McGill and Beatty list the four main things that learning set members do as presenting, supporting, preparing and reviewing (McGill & Beatty 1995). In AROW learning sets these four activities happen by e-mail, with some learning sets also meeting face to face. The e-mail process encourages reflective dialogue, rather than debate or discussion. A skilled facilitator can enhance this process, whereby students construct their own meanings from their reading, experience, dialogue and reflection. AROW encourages students to re-examine, reflect and reconstruct their personal systems of meaning.

AROW recognises that each student produces meaning and knowledge in his or her own head. This understanding rejects the model of the university as a factory for production and distribution of knowledge. This has implications for systems of meaning. Meaning is not about a 'product' that can be commodified and sold, but is about understanding in the minds of people.

Systems of meaning are important to organisational change. Strategic planning literature encourages change agents to aim for agreement on improvement strategies (Goodstein et al 1993; Lewis 1995). A focus on systems of meaning directs our attention to the sense we make of words and events; to value systems and ideologies; and the coherence, contradiction or incongruity of thoughts, feelings, values and actions (Watzlawick et al 1967) in organisational contexts. Flood (1999) offers a continuum of agreement ranging from consensus through accommodation to toleration of diversity.

When I introduced action research and systemic thinking into a science based faculty, I made no attempt to secure consensus or accommodation from members of the faculty with different values and knowledge about teaching and research. I did not attempt to manage polarised viewpoints, but worked to build a community of interest and practice around action research. In 1995 and 1996 there were very few academics in the faculty with an interest in action research. These few were busy with other projects, or their career interests did not lead them to offer practical support.

The liberal university is tolerant of diversity, especially if new or changing elements do not make demands for change on older or more stable elements. The use of the World Wide Web and email for communication with students and colleagues off-campus meant that AROW could develop as an inconspicuous element in the organisation, without demanding consensus, agreement or even accommodation from academics who were committed to scientific method.

Toleration provided a nursery in which AROW was permitted to grow. As AROW grew and developed, the institution came to accommodate this internal change. More recently key members of the faculty have come to recognise some advantages and opportunities that AROW and action inquiry can offer the institution. But this does not imply agreement or consensus about action inquiry or its place in the faculty. The introduction of new elements in an organisation and the process of change always involve questions of power and local politics.

Power

Power is an element in all relationships, and is exercised in subtle as well as obvious ways. Knowledge is important in the university, which is a key institution in determining what counts as valid knowledge in society. People in senior academic positions determine what is to be counted as valid knowledge. The dominant systems of knowledge support and enhance the power of some people, and maintain the exploitation and powerlessness of others, so systems of knowledge have implications for what is fair and unfair inside the university, and in the wider society.

AROW operates within a system of knowledge-power that privileges reductionism, positivism and experimental design research. At the same time action research and systemic knowledge are tolerated in an institution proclaiming liberal values and academic freedom. The institution ambiguously provides a space within which AROW can operate, and simultaneously withholds the resources needed for it to thrive.

The systems of knowledge and power within the faculty discount the value of systemic thinking and action research. At the same time, the location of AROW within a major university endows action inquiry a status that carries certain authority and validity. After establishing it in the 'cracks' of the university structure, and keeping it alive for five years, AROW is moving towards the status of an established program in a major university. As a strategy for organisational change, AROW can be presented as a normal part of the university program. This assists acceptance both inside and outside the university. Through the strategy of not attempting to change the organisation as a whole, AROW has reached a point where claims can be made that the faculty includes an established program for action inquiry and systemic thinking, that sits beside programs of scientific positivism and reductionism. To this extent the character of the faculty as a whole can be described as changing. I used a strategy of avoiding direct confrontation with established systems of knowledge-power, and working to establish a complimentary system to achieve this.

In a climate of shrinking resources and increasing commercialisation, web-based delivery and the adaptation of learning sets to support graduate courses were welcomed as a way to offer flexible learning into new markets. Strategies for learning that were developed in AROW have been adapted to other activities. This instrumental value enhances the value of AROW to people in positions of power in the faculty.

Within AROW learning strategies were adopted with specific attention to issues of knowledge-power. Systems of knowledge-power can be used to reinforce patterns of dominance, or to move towards fairer relationships. Flood points to two ways to do this. We can raise the awareness of privileged people, so that they may decide to operate in ways that are fairer. Alternatively, we may work to develop the resilience of vulnerable people, so they are better able to empower themselves (Flood 1999 p119).

Many AROW students are in leadership positions within privileged professional elites. Some are from disadvantaged backgrounds, now seeking upward mobility. The facilitation style and participatory emphasis in AROW offers an alternative to these members of a knowledge-power elite. In AROW there is no attempt to establish knowledge on the basis of authority or power. There is no attempt to achieve consensus or shared meaning among participants, but an attempt to gain understanding of the range of meanings that can be attached to key concepts, and an appreciation of difference.

Students learn in diverse ways. Some AROW participants engage in action learning, some work on action research projects, and others engage in related forms of action inquiry (Tripp 1996), including collaborative learning, reflective practice or other action inquiry projects. Students engaged on different forms of action inquiry may belong to a single learning set. There is no single definition of action inquiry or action research to which students are expected to subscribe.

The AROW learning set becomes a self-reflective community (Carr & Kemmis 1986). Each learning set participant is concerned with the transformation of his or her own situation, typically in two dimensions. He or she is engaged in a search for personal transformation through education, and at the same time most participants are actively working for transformation of their workplaces or professional practice. These dimensions relate directly to the twin aims of action inquiry. Learning sets bring people from different professions, workplaces and nations together, to work on varied projects. Participants are required to engage in critical reflection on other people's projects, and receive feedback from people in other professions, workplaces, cultures or countries. This ensures that action inquiry in AROW is not only concerned with transformation of the participant's own local situation. Participants are challenged to reflect on their own learning and action in relation to other projects, and to consider the relationships between problems and situations that are not usually brought into the same context.

As a strategy for improvement AROW introduced a form of inquiry and strategies for learning that tend to increase fairness in an institution that creates privileged elites. Introducing action inquiry into this setting is an opportunity to influence those who may occupy positions of power, and contribute to the definition of what counts as knowledge in the future (following their graduation). Establishing and maintaining AROW within the university is an act of resistance to established regimes of knowledge-power.

The combination of action learning and inquiry with international discussion in facilitated learning sets, supporting each other's learning across national and ethnic boundaries is a tool for international understanding, interdisciplinary dialogue and critical inquiry.

Summary

Action inquiry includes a number of processes for learning, research and change characterised by critical inquiry, systems thinking and feedback cycles of action and reflection. Action Research On Web (AROW) is a system designed to introduce change into a university faculty through action, learning and research. In seven years the system has grown into a complex system including a web site, electronic publications, email and face-to-face learning sets, workshops and action research projects. Collaborative relationships have been forged with Australian and overseas project partners.

Action learning and action research are robust practices. The story of AROW demonstrates that they can be used with few resources to exert leverage for change on large organisations, without the commitment of senior decision makers. Strategies for change can be analysed in terms of process, structure, meaning and power. Although actual practice in AROW has been messier than this short description might imply, systemic thinking, action in several sub-systems at once, and viewing the situation through multiple 'windows' enabled change to be exerted from a relatively junior position within a large organisation.

Internet technology has facilitated communication, and permitted collaborative, learning and supportive relationships to develop. Much of what has been learned during this project is embedded, in one way or another, on the Action Research on Web site, which readers are invited to visit at www.cchs.usyd.edu.au/arow.

Acknowledgment

I wish to thank all who have contributed to the development of Action Research On Web, especially AROW students, and collaborative partner in Singapore, Australia and Africa. Special thanks to Bob Dick and Shankar Sankaran.

Bibliography

Argyris, C & Schon, D (1978) *Organisational Learning: A theory of action prespective.* Reading: Addison-Wesley

Campbell, A (2000). *Psyberspace*: The University of Sydney (available online: http://www.cchs.usyd.edu.au/bach/psyberspace – accessed 1 May 2001).

Carr, W & Kemmis, S (1986) *Becoming Critical: Education, knowledge and Action Research.* Geelong: Deakin University

Davis, R.H. Alexander, LT & Yelon, SL (1974) *Learning System Design: An approach to the improvement of instruction.* New York: McGraw-Hill

Dick, B (Moderator) (2001) *Arlist.* Email Action Research Mailing List. Southern Cross University (available online: arlist@scu.edu.au)

Faculty of Health Sciences (2000) *Postgraduate Handbook 2000.* Sydney: The University of Sydney

Flood, RL (1999) *Rethinking the Fifth Discipline: Learning within the unknowable.* London: Routledge

Goodstein, LD, Nolan, TM & Pfeiffer, JW (1993) *Applied Strategic Planning: A comprehensive guide.* Amsterdam: Pfeiffer

Hughes, I (1996) *Action Research Electronic Reader.* The University of Sydney (available online: http://www.cchs.usyd.edu.au/arow/reader – accessed 1 Jan 2001)

Hughes, I (1997) *Introduction to Action Research Electronic Reader.* The University of Sydney (available online: http://www.cchs.usyd.edu.au/arow/reader/rintro.htm – accessed 1 Jan 2001)

Hughes, I (2001a) *Action Research e-Reports.* Sydney: The University of Sydney (available online: http://www.cchs.usyd.edu.au/arow/arer/ – accessed 1 Jan 2001)

Hughes, I (2001b) Teaching Action Research On Web. *Information Technology and Society.* 4(3) pp64–71

Lewis, JP (1995) *The Project Manager's Desk Reference.* Chicago: Irwin

McGill, I & Beaty, L (1995) *Action Learning: A practitioner's guide.* London: Kogan Page

Porter, LR (1997) *Creating the Virtual Classroom.* New York: John Wiley

Revans, R (1982) *The Origins and Growth of Action Learning.* Bikley: Chartwell-Bratt

Senge, P (1990) *The Fifth Discipline: The art and practice of the learning organisation.* New York: Doubleday-Currency

Senge, P, Cambron-McCabe, N, Lucas, T, Smith, B, Dutton, J & Kleiner, A (2000) *Schools That Learn.* London: Nicholas Brealey

Tripp, D (1996). *Action Inquiry.* (available online: www.parnetorg/PARchive/docs/tripp_96/ – accessed 1 May 2000)

Watzlawick, P, Beavin, JH & Jackson, DD (1967) *Pragmatics of Human Communication: A study of patterns, pathologies and paradoxes.* New York: Norton.

Elisabeth Wilson-Evered & Charmine EJ Härtel

Introduction

Action research is a normative model for learning and for planned change (French & Bell 1990). In action learning programs, participants learn from their own experience and through questioning what they do, what they believe and what can be done to make their actions and processes more effective (Mumford 1991). In this chapter, we share a case study of how one hospital used an action learning framework in the design and implementation of a planned organisational change program aimed at improving morale and innovation and preparing staff for an anticipated merger. The case represents a unique illustration of how the integration of action research, empirical investigation and organisational development (OD) can aid practitioners to secure desired changes in their organisations.

Theoretical Foundations

This case study, presented from the practitioner perspective, is under the rubric of organisational development (OD) which may be defined as:

> ...a process of planned system change that attempts to make organisations (viewed as social-technical systems) better able to attain their short-and long-term objectives. This is achieved by teaching the organisation members to manage their organisation processes, structures, and culture more effectively.
>
> (French, Bell & Zawacki 1994 p7)

We acknowledge that the approach we adopt is one of many possible applications of OD and action research (French & Bell 1990; Reason 1999). We used a model of action research applied to OD because our case study was a behavioural intervention (French & Bell 1990). Techniques of group facilitation including the FIDO model were derived from the work and teaching of Bob Dick (1991). The *processes*, both subtle and obvious, that occurred in, around and within the project, were enabled and enhanced through incorporating action learning concepts and principles.

We based our project design on the principles of participative (action) research (Park 1999; Reason 1999) and adult learning (Knowles 1990). Action learning and action research methods were used to ensure that affected personnel played a key role in what happened in their workplace (Reason 1999). In keeping with the tradition of Revans (1976) on action learning in hospitals, we employed both surveys and learning groups in order to engage action and create learning opportunities among staff.

In conducting the project, which became known later as the Organisational Improvement Initiative, we integrated the work of a number of theorists, researcher-practitioners and teachers. Our perspective on innovation and teams including team reflexivity is drawn from the extraordinary insight, research and interventions of Michael West and his various colleagues (1987; 1990; 1994; 1997; 1998; 2000). With respect to leadership style to support innovation and change, we argue for the usefulness of the concepts of transformational leadership (Bass 1998; Kanter 1997; Parry 1999). Our techniques on process consultancy were derived from the work of Edgar Schein (1987). Data was collected and interpreted using the notions of reflection in action, organisational defences, theory of action and single and double loop learning (Argyris 1990; Lichtenstein 2000; Schon 1995; Swift & West 1998).

Action Research Model

The action research model proposed by French and Bell (1990 p100) informed the project strategy:

> The key aspects of the model *are diagnosis, data gathering, feedback to the client group, data discussion by the client group, action planning and action.* The sequence tends to be cyclical with the focus on new or advanced problems as the client group learns to work more effectively together.

The initiative was project managed by the first author who was a member of the larger organisation. The day-to-day management of the project was conducted according to basic project management methodology (Duncan 1996). Traditional project management and action approaches have worked effectively when juxtaposed as evidenced in large scale change interventions at the National Aeronautical and Space Administration (NASA) (Kotnour, Matkovich & Ellison 1999).

Innovation at the Hospital

No organisation can protect itself from change – rather, people must learn to be change-adept (Argyris 1990; Kanter 1997). However, in the unrelenting push to increase quality and cut costs, adapting to change is not enough (Savitz, Kaluzny, Kelly & Tew 2000). Companies need to anticipate or better create the change so that others may follow (McLaughlin & Kaluzny 2000). How can organisations enable and harness the creativity of their human resources? How can people learn to be creative and to support innovation in others? The action research approach described in this chapter provides insight on how to achieve these aims.

Exigency for Innovation

Managers are often pressured to find ways of enabling people to be creative in order to improve the value and job satisfaction of this expensive resource (Kotter 1999). This means more than incremental innovation; it means encouraging people to transform what they do (radical innovation) and produce a new state of the art (Van de Ven, Polley, Garud & Venkataraman 1999). Liberating people to envision new possibilities requires a workplace characterised by high morale, imagination, enthusiasm, energy, transformational leadership (Bass 1998; Parry 1999) and a climate for innovation (Kanter 1997; Shamir, Zakay, Breinin & Popper 1998; West 1997; Wilson-Evered, Härtel & Neale 2001).

Innovation for the purpose of this case study is defined as the intentional introduction of ideas, systems, methods, products, procedures or processes *new* to the unit of adoption and designed to significantly *benefit* a target (West & Farr 1990). For a hospital this means that although one area may have implemented a new system such as team planning sessions or a clinical education program or patient support groups, these are still considered innovations when they are planned and implemented by other staff in a different area.

Older more successful organisations like the subject of our case study are likely to have institutionalised systems and structures that inhibit innovation (Van De Ven 1986). The case hospital had experienced peaks of success in its 60 years (Patrick 1988). However, some evidence of decline was apparent in a reduction of patients attending the hospital. At the time, many of the senior staff and managers had commenced working at the hospital in the 1970s, having worked their way up through the system. The hospital was undergoing redevelopment (being rebuilt and integrated with a larger facility) which meant an imperative for innovation among all groups. Consequently, existing systems, structures, procedures and processes had to be reviewed and created afresh for the new facility. No individual, group or department was exempt from the need to effect significant change.

Context and Background Initiative

The health facility, a centre for specialised research and teaching, comprised 200 beds and 970 staff. It had a long tradition of providing care to the community of women and infants and was tightly circumscribed within this ethos for many years. Changes in the health care system meant that facilities such as this were opened to external scrutiny in an effort to secure the best possible value for the health dollar. The message to staff, common in most organisations, was to find ways of increasing quality without increasing (preferably reducing) costs (Argyris 1999; McLaughlin & Kaluzny 2000; Revans 1976; Savitz et al 2000).

Project Overview

Diagnosis and data gathering

Conversations with staff, individually and in groups, indicated that many were distressed about a number of issues. The most common report was feeling unappreciated, overworked and deprived of information and involvement in matters that significantly affected them. Staff raised concerns that the low morale was negatively impacting on patient care and enthusiasm in the workplace. Line managers echoed the concerns and the message eventually reached senior management.

Unlike many change initiatives, senior management did not initiate this project, although considerable work was invested in gaining their commitment and sponsorship. The project, which was initiated by staff groups, however, was concordant with the newly appointed CEO's organisation development strategy. Because of this and the fact that the hospital prided itself in being caring and supportive of staff and patients, the executive group cautiously accepted the need for a special project to explore the issues and possible interventions. Staff took an integral role in designing the main project and the subprojects. Among their roles was a responsibility to ensure the ecological validity of processes and appropriateness of language used in communications and data gathering instruments.

A summary of the full project scope is presented in Figure 18.1.

Fig 18.1: Project Overview

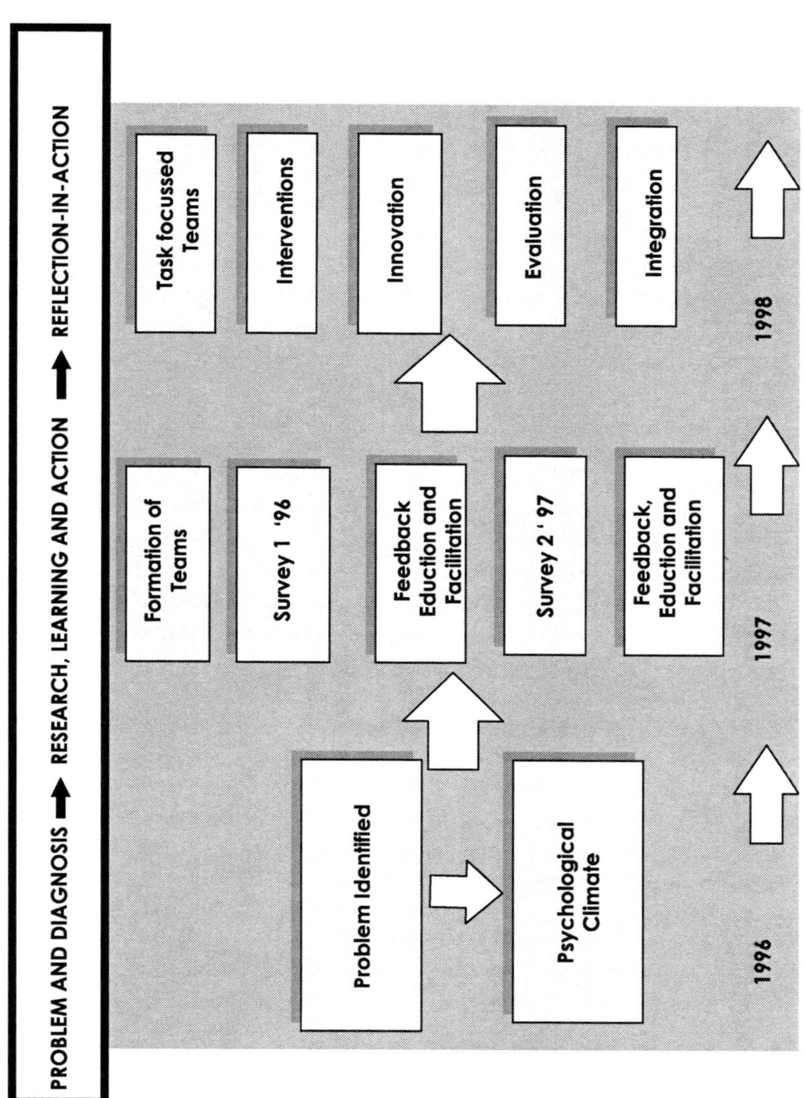

Note: Multiple sources of information were gathered at different points in time by multiple groups and involved multiple cycles of reflection-in-action. Finally, the knowledge became integrated within organisational systems, processes and language.

Project team infrastructure

Employee participation in decision making is important in its effects on performance, innovation, responses to downsizing, change acceptance, commitment and job satisfaction (Martin, Parsons & Bennett 1995; Sagie & Koslowski 1994). The importance of participation from all levels and professions was highlighted and confirmed throughout the project (Kotnour et. al 1999). Staff often spoke of the organisation as a community or a family, and that inclusion in the organisation was very important to them.

The contention that people support what they create is axiomatic in action science and organisational development (Putman, 1999). Such a belief is highly congruent with the collaborative aspect of action research (French & Bell 1990 p104) and participative action research, which aims to generate both knowledge *and* produce action and practical outcomes (Park 1999; Reason 1999). The choice of project team infrastructure was based, therefore, on how people wanted participation to be practiced (Kotnour et al 1999). The infrastructure is diagrammatically represented in Figure 18.2.

The strategic direction of the project was coordinated by the strategic team, which consisted of senior managers chaired by the senior executive of the hospital. The strategic team's responsibility was to ensure that the

Fig 18.2: Project Team Infrastructure to Ensure Representation and Participation.

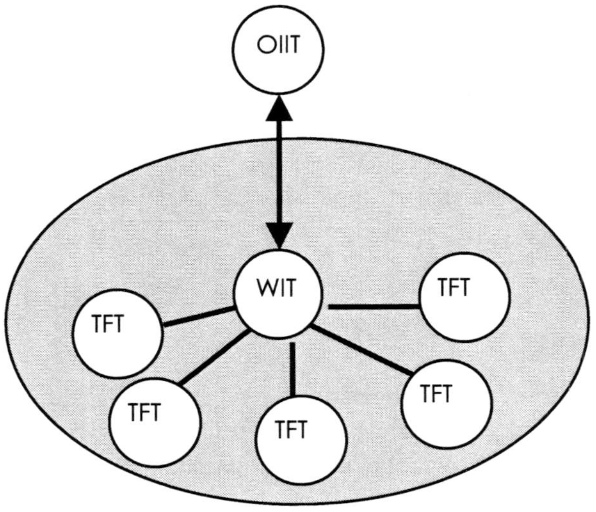

OIIT = organisation improvement implementation team (strategic focus)

WIT = workplace improvement team (action focus)

TFT = task focused teams

Organisational Improvement Initiative both informed and was integrated with the organisation's strategic goals and took into account information collected by the action teams. This approach led to the identification of three key performance indicators for the project: an increase in staff morale, an increase in staff satisfaction and an increase in staff innovation.

The strategic decisions reached by the strategic team were informed and implemented by action teams, which comprised the workplace improvement team and its five supporting task focused teams. The workplace improvement team comprised line managers and staff from the coalface. Meetings were typically volatile, vocal and action oriented. The diverse group ensured that challenges and disconfirming evidence surfaced at all project meetings (Dick 1991 p255). Finally, ad hoc teams were established when the need arose to act on information.

An open invitation to join the action planning groups and participate at any stage in the project lifecycle was issued. Members of teams actively encouraged colleagues to participate when an area was under-represented. Opportunities for membership also arose when a nominated person left the organisation or failed to attend due to work pressures. Indeed, anyone who offered ideas or showed an interest in making changes was quickly coopted on to teams.

Learning and Action

The ability of organisations to learn from their mistakes and successes and learn how to understand and improve processes is vital for survival (Brown 1991). An important step, therefore, is for leaders and line managers to examine their espoused theories – what they say is happening – compared with what is actually demonstrated by their actions (Korth 2000). These processes are representative of Argyris' (1990) theory of action.

Argyris and Schon (1978) argued that organisations need to develop learning systems so that single and double-loop approaches are used appropriately (Korth 2000). Minimal change occurs with single loop learning in which the organisation maintains its current focus and style. Double-loop learning, on the other hand, requires that the organisation examine its underlying beliefs, values and culture and the way in which they are interpreted into systems, policies and objectives and then makes changes. The project described here aspired to promote double loop learning.

Teaming up for Action

Not all groups were effective in producing action and achieving outcomes. Possible reasons for the different outcomes include an inability to apply group skills and knowledge to the task, lacking the skill set required for the task, problematic group dynamics, personality clashes, ineffective leadership, misunderstanding of the tasks, lack of motivation and lack of intrinsic or extrinsic rewards (West 1994). The critical success ingredient for these groups was enthusiasm and willingness to learn on the part of the participants. Leaders that encouraged new ideas, stimulated thinking about work in different ways, motivated people to act and inspired them to achieve a shared vision achieved better results (Wilson-Evered, Härtel & Neale, 2001. These are attributes of transformational leaders who consider staff and promote their development rather than seek personal recognition (Bass 1998, Parry 1999). Further, the importance of feelings and information were acknowledged. Accordingly, we integrated the Feelings, Information, Decisions and Outcomes (FIDO) model (Dick 1991) in our meeting processes

Enabling Team Processes Using FIDO

The order of the terms in the FIDO model represents the flow of a group process (Dick 1991 p23). The FIDO model is a very useful tool for group facilitation. It provides a framework for understanding individual reactions, the group process and gives a guide to encourage effective problem solving. In brief, feelings (F) are dealt with first in meetings as they influence individuals' engagement and commitment. At most meetings, negative feelings towards the organisation and frustration featured. Consequently, opportunities were provided to express these (F) feelings at the beginning of meetings. Moving through the negativity meant work could begin on using the (I) information that had been collected. Information brought to the meetings had to be specific, adequate, accurate and relevant and understood by the group, then it was used to inform (D) decisions (Dick 1991 p23) in order to achieve (O) agreed outcomes.

Apart from the FIDO process, a number of other group norms were discussed and employed according to West's (1990) theory of group innovation. These processes were as follows:

-*support for new ideas* and building a 'yes' culture so that when ideas are offered they are supported and encouraged both verbally and practically – the group actively supported each other's ideas and became excited by developing and implementing them

-*task orientation* where the group share concerns for excellence and quality – participants were enthusiastic about their group project and developed a sense of pride in their processes and outcomes; members worked very hard whilst having to achieve the heavy and demanding workload common in hospitals

-*vision* which serves as a motivating force and a higher order goal – the participants of these groups were working to create interventions to benefit the whole organisation as well as implementing innovations in their workplace

-*participative safety* where involvement in decision making is enabled and reinforced in an environment that is non-threatening (Anderson & West 1998; Bunce & West 1995; West 1997) – the group atmosphere was characterised by encouragement and support for diversity of ideas and contribution

-*team reflexivity* or the 'extent to which a team reflects on and modifies its objectives, strategies and processes in relation to its task-functional environment' (Schon 1995; Swift & West 1998 p2).

The purpose of the groups was to design and implement innovations for enhancing identified aspects of climate across the whole organisation as listed below:

-Participative Decision Making
-Reward and Recognition
-Recognition of and Support for Innovation
-Communication
-Team Building
-Change Management (this group did not establish an action plan)
-Linking Performance Data.

The groups reported considerable satisfaction from working on these projects. Some were given project management support, others worked independently (Schein 1987) while project staff led the linking performance data aspect. A summary of the creative output of the task-focused teams is provided in Table 18.1 below.

Table 18.1: Summary of Output

Project Title	Intervention	Outcome	Evaluation
Participative Decision Making (PDM)	A table was drawn up of all areas where staff felt they should be included in the decision making process. It was attached to a memo highlighting findings and importance of PDM	Document sent to executive who replied by memo, acknowledging the importance of matters but that the senior team would decide on such matters.	No formal evaluation Group Reflection and debriefing
Reward and Recognition	Areas that had made improvements between surveys one and two were recognised at a public ceremony that provided hot lunch with drinks, open to all staff. Certificate and plaque and a formal thankyou by the senior executive occurred, and book tokens were awarded to special categories such as most improved areas across all dimensions	Improved understanding across the organization of the work and creativity of different work areas. Provided encouragement to areas Staff felt pride and pleasure in their achievements	Survey of staff opinions about the Reward subproject was favourable
Support for and Record of Innovations	A record was made of all innovations by work area by year in the year following the survey (97 and 98). Areas were encouraged to present their innovations at meetings.	All innovations were recorded and published in separate reports for both years. Reports were distributed to all senior staff	Staff and industry experts rated the innovations in terms of novelty, magnitude, radicalness and effectiveness and benefit to patients, staff well being and team function or administrative efficiency
Communication	A communication strategy was proposed from which a team briefing process was implemented. All decisions made by executive were summarised on a briefing sheet. The information sheet and its contents were also verbally reported to next level managers. This process was repeated to all levels of staff. The process then returned through the levels with added comments, questions and issues within two weeks. Management publicised staff questions and executive response in the hospital newsletter.	Improvements in information circulation were achieved. Some roadblocks were described and short comings were discovered from discussions with staff	A survey of the effectiveness of team brief, uncovered strengths, weaknesses and the roadblocks and successes. The senior staff in the identified areas were tasked with exposing and removing roadblocks
Team Building	A group of staff brainstormed ideas for improving relationships and communication across teams.	Team identification process for work area was erected at the entrance to the area. A team collage was produced and presented in a poster and exhibited around the organization	From verbal feedback, the process improved relationships among teams.

Freeing up Innovation

Innovations occurred at a number of levels. First, the strategic group implemented a number of new initiatives, such as leadership development programs and individual development, which aligned the initiative with the overall organisational development program. Transformational leadership was considered critical for stimulating innovation and improving morale. The executive group also published a pamphlet on the findings of the initiative in which they recorded their commitment to action across all key aspects of the organisational climate. Leadership action was demonstrated and modelled by integrating processes, learnings and information from the initiative's key strategic programs. People issues were accepted as important for achieving organisational outcomes.

Second, analysis of the record of all innovations revealed a clear increase in the number of innovations implemented across all work groups. Furthermore, survey and focus group information demonstrated incremental improvement in perceptions of leadership, morale and other aspects of the work group climate for most work groups. Organisational learning was evident by an improvement and innovation policy and supporting procedures that were collaboratively developed by management, staff and union groups (see Appendix A). Finally, the task focused teams brought together diverse groups in unusually challenging problem solving exercises (eg. how to improve participative decision making across the hospital?). The groups were able to implement innovations that made a difference to people in the organisation and flowed on to their customers (Wilson-Evered et al 2001a, 2001b).

Discussion

From a modest endeavour to respond to staff concerns about declining morale, the project grew into an organisation-wide improvement initiative that produced an increase in innovation and encouraged transformational leadership. Overall achievements are attributable, in part, to the 'small wins' made by work groups and task-focused learning groups (Kotter 1999; Weick 1984). Staff participation and potency in and their championship of facets of the project was a central component of the methodology. We found support for the tenet that putting people first leads to competitive advantage (Pfeffer 1998).

In closing, we would like to leave you with the paradox posed by Argyris (1999) as a possible explanation for why some areas remained sceptical about the importance of focusing on 'soft processes'. If managers do not discuss their defensive routines, these routines will persist and proliferate. On the other hand, if they do discuss them, they may be penalized for doing so. In this way, defensive routines are shielded from change (Argyris 1999). The increasingly sophisticated and diverse ways of studying and applying action learning research hold the promise of unraveling this paradox and exposing new ways to stimulate action leading to organisational innovation.

Acknowledgments

We would like to thank the staff and management of the hospital for their encouragement and participation and particularly their challenges, which though perplexing at times, enhanced our learning. We are also grateful for the contribution of project officers particularly, Susan Pienaar and Stephanie Boldeman, and are indebted to our teachers.

Bibliography

Anderson, NR & MA West (1998) 'Measuring climate for workgroup innovation: development and validation of the team climate inventory' in *Journal of Organizational Behavior* 19, pp235–258

Argyris, C & D Schon (1978) *Organizational Learning: A theory of action perspective.* Reading: Addison-Wesley

Argyris, C (1990) *Overcoming Organizational Defenses: Facilitating organizational learning.* Boston: Allyn & Bacon

Argyris, C (1999) 'The next challenge for TQM – taking the offensive on defensive reasoning' in *The Journal for Quality and Participation.* 22(6), pp41–43

Bass, BM (1998) *Transformational Leadership: Industrial, military and educational impact.* Mahwah: Lawrence Erlbaum Associates Inc

Brown, T (1991) 'Andy Van de Ven: Why Companies Don't Learn' in *Industry-Week.* 240(16), Aug 19, pp36–43

Bunce, DA & MA West (1995) 'Self perceptions and perceptions of group climate as predictors of individual innovation at work' in *Applied Psychology: An international review.* 44(3), pp119–215

Dick, R (1991) *Helping Groups to be Effective: Skills, processes and concepts for group facilitation.* Brisbane: Interchange

Duncan, WR (1996) *A Guide to the Project Management Body of Knowledge.* Upper Derby: Project Management Institute

French, WL & CH Bell (1990) *Organizational Development: Behavioral science interventions for organization improvement.* Englewood Cliffs: Prentice-Hall

French, WL, Bell, CH & Zawacki RA (eds) (1994). *Organization Development and Transformation: Managing effective change.* 4th ed. Homewood: Richard D Irwin

Kanter, RM (1997) *Rosabeth Moss Kanter on the Frontiers of Management.* Boston: Harvard Business School Press

Knowles, M (1990) *The Adult Learner: A neglected species.* Houston: Gulf Publishing

Korth, SJ (2000) 'Single and double loop learning: Exploring the potential influence of cognitive style' in *Organization Development Journal.* 18(3), pp87–98

Kotnour, TJ, Matkovich & Ellison, R (1999) 'Establishing a change infrastructure through teams' in *Engineering Management Journal.* 11(3), pp25–30

Kotter, JP (1999) 'Leading change: The eight steps to transformation' in Conger, JA, Spreitzer, GM & Lawler, EE (eds) *Leader's Change Handbook: An essential guide to setting direction and taking action.* pp87–99. San Francisco: Jossey Bass Inc

Lichtenstein, BMB (2000) 'Generative knowledge and self-organized learning: reflecting on Don Schon's research' in *Journal of Management Inquiry.* 9(1), pp47–54

Martin, CL, Parsons, CK & Bennett, N (1995) 'The Influence of employee involvement program membership during downsizing: Attitude toward the employer and union' in *Journal of Management.* 21(5), pp879–890

McLaughlin, CP & Kaluzny, AD (2000) 'Building client centered systems of care: choosing a process direction for the next century' in *Health Care Management Review.* 25(1), pp73–82

Mumford, A (1991) 'Learning in Action' in *Personnel Management.* 23(7), p34

Park, P (1999) 'People, knowledge, and change in participatory research' in *Management Learning.* 30(2), pp141–157

Parry, K (1999) *Transformational Leadership: Developing an enterprising management culture.* Sydney: Business and Professional Publishing

Patrick, R (1988) *The Royal Women's Hospital, Brisbane.* Brisbane: Boolarong Publications

Pfeffer, J (1998) *The Human Equation: Building profits by putting people first.* Boston: Harvard Business School Press

Putman, RW (1999) 'Transforming social practice: An action science perspective' in *Management Learning.* 30(2), pp177–187

Reason, P (1999) 'Integrating action and reflection through cooperative enquiry' in *Management Learning.* 30(2), pp207–226

Revans, RW (1976) *Action Learning in Hospitals: Diagnosis and therapy.* Maidenhead: McGraw-Hill

Sagie, A & Koslowksy, M (1994) 'Organizational attitudes and behaviours as a function of participation in strategic and tactical change decisions: An application of path-goal theory' in *Journal of Organizational Behaviour.* 15, pp37–47

Savitz, LA, Kaluzny, AD, Kelly, DL & Tew, DM (2000) 'A life cycle model of continuous clinical process innovation/Practitioner application' in *Journal of Healthcare Management.* 45(5), pp307–316

Schein, EH (1987) *Process Consultation: Lessons for managers and consultants.* Reading: Addison-Wesley

Schon, DA (1995) *The Reflective Practitioner: How professionals think in action.* Aldershot: Arena

Shamir, B, Zakay, E, Breinin, E & Popper, M (1998) 'Correlates of charismatic behaviour in military unit, unit characteristics and superiors in appraisal of leader performance' in *Academy of Management Journal.* 41(4), pp387–410

Swift, TA & West, MA (1998) *Reflexivity and Group Processes: Research and practice.* Sheffield: ESRC Centre for Organization and Innovation, University of Sheffield

Van de Ven, AH (1986) 'Central problems in the management of innovation' in *Management Science.* 32, pp590–607

Van de Ven, AH, Polley, DE, Garud, R & Venkataraman, S (1999) *The Innovation Journey.* New York: Oxford University Press

Weick, KE (1984) 'Small wins: Redefining the scale of social problems' in *American Psychologist.* 39(1), pp40–49

West, MA (1990) 'The social psychology of innovation in groups' in West, M & Farr, JL (eds) *Innovation and Creativity at Work: Psychological and organizational strategies.* Chichester: John Wiley & Sons.

West, MA & Farr, JL (1990) 'Innovation at work' in *Innovation and Creativity at Work: Psychological and organizational strategies.* pp3–13. West, MA & Farr, JL (eds) Chichester: John Wiley & Sons

West, MA (1997) *Developing Creativity in Organizations.* Leicester: BPS Books

Wilson-Evered, E, Dall, PJ & Neale, M (2001a) 'The influence of leadership on innovation at work' in Parry, K (ed) *Leadership in the Antipodes: Findings, implications and a leader profile.* Wellington: Victoria University Institute of Policy Studies (in Press)

Wilson-Evered, E, Härtel, CEJ & Neale, M (2001b) 'A longitudinal study of work group innovation: The importance of transformational leadership and morale' in *Academy of Health Care Management* 2 (in press).

(Note: I wish to thank Jacqueline Budgeon, EB Secretariat, for her work and permission to use these documents.)

Appendix A: Improvement and Innovation Policy with Supporting Procedures

Policy

Improvement and Innovation

Policy

The Health Service recognises the importance of encouraging innovation and improvement in all work activities. Improvement and innovation are best achieved through staff and managers sharing responsibility for involvement and consultation. All staff are encouraged to identify improvement initiatives and innovations which affect work practices, efficiency, cost and quality of service delivery. Managers will facilitate the development of an improvement culture through the development of new ideas. Monitoring, evaluation and continued refining of the initiative are considered important to make the health facilities leaders in standards of health care and to demonstrate accountability for the best use of resources.

Principles

1. Managers and Supervisors have a responsibility to foster the philosophy of continuous quality improvement through innovations, procedural improvements and group learning by providing support and encouragement for new ideas. Staff members initiating improvements must be kept involved during the development of the improvement initiative.

2. Any staff member or work team has the right to bring issues about work procedures, practices or processes that will improve the standard of patient care or service delivery, to the attention of the relevant manager. Staff members are encouraged to develop new procedures and to work collaboratively with other work units to achieve the optimum outcome. Once the idea has been developed existing processes for policy and procedure development should be followed.

3. Depending on circumstances, it may be appropriate for the issue to be discussed in work group meetings for the ideas to be explored and developed. For the outcome to be successful, sufficient work time and resources may be required such as the provision of relevant statistical, financial or other material for analysis and development of the issue.

4. Where the issue involves the service provision of another work unit, the manager may institute discussions with other work areas or form an interdepartmental improvement group from members of all of the work units affected, to resolve the issue.

5. Where new procedures have been decided upon processes for approval, implementation and education of staff should be followed.

6. Evidence of gains and improvements through monitoring, assessment, action, evaluation and feedback to staff shall be documented to demonstrate improvement of service delivery and customer/patient satisfaction. Cost and economy should be a consideration in the development of all improvement initiatives and through the monitoring and evaluation process.

(Advice and clarification of this policy can be gained by contacting The Quality Management Unit or the Enterprise Bargaining Secretariat)

Checklist For Improvement And Innovation Policy

The importance of developing new ideas can not be overstated because their outcomes will form the basis of improvement. Supporting new ideas and innovation is best achieved though encouraging teamwork and open communication.This verbal encouragement must be reinforced in practical ways by providing time, resources and cooperation for the development of new ideas. Conflict and debate are healthy aspects of work life and often generate improvement ideas. Improvement and innovation should be used to develop RBH&DHS into leaders in health care rather than being forced to change because of economic constraints. Not all new ideas however will be successful, cost-effective or have positive outcomes, nevertheless, it is important to constantly strive to learn from these experiences and create an environment where the development of improvement initiatives and innovations are everyday activities.

√ 1. Checklist tips for creating the right environment for new ideas

-Is the managerial style of the area democratic and supportive of new ideas by demonstrating openness to change?

-Are all ideas coming forward being accepted in a non-judgmental way?

-Are all sections of the work force, including minority groups encouraged to participate in developing new ideas?

-Is there a regular meeting/forum where staff can share information face to face?

-Is there a meeting/forum in the workplace where staff can express their views and opinions?

-Are all ideas listened to, even if they are a minority view?

√ 2. Checklist tips on ways to support Innovation

-Are new ideas being actively developed so they can be converted into practical solutions?

-Is active support for new ideas demonstrated by management providing work time, resources and cooperation for their development?

-Are staff involved in the development and implementation of the idea?

-Have the individuals or work groups received praise, been thanked or provided with other forms of recognition such as an award, for their work on the project?
-Do staff or team members have influence over decision making about local work improvement activities?
-Have staff been encouraged to look at new ways of doing the job or changed hours of operating to improve efficiency and work flows?

√ 3. Checklist tips on staff participation and team work

-Are staff being encouraged to participate and be committed to change projects to improve work procedures?
-Have staff been provided with the opportunity to be involved in cooperative work with other work units or staff members or improvement projects?
-Is conflict worked out in vigorous and open ways? Is debate seen as constructive?
-Have all staff been informed about the details of the changes and the effects of the changes?
-Have staff been provided with sufficient training to equip them to implement new ways of working? Has consideration been given to staff who may have specific training needs?

√ 4. Checklist tips on work group objectives

-Does the team or work group have clear objectives to work toward?
-Does management and the work group agree with and understand the objectives?
-Are the objectives realistic and achievable?
-Is the group committed to the objectives?
-Are the group objectives in line with those of the District Health Service?

√ 5. Checklist tips on monitoring, evaluating and reporting

-Have effective mechanisms been put in place to monitor the implementation and measure outcomes of the new process/procedure?
-Are all relevant people involved in the review process?
-Will the review process take into account the effect of changes on staff?
-Have cost and economy of the new process/procedure been calculated and documented?
-Has the new procedure been formally evaluated within the work group to ensure benefits flow from the changes?
-Has fine tuning of the new procedure been undertaken?
-Have details of the improvement or innovation been documented and sent to the Quality Management Unit for inclusion in the data base?

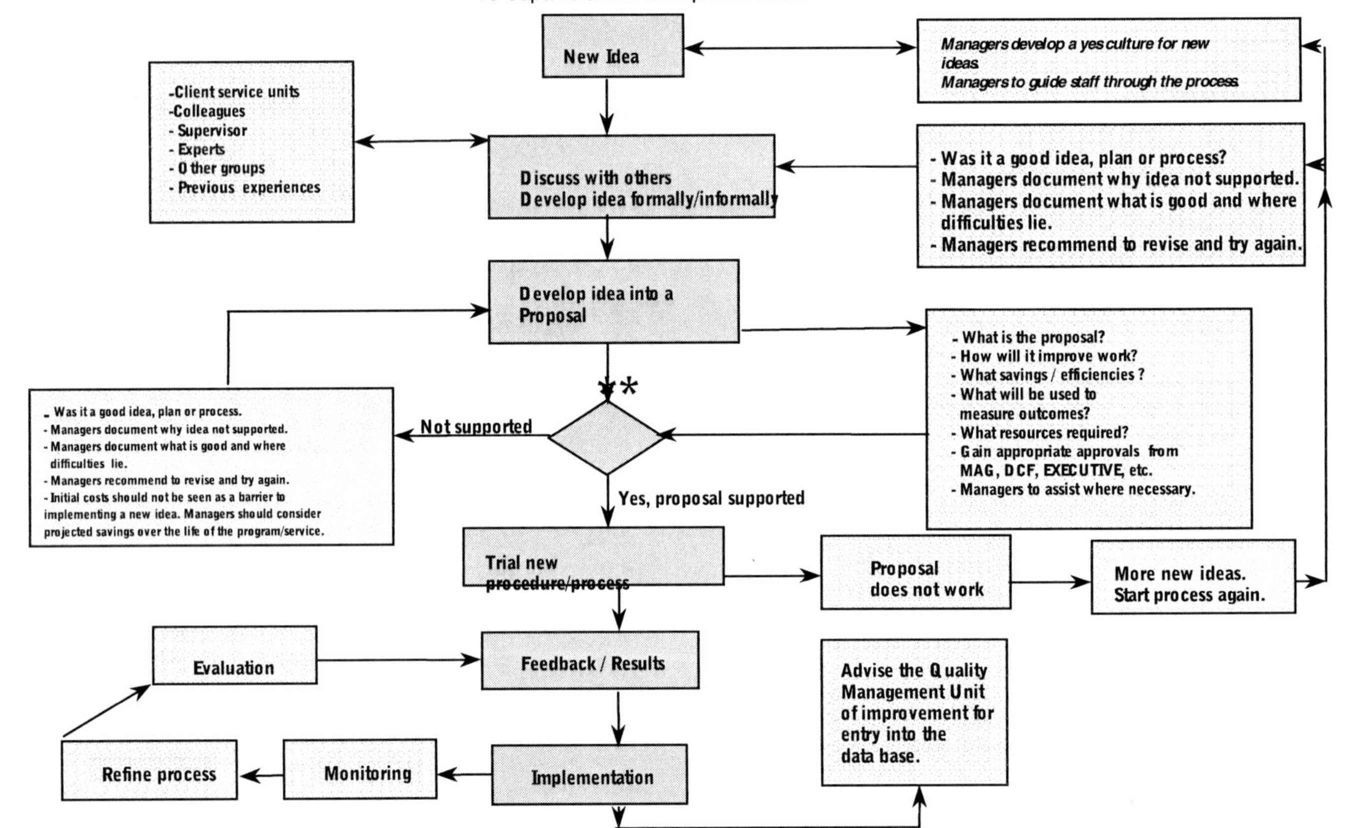

*If for whatever reason the idea can not be considered at a local level it may be referred to the Quality Committee

Action Reflection Learning (ARL™) in Thailand: Defying Cultural Differences

Isabel Rimanoczy

Introduction

This chapter describes an ARL™ experience with the Thailand-based executive team of a multinational company. The Chief Executive Officer (CEO), the only Western executive, who had spent three years in that function, had been appointed as a CEO in another country. He was interested in: (a) ensuring a smooth transition for the team and their new leader, (b) getting feedback from his executive team on his own performance, and (c) giving feedback to team members to help improve their future performance.

The CEO seriously doubted that a 'democratic' and 'open' approach like Action Reflection Learning (ARL) could be implemented in a traditionally hierarchical society, where straight feedback, critical observations and 'left column' thoughts are socially unacceptable between peers and superiors.

The experience showed that an ARL based intervention was possible in this culture, that the values supporting the model transcended cultural differences and that success is very much conditioned by the intervention's design.

The Case

Background

In 1998 the CEO of a multinational corporation in Thailand invited one of my partners and me to help him prepare a smooth transition from his current assignment to a new position in another Asian country. He had been the only Western executive in the Thai subsidiary, and he had experienced many cultural challenges with his executive team. He sensed that he had failed in the past to extract learnings from those experiences and provide feedback on his performance as a leader of the team and organisation.

He felt that it was now important for him to reflect on those experiences, to draw meaning from them, and to use the learnings to prepare him for his new assignment. He felt that if he could persuade his executive team that he needed their honest and actionable feedback, he would benefit enormously from their response. In preparing to leave, he wanted, too, to prepare his team for a good start with his successor, the incoming CEO, by giving them feedback based on his own experience with them, so that they could be helped to work effectively with their new leader.

He had, however, many doubts that the Action Reflection Learning approach, based as it was on transparent feedback, democratic thinking and candid questioning would be possible in a very traditional culture, where hierarchies were very much respected, and where saving face is often viewed as more important than voicing one's true feelings about another member of the team.

Preparation

We began by meeting with D (the CEO) to define what outcomes he wanted from this intervention. We listened to his assumptions about what might happen during the intervention, and got his agreement to have us challenge the feelings and data on which he based them. With his active participation – a basic tenet of our process – we designed a meeting that would help him to both receive and to give feedback.

He felt comfortable with the design and we clarified what his role would be during the one-day meeting. He was the team leader and as such was to lead the meeting. My partner and I were to act as Learning Coaches, helping the group to work on the task and to learn from it, and supporting the entire team as it navigated the potentially difficult rapids of an unfamiliar cross-cultural experience.

Meeting

The meeting began with D introducing us to the executive team, and stating the objectives of the meeting. We then showed an outline of the agenda, and asked everyone to take a moment of silent reflection to write down his/her expectations from the meeting (Stop /Reflect / Write/ Report). We asked the members to read their reflections out loud, thereby taking the first step in accepting some ownership of the process, and in influencing the outcomes of the session.

Then we introduced the process of setting norms, stated the rationale for the procedure, and invited everyone in the room to write down one norm that we should respect during the session, based upon their former experiences of what helped in other meetings.

After that D talked to his team about his need to learn from his performance as a leader. He positioned his request by stating that he wanted them to give him a 'good-bye' gift, one that was to help him in his next career step, and one that would identify the behaviours that he should continue to do because they were very helpful, and those behaviours that he should consider changing in his next assignment. He, in turn, offered a similar 'gift', to help them in their integration with the next Western CEO they would have.

We provided instructions on how to proceed. We asked D to go to a separate room for the next part of the session, and gave both him and the team the same assignment. First, the team took time for individual reflection on what they would say to D on his return to the room, then they exchanged their thoughts and recorded a summary on a flip chart. The team decided what to present and chose a spokesperson, the oldest member of the team, as a sign of respect for seniority.

The CEO did the same exercise in another room. When he came back into the room, the team was very excited to share their feedback with him – they liked both the idea of the 'gift', and also the notion that past experience could be seen as a lesson for the future.

We decided that D would give his feedback first. The respect for hierarchies is high in this culture, and the feedback exchange was already a challenge to their habits. So we decided to begin with D, as a way to lower the anxiety and begin in a way they were more 'used to'. Then both he and the team members would use the concept of a 'fishbowl' as the device for providing the data. D began with his feedback to his team in a conversation with the two of us while his team listened in the 'fishbowl' setting. Afterwards they asked questions for clarification only.

Then the team had a fishbowl conversation with the two of us while D listened carefully, taking notes on the issues where he wanted to get more information later. He practised active listening, for which we had coached him before the meeting.

We ended with a session of Reflection and Dialogue, sitting in a circle, with the question 'What have we learned from this experience and how do we feel'? This introduced a new way of communication among the executive team, as they had never had the experience of taking a silent time for reflection in the work setting, nor were they used to extract lessons from a regular meeting.

The spirits were high. They all felt very honoured to be able to give such a gift to their leader, and they discovered a way to give feedback by phrasing it in a positive, constructive way: highlighting what the person did *well*, and instead of stating 'this is what you do badly' suggesting instead 'this is what you could consider doing differently'.

Debrief

What happened here? We used a design based on ARL.

ARL is a modified version of Action Learning developed in the mid-80s by LIM partners and their colleagues from MiL in Sweden. From their experience, learning does not automatically result from action. For the learning to occur, an intermediate step is essential the awareness of what has happened in the action phase. Awareness is rarely a spontaneous event (Aha-Erlebnis); it requires an intellectual process thinking about an action. For awareness to take place, it is necessary to do a pause in the action and introduce a challenging question to promote reflection on what has happened.

Thus, reflection was found to have a major role in this Action Learning process.

As a consequence of this, a learning-cycle was defined:

5 - New Ation

1 - Reflection

4 - Plan

Ation

2 - Awareness

3 - Need

' Rimanoczy, 2001

Each phase is supported by different interventions and tools to reach depth and efficiency of the cycle. A Learning Coach who is trained to see the just-in-time learning opportunities guides the learner/s along the cycle and introduces tools and concepts to optimize the process of working on a task.

What were the key ARL elements that we used?

Question-driven process

ARL is a question-driven process, and the posing of the appropriate question is the key element of the gaining awareness. The principle supporting this is that people have the knowledge to find their own answers, but need to be asked insightful questions to be able to find those answers.

Questions have the capability to generate insight when:

- -They are not leading . They don't disclose the intention/opinion of the person who is asking.
- -They are exploratory: They expand the information and usually begin with How? What? Why? When?
- -They assume the person knows: What was behind your thinking when...? What do you think the reasons are for...? What are potential options?
- -Challenging: They uncover assumptions: Is this an assumption or a fact?
- -They connect with the past experience: What have you learned about similar situations in the past?
- -They demand clarifications, not assuming the meaning: What do you mean by...?

In our role of Learning Coaches we explored, together with the client, what were the best questions to ask in order to achieve his desired outcomes of feedback exchange. This took us into learning from the past, as we asked the participants to reflect on their past years together and express what behaviours, attitudes and actions should be kept and which needed to be changed.

Balance task and learning

For real learning to take place, as much attention needed to be given to the team's task (the 'real life') as to the *learning* that can be extracted from that 'reality'. In this case, we linked their real transition with the lessons about giving and receiving feedback, to the norms that served as guides for a more informed meeting, and with the other tools and concepts we introduced.

Learning styles

According to McCarthy's (1996) findings, everyone has a preferred learning style. Some go after the 'Why?' and are interested in knowing the purpose and rationale of what they will do. Others are more interested in the 'What?' – what will be done? what are the data? and the theories behind it? Some are oriented towards the 'How?' and are curious about the mechanics – *how* things will be done, and others finally are more interested in the 'So what?', which is a pragmatic stance geared towards the actual application of the learning – what can I do with this? In our session we paid attention to the four learning styles (Why? What? How? So what?) in the way we introduced each activity, by explaining what we would do, why, how and so what that would mean for them. This, we felt, was critical, because, given the unfamiliar terrain, it was essential that the participants be as clear as possible about why and how we were asking them to stretch in order to achieve the goals of the intervention.

Learning Coach

The Learning Coach is another key component of an ARL design, and two of them were present in the workshop we described. A Learning Coach has many different roles in a learning process. Certain of the more important ones are that:

- -he/she is focused on the process and therefore will act as a 'mirror' asking questions that help the learner to see him/herself (reflection à awareness)
- -he/she provides the Just-In-Time tools and concepts
- -he/she helps the individual/teams apply lessons to their daily work life – that is, to transfer the learning to other situations and ensure that the insights gained continue to illuminate the participants' daily work life.

Just In Time learning

One of the principles on which ARL is based is that learning happens best when the person is in the middle of the problem/situation. At this moment the potential for the assimilation of new thinking is highest, therefore all the concepts or tools the Learning Coaches introduced during the session were 'just in time' in relation to what was happening in the room.

Exchange of learning

When learning can be exchanged with others, the learning process is multiplied and accelerated. In the design of the session, we promoted the moments of individual reflection and the exchange of the learning among the team members to ensure that the learning became internalised within team members.

Writing thoughts

While questions invite reflection, the pen and paper combination enables the expression of thoughts that we didn't think we had. Writing is a major component of the ARL designs, and we used it during the workshop at several points, asking the managers to take some time to write down their answers to the questions we asked, to sharing them with colleagues, to exchanging insights gleaned from listening to other views.

Systemic approach

Real change is only possible when we approach a behaviour from a system's perspective, that is, paying attention to the various connections to other systems. In an ARL design, we focus on the personal and the professional implications of the participants, on the team impact, on the organisational and business impact.

The Learning Coaches helped the team and its leader to identify the multiple perspectives that needed to be considered to ensure a smooth transition.

Appreciative approach

The appreciative attitude (Cooperrider 1999) of the Learning Coaches was key to building trust and a non-judging, safe environment. This transferred confidence into the team and helped them to take some risks expressing their ideas and thoughts about their boss.

Conclusions

This experienced showed us that given a certain design, the Thai culture can be open to an Action Reflection Learning experience. We believe that, given the awareness of national sensibilities, and given the intentional explanation of purpose, this is a 'Western' process that can cross national and ethnic borders. This was our first experience with its successful use in the Thai culture.

The ARL element that was missing was the sequential learning, meaning that as change of behaviours requires time, it is important to try out something new, getting feedback, trying it out again and again to effectively assimilate it. In this case we were not able to continue the process, which would have required meeting with the incoming leader, working with him, setting mutual expectations (between his role and the team), applying the lessons learned with the departing CEO, using the new approach for giving and receiving feedback, and finally reflecting and exchanging lessons.

Bibliography

McCarthy, B (1996) *About Learning.* Barrington: Excel Inc

Cooperrider, D et al (1999) *Appreciative Inquiry: Rethinking human organization toward a positive theory of change.* Champaign: Stipes Publishing

Goldberg, M (1988) *The Art of Questions.* New York: John Wiley & Sons

Rimanoczy, I 'The Learning Coach' in *What is ALR?* www.limltd.com

Implementing Business Continuity Planning in an International Bank Using Action Research

Goh Moh Heng

Introduction

This chapter outlines the application of action research in the implementation of Business Continuity Plans for banks. It is based on my doctoral research (Goh 1999). The research integrated theory and practice, and in particular, qualitative research and professional practice. The research started off with the development of an implementation model using meta-analysis and this implementation was tested using action research as the key research methodology. The research contributed to the establishment of a proven method in developing business continuity plans for financial institutions such as banks.

Business Continuity Planning or BCP is the process of developing a comprehensive plan that minimises the effect of a disaster to an organisation's key businesses. This plan assures organisations that their critical businesses continue immediately upon any a major disruption.

Purpose of research

I began my research by addressing the focal question: 'How can I use an action research intervention to develop business continuity plans within an international bank setting?' The research was based on case studies on branches within Standard Chartered Bank Asia specifically in Hong Kong, Malaysia and Indonesia. In particular, the research examined the steps needed to implement business continuity plans for all countries within Asia. These plans were meant to help the Bank to resume its critical business processes to continue in a controlled manner during a disruption to its normal business operations.

What was my thematic concern?

The research began with my thematic concern, which was 'developing and sustaining a business continuity program for an international bank'. The concern was triggered by the lack of available information and standards on the development of business continuity planning for international banks such as Standard Chartered Bank. Most of this information was proprietary to professional firms and was not available in the public domain. Existing knowledge that was available emphasised using a computer system recovery approach rather than a business recovery approach. Hence, this research project was initiated with the intent of investigating the development of Business Continuity Plans and how they can be implemented in an international bank. The intent was to capitalise on the talents and ideas of global team members (identified as internal consultants and co-researchers) within the Security Risk Management area of Standard Chartered Bank.

In order to perform my research in a natural setting and free from artificiality or the need to alter my natural environment, I used action research to provide a normal and natural research paradigm. Bob Dick

(1993a) has emphasised that action research can provide adequate rigour in a natural environment.

Can I function both as a manager and as a researcher?

One of my dilemmas while performing the research was how I could function both as a researcher and as a manager. In order to perform my research, I had to pursue the following goals simultaneously:

-Action a change as a manager in the bank.
-Research and understanding as a researcher.

My aim was to integrate the two goals such that change was informed by understanding and intervening in a changing system enhanced understanding.

In order to perform this dual function during the same working day, one of the key success factors was to convince my superior that the research conducted would not disrupt my function as a manager. Rather, it will further improve the work environment and the business continuity planning program for the bank. Fortunately, my superior acceded to my request and even agreed to be my co-researcher.

What was my implementation model?

The research began with a meta-analysis of the business continuity planning literature, which yielded business continuity planning methodology model. The analysis found that the majority of the practitioners organise their methodologies into the following general phases:

-Project Planning
-Business Impact Analysis
-Recovery Strategy
-Plan Development
-Training and Testing
-Maintenance.

A graphical representation of the resultant Bank's Business Continuity Planning (BCP) methodology model is appended below as Figure 20.1.

Fig 20.1: BCP Implementation Model

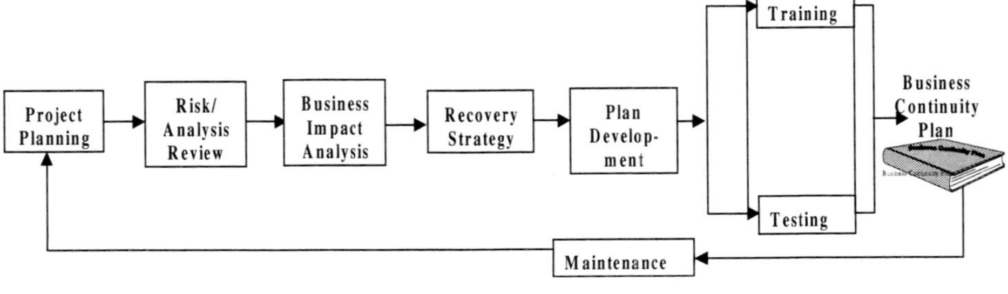

Research Method

What was the uniqueness of my inquiry and environment?

I was primarily interested in the development of the business continuity planning process in a banking environment. My bank was constantly undergoing turbulent changes and re-organisation; most of my co-researchers changed during the research duration. In spite of these challenges, I continued as the primary instrument for data collection and analysis and was able to conduct my fieldwork and the collection of data under normal conditions within the boundaries set by my working environment.

The topic of this study was a new area of inquiry. The literature search based on an extensive database searches and the use of the Internet was at its infancy stage during the mid 1990s. It revealed no reported studies or examples of the use of qualitative research or action research methods in the design and implementation of business continuity planning program for banks.

A review of the literature of the past two decades showed that the research problem area was immature and that there was a conspicuous lack of theory and prior research.

What is an Action Research design?

In my approach, there are two key features of action research processes; they are cyclical and each cycle alternates between action and critical reflection. Because they are cyclical, the later cycles can build upon the understanding that arises from the earlier cycles. The data and interpretations arising in the earlier cycles can also be tested and refined in later cycles. The action research process is shown in Figure 20.2.

Fig 20.2: Action Research Spiral

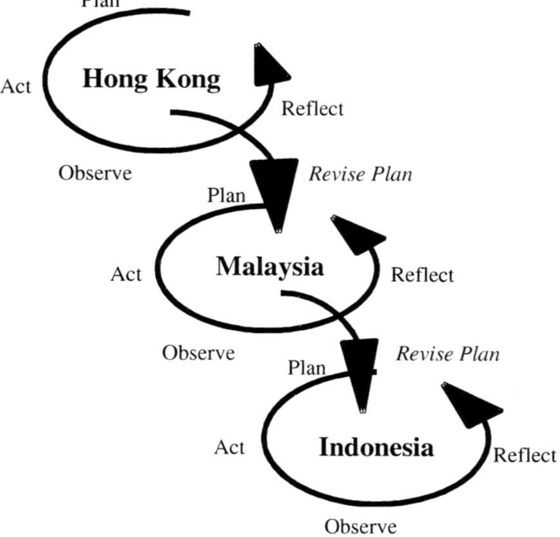

In essence, the characteristic cycle as shown above was used in the action research design as follows:

- *-Plan.* The exploration and general *plan.* Initially I adopted an investigative stance where an understanding of a problem is developed and plans are made for some form of intervention strategy.
- *-Act.* The *action* in action research. I carried out the intervention.
- *-Observe.* The monitoring the implementation by *observation.* During the time of the intervention, pertinent observations are collected in various forms.
- *-Reflect. Reflection* and revision. I carried out new intervention strategies and the cyclical process repeated, continuing until a sufficient understanding of the problem was achieved.

Critical reflection in turn has two main components: reviewing what happened in the previous cycle so as to draw insight from it, and planning what to do in the next cycle. The use of critical reflection in each cycle also allows action and understanding to be integrated.

This cycle of plan-act-observe-reflect is applied throughout the business continuity planning methodology. Figure 20.3 is a detailed representation of the cyclical process within the business continuity planning methodology. On completion of one cycle, this cyclical process was repeated over the next cycle in the next country.

Fig 20.3: Action Research Cyclic Process with the BCP Implementation Model

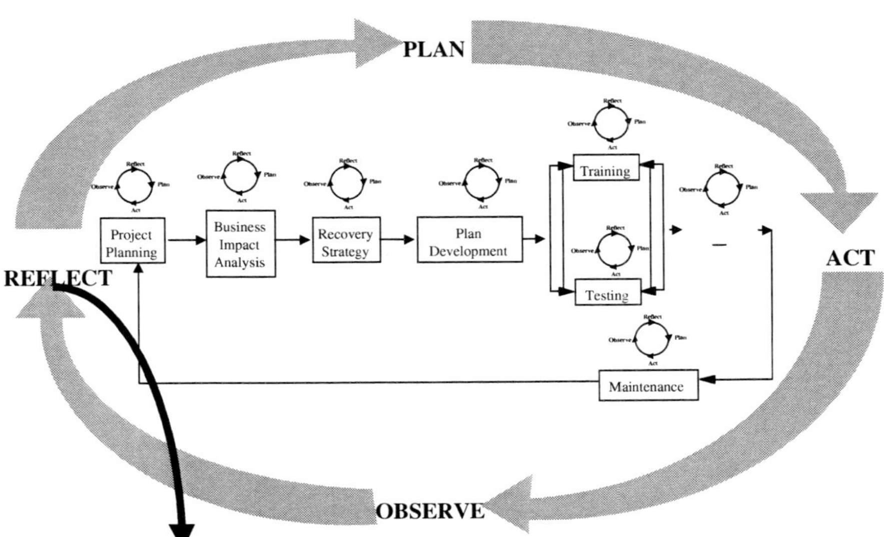

Interpretation of data

During the research process, I often asked the following questions on the interpretation of data: What data should I include? What form should they take? Where should I put them? How do I combine my interpretation with my data? The answer came from one of Strauss' (1987) comments that one of the issues in interpretation is the ratio of interpretation spent to data collated.

My interpretation of my data was conducted in the following ways:

1. *Use of multiple cycles to disconfirm.* Dick (1993b) advocates the need to develop an interpretation approach from the start so that more time and more cycles are available to test it thoroughly. At each cycle, I constantly tried to disconfirm the emerging interpretations. The use of many short cycles provided me with more opportunities to disconfirm.

   An example of an interpretation is *the selection process of the Business Continuity Manager* for each country. Initially, I had allowed the country manager to appoint his senior bank officer as the project manager. I found that the appointed manager was not the most suitable project manager. This was true in the context of Hong Kong as the senior bank officer was experienced but was due for retirement immediately after the project.

   The cycle of selecting a Business Continuity Manager provided disconfirming evidence that the country manager may be able to make better choices given certain guidance. In the second cycle, in addition to the necessity for the Business Continuity Manager to be a senior bank officer, a list of preferred profiles of a Business Continuity Manager was included as part of the selection criteria. The reflection on the need to have a stringent profile for the Business Continuity Managers resulted in the selection of suitable Business Continuity Manager for Brunei (not included as a case study) and for Malaysia. It showed that the appointed senior bank officers with the 'improved' criteria met most of the requirements in all subsequent selection process.
2. *Critique and refine methods at the end of each cycle.* The entire business continuity planning implementation model was critiqued after each implementation and the model was refined. The refinements and changes made to the implementation

model after each cycle were documented. This is possible when both data collection and interpretations are included in each cycle, and both data and interpretation can be tested in the later cycles.

Whether the cycle is minor or major, data are interpreted and documented. The detailed documentation of my reflections and changes to the business continuity planning implementation model were used as evidence. The documentation was compiled as a workbook and it was made available to all Business Continuity Managers to be disseminated during regional workshops. This workbook was also used as a development standard during the implementation at each new branch.

Divergent data can be specifically sought out as it increases the chances of any piece of data or interpretation being challenged by other data. One noticeable example of divergent data is the usefulness of the specialised PC-based software for writing business continuity plans. The initial feedback was positive but as the staff members were replaced over time, the positive feedback began to turn 'negative.' The constant challenges from the Business Continuity Managers and the appointed staff members within each branch indicated that using the specialised BCP software may not be the correct direction to go for the business continuity program.

3. *The literature review can be used as a further source of disconfirmation.* The literature review was used as a source of disconfirmation. An example from the literature reviewed showed the advocating of corporate-wide business recovery plan by Delvin (1994) and Jackson (1995) to include the recovery of all the workstations and microcomputers in the event of a disruption. The disconfirming evidence was that practitioners understood the need to develop the plans from the business or corporate wide perspective but the fundamental mode of development was still via the computer recovery method. The evidence is supported in the review of thirty-four business continuity planning implementation models.

These three methods were used during the interpretation of data. The interpretation and the data relevant to its confirmation and disconfirmation were documented during each implementation phase.

How were project journals and logs kept?

To assist in the data collection, I have utilised logs and project journals and it is titled 'Action Research Log'. The logs contain records of transcripts of my observations, reflections and records that are supported by current project documentation.

A routine for reflective writing was followed to ensure that I kept track of my findings. The journals identified by Kemmis and McTaggart (1992) included the types of reflections, which are related to the thematic concern.

These action research logs are my notes and reflections and according to Kemmis and McTaggart, these logs are:

- 'On changing uses of language and the development of more coherent discourse'. I was able to operationalise this as being the thematic concern that I was studying; both my co-researchers' and my language and discourse; and the way they relate to the wider context of language and discourse of my workplace and the world around it.
- 'About changing activities' in my environment, and the emergence of more coherently described and justified business continuity planning practices. It relates to the constant relationship with my co-researchers' and my activities, and in relation to the wider context of circumstances, constraints and opportunities in and beyond my workplace.
- 'About changing social relationship among those involved in the setting and any emerging changes to the formal organisation structure' – both in relation to my co-researchers' and myself, and as they are framed in the wider structure of social relationships of my workplace and beyond.

Triangulation

I conducted 'Triangulation' according to Chadwick et al (1984). Their definition was:

The search for consistency of findings from different observers, observing instruments, methods of observation, times, places and research situations.

Triangulation is one of the main strategies to increase confidence in the data and the interpretations and it is used in this research. According to Dick (1996), the most important strategy is the use of multiple sources of information within a cycle. During this research, a variety of data was created by methods indicated in the 'Data Collection Strategies' section. Winter (1989) stressed that a situation can be investigated using a number of different methods, each of which can partly transcend its own limitation by functioning as a point of comparison with another.

How is triangulation applied?

One such example of triangulation was the process of collating Business Impact Analysis. In the following three specific areas, the co-researchers from all three countries, working in different environments, came to the same conclusions. The source of data came from:

- -my review of the Business Impact Analysis report received from the countries
- -the observations recorded by my co-researchers during the planning, action, observation and reflection cycles of the Business Continuity Planning program
- -the sharing of these reflections among the participants during the workshops.

Contribution

My initial contribution was business continuity planning implementation model, which is synthesised from the thorough review of existing literature. The major contribution is the contribution of a proven and workable model to literature using action research. Another contribution is that the outcomes of the research were made known in the public domain. This will contribute to the limited research literature currently available in the area of business continuity planning. My research also contributed to the field of action research beyond traditional areas, where it is used, such as education and nursing.

Conclusion

I have summarised, in this chapter, an overview of the use of action research starting from the thematic concern, the research design, the research methods such as triangulation, action research logs and interpretation of data, and finally the outcomes. The successful completion of this research and the implementation of business continuity plans for most countries in Asia has proved that action research is a suitable research methodology for an ever-changing environment such as a bank. This research was accepted as a doctoral thesis in April 1999.

In retrospect, I felt that the use of action research in implementing business continuity planning most suitable for an organisation that is constantly undergoing changes.

Bibliography

Chadwick, BA, Bahr, HM & Albrecht, SL (1984) *Social Science Research Methods.* New Jersey: Prentice-Hall

Devlin, ES, Emerson CH & Wrobel, LA (1994) *Business Resumption Planning.* Boston: Auerbach Publications

Dick, B (1993a) *Rigour and Relevance in Action Research.* (available online: http://www.scu.edu.au/schools/gcm/ar/arp/)

Dick, B (1993b) *You Want to Do an Action Research Thesis?* Brisbane: Interchange

Dick, B (1996) *Rigour in Action Research.* (available online: http://www.scu.edu.au/schools/gcm/ar/arp/)

Goh, MH (1999) *Business Continuity Planning for Banks in Asia: A case study in Standard Chartered Bank.* PhD thesis. Adelaide: University of South Australia

Kemmis, S & McTaggart, R (1992) *The Action Research Planner.* 3rd edition. Geelong: Deakin University

Jackson, CB (1995) 'Case Study: How to rapidly develop unit business continuity plans' in *Computer Security Journal.* pp25-p–34

Strauss, AL (1987) *Qualitative Analysis for Social Scientists.* Cambridge: Cambridge University Press

Winter, R (1989) *Learning from Experience?: Principles and practice in Action Research.* London: The Falmer Press.

Richard Kwok

Introduction

I used Action Learning and Action Research to improve the effectiveness of the design process in my engineering organisation.

My research started with my working with my team members, and then widening the circle to the entire department and subsequently extending it to my customers as well. The outcomes of my research demonstrated that action learning and action research could be an effective methodology in changing processes, and enhancing system implementation and work practices in an engineering organisation.

I developed an interpretative model of change through the reflective process that accompanied the various intervention processes in the organisation.

One of the contributions of my research was the development of a change model showing that:

Effective change is a function of:

-flexibility
-multiplicity of objectives
-camouflaging change using culturally appropriate methods
-driven by data and status
-effective participation
-interaction
-control of the overall environment.

The Situation

At the time of the research, about 158 designers worked in the design department of my company. This group of designers was not easy to manage, as job opportunities outside were plentiful and their expectations from their job was high. On the other hand, the company was aggressively moving into regionalisation. Competition was stiff and the company had to acquire new design tools and processes such as re-engineering and concurrent engineering processes to improve the efficiency of the design process. New project management systems such as budgeting, scheduling and the formation of subject specialist groups were also introduced to execute large-scale projects using a matrix organisation.

Concurrently, the company also wanted the design department to adopt the ISO 9001 and ISO 9002 system in the design process. After two-and-a-half-years of hard work, we were awarded ISO 9001 and ISO 9002 certification. However, the designers felt that they were spending too much time filling out forms and had less time for design work. All these problems led to the slowing down of the design process with many bottlenecks at different stages of design at their electronic drawing board. This also led to frustration and the resignation rate for the designers shot up to 25 percent in 1994 from a normal rate of 12 percent. It was at this time that I started my research.

Besides being the researcher I was also the group head in the Design Department. I was responsible for all design and development activities in my group, which included quality assurance, design, manufacturability and safety of all the development work carried out by my design team members. I was also required to ensure that the operation and work practices adopted by my group members conformed to company policy.

Hence, I was directly responsible for the productivity of my team members in the design department and had a direct involvement in the improvement of the efficiency of the management of technology and the change process.

At this time the management said to me that in the near future I was needed to manage a new, large and demanding development program to integrate some sophisticated technology systems in a very short time frame and with a limited development budget. When I took over this program, I had to perform three roles:

-As a group head to take care of my group of designers.
-As a project chief engineer to take charge of all technical functions of the new program.
-As a program manager to be responsible for the program schedule and all the contractual terms and conditions.

What did I do?

I wanted to successfully execute the new program and I was desperately seeking solutions to improve the working condition, the thinking process of the designers and the entire project management system in the Design Department.

Under such circumstances, I used Action Learning (AL) and Action Research (AR) to improve the project management system in technology management and introduce a change process in my engineering organisation.

Prior to embarking on my research the engineers in the department, including myself believed that all engineering problems could be resolved through engineering solutions. At the same time, I felt strongly that we had to do something to assist the designers to solve or minimise their frustration with the Computer-Aided Engineering and Computer-Aided Manufacturing (CADCAM) systems. To the system administrators in the CADCAM Section, everything that the designers wanted to do was available in the manual and could be easily retrieved from the system. Training had also been provided to the designers. What more did the designers need?

I divided my research into four learning phases. Each phase was distinctly divided by different time frames, levels of maturity in learning, skill sets required and involvement of groups. It was interesting to note that to bring about the change that I was proposing I had to break the traditional organisational structure and its top-down approach. To achieve this I approached it by exerting influence through setting up events with a purpose for all stakeholders to include them as part of useful members to implement the change.

I was looking for practical methods for implementing effective change in my organisation. Two areas of literature provided ideas for me to develop my change model. These were the literature on learning organisations and change management. I found it difficult to apply the principles derived from these literatures directly to my situation and had to modify them to make them relevant to my context to be effective.

The interpretative model of effective change that I developed through my research represents the combination of Lewin's (1951) method, team building strategies, strategic interventions, action research and action learning methodologies. It also shares some commonalties with other researchers too. For instance, my model is similar to the work cells reported by Socio-technical systems (STS) researcher Lee (1997). I also extended and modified the Total Quality Management (TQM) and STS method in my research. My method of change involved the issues of flexibility, ownership and customer satisfaction. Manz and Stewart (1997) have demonstrated this involvement in earlier research.

I also introduced collaborative participation of stakeholders. This has been demonstrated to have positive results in dealing with complex situations of computer aided engineering technologies (Purser 1992). My model also considered open communication, trust and ownership of results (Kerr 1991) and action orientation rather than planning (Keffeler 1991), which are essential for successful change management. Thus my interpretative model reflects an integrated interpretative model of change that incorporates very successful parameters of change that have been previously used. However, to my knowledge, this was the first time that all these theories were put together to apply successfully to an engineering organisation in Singapore.

The model that I derived can be represented by a formula:

Effective Change:
Echange f F x Om x Cc x D x Pe x Ec

Where:
F= flexibility
Om =
multiple objectives
Cc =
camouflage using culturally appropriate method
D =
data or status driven
Pe =
effective participation
Ec =
control of overall environment
where:
fdenotes 'function of'
x denotes 'interaction'

With processes introduced based on the literature and the AR process, an understanding of the situation developed as events unfolded. The cycles within cycles model that I introduced resembled the model proposed by Perry and Zuber-Skerrit (1991). The AR model in Figure 21.1 summarises the various phases of learning from independent observation to team interaction and on to forming a collaborative partnership.

Fig 21.1: Action Research Cycles Model

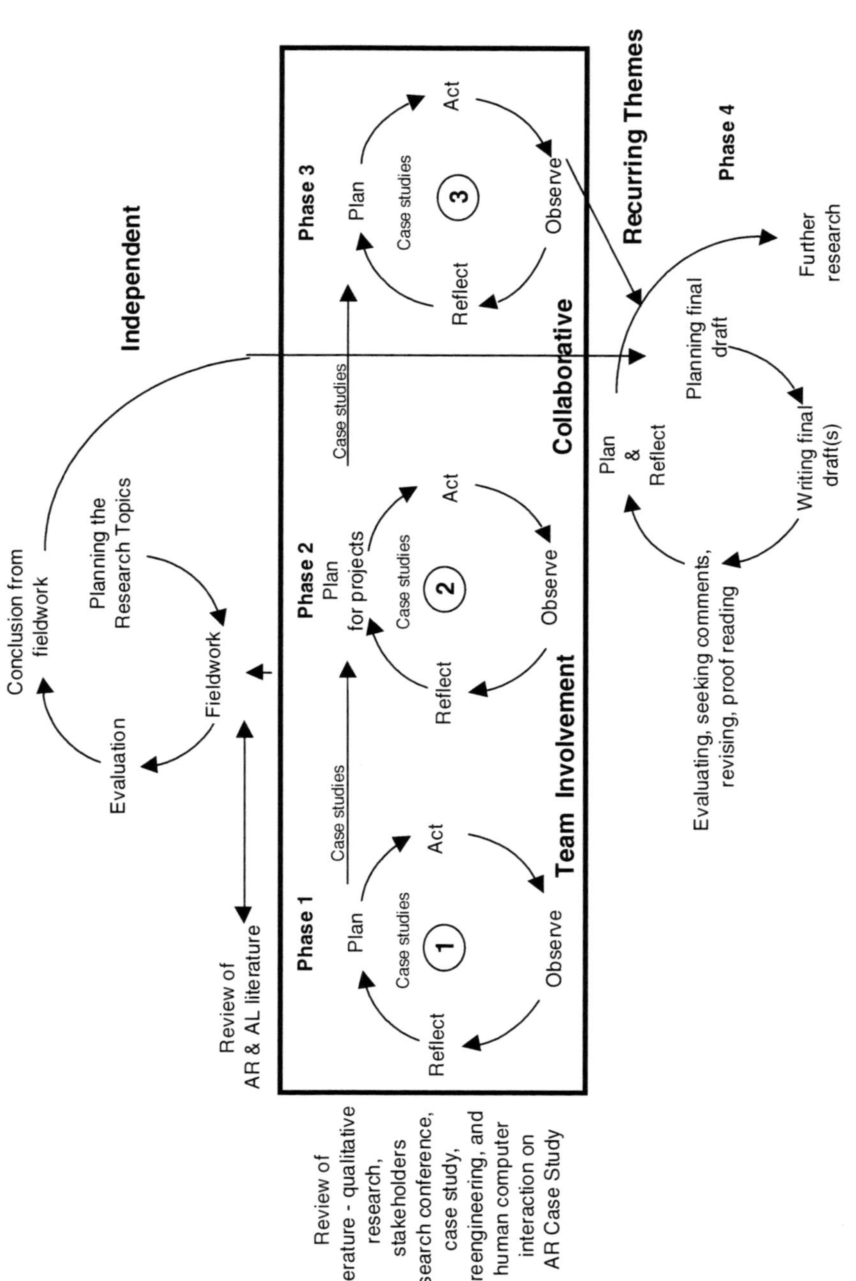

Action Learning Cycles

Phase One (March 1994 to September 1995)

The entire research took four years. I began this phase with my immediate team members within the group of engineers and designers I was in charge of. During the first phase of learning, project team members who used action learning activities felt that they were gaining more confidence in project management and a sense of joint responsibility developed within the team. They also felt that as a team they were now able to handle more complex issues and ready to assist me in the facilitation role for the next learning phase. Some of the activities that we went through are summarised as follows:

a) Engineering Retreat (1)

I started it in a small way by involving few of my staff members within my group. They were chosen because they were my key stakeholders and they would constitute the system and configuration section of my new development program. Initially, the management and myself felt that the problems were technical in nature. However, the retreat provided me with insights into the problems I was up against. I started to notice some social elements in the whole issue and also noticed that there was a low level of participation and some resentment from the participants. The participants also felt that retreat was a 'NATO', ('NATO' in our local context = No Action, But Talk Only) exercise and were sceptical about its effectiveness.

Immediately after the retreat, I began exploring the possibility of using some forms of action learning processes to improve the level of participation. I realised that the issue of participation had to be improved.

b) Search Conference

Soon after this I sought help from some of my colleagues to conduct a search conference, involving all staff members in the department with support from the project management section. I called it a focus interview because the team members might not be comfortable with the term 'search conference'. Through this search conference, I compiled a total of *111* problems. Based on that data, management acknowledged the fact that there was a real crisis and decided to seek help from an external consultant.

Now, I started to question myself. Was it flexibility that fostered participation? For example replacing the term 'search conference' to the more familiar term 'focus interview' enabled me to bring participants together to generate data. By using the data, we were able to successfully make the management acknowledge the real situation. I also started to feel that the problems I was handling were beyond just technical problems, and possibly involved a social dimension. Through this exercise, I found that the level of participation was much higher than had been the case for the retreat. Perhaps the search conference methodology enabled the participants to discuss, reflect and communicate their deliberations. As a consequence I began to see participation as a tool for effective change.

c) IPD Consultant

To solve the problem explained earlier, the management chose the option of using a consultant as a quick-fix solution. I was very sceptical as to whether it would work. I had no option other than to work along with the Integrated Product Design (IPD) consultant but I felt uneasy about management's decision. I was not involved directly and had no control over the situation. I adopted a wait-and-see approach and resorted to participant observation and critical reflection throughout the process.

The consultant first interviewed all the relevant personnel suggested by the head of CADCAM Section. Through the interviews, the consultant established a set of information for each functional role in terms of their inputs and output parameters, constraints or limitations, problems, supporting tools, mechanisms, systems, and the feedback needed for effective performance. The outputs of identifying all the existing processes by the consultant were termed 'As-Is process'. This information was transferred into a template, known as the 'As-Is process' table and the completed table was sent back to the participants for feedback and clarification. After two to three iterations, the IPD consultants proposed a 'To-Be process ' and this process also went through two to three iterations with all the participants and a final version was established. Once all the 'To-Be processes' were in place, all the functional roles were merged together in an integrated model to generate the so-called 'integrated product development' IPD in short. That was the consultant's claim.

In the next step, the IPD consultant gathered the designers together to conduct a role-play and simulation test to check the proposed system prior to implementation. However, the outcomes generated by the IPD consultant led to more frustration and turned the concurrent engineering to 'concussion engineering'.

From this observation, I realised that just getting people together to participate was not enough. Perhaps, it required a more strategic approach and definitely some form of social approach. Thus, I was convinced about the importance of the socio-technical nature of the problems faced by designers in my organisation. This was particularly evident when the IPD consultant did not show sufficient consideration for human computer interaction. Users were very unhappy and reluctant to use the system even though they had participated in the entire development process.

Phase Two (July 1995 to January 1996)

In Phase Two of the learning, I went through another three case studies. During this phase of learning, I could see the level of learning had extended to other functional groups and the level of participation increased, especially for the other functional groups from partial involvement to full involvement. As for myself, I was now focusing on the strategic and operational management of the whole change process and had delegated almost all the facilitation work to my team members.

Phase Three (February 1996 to July 1997)

Phase Three of the learning involved two case studies. During this phase of learning, I handed over the operational management and facilitation to my team members who worked with the whole project team, ie. including the customers.

It was interesting to note that during this learning phase, I saw a greater understanding among project team members about the need for sharing, learning, and handling problems. This was evidenced in the open sharing within the taskforce and the self-generated nature during the course of the case studies. I was now taking care of strategic management only, ie. managing the strategic part of the planning process at this phase.

Phase Four (August 1997 to March 1998)

In the fourth or final learning phase of my research, I conducted a workshop session with the project team members. At the workshop, the team members and I discussed all the processes developed on the Project Management process.

It was interesting to note that during this learning phase, I found greater co-operation among project team members in sharing, learning and handling problems. The core team members became capable of managing the whole project on their own. They also exhibited the capability of facilitating team members and conducting both the operational and strategic management functions. I also noticed that learning diffused to other project teams and had significantly improved the morale of the whole department. The resignation rate for the design department had dropped to 13 percent by June 1997 from a high of 25 percent a year before. On many occasions, solutions were developed through the project team members *as well as our customers*.

Lessons Learnt From the Case

It was after my four years of research and active involvement with my team members, I started to understand the important of socio-technical issues and it also changed my outlook in life. Through this process, I also found a *new solution* in making people work effectively and collaboratively together, a process, that I called *Collaborative Engineering*. The entire process was so successful that by using this process, we in the design team for the first time could deliver our development program on schedule and within budgets. The team members presented our findings to the top management. It was accepted in 1997 as the best process improvement program and the team members were given S$10,000 for the top award that year.

My research was successful and had generated both management and research outcomes, such as:

1. I was able to integrate very successful change management programs and extend them to my engineering organisation.
2. The framework was grounded both in theory and in practice and my research demonstrated that it is useful in change management. This also provides new and innovative research directions in management.
3. A free and open communication process contributed greatly to the management of technology. This is evidenced by the effectiveness of the change process. I have demonstrated that the following were contributing factors: Effective participation, transparency of the data, and free and open communication in a non-threatening atmosphere.
4. The management brought in the IPD consultant to fix all our system related problems, but the consultant seemed to have a different perspective of the whole

process and did not address cultural and socio-technical issues confronting the designers. Hence, this led to more frustration. In such a precarious situation, I found that action learning was an effective tool to enable the designers to solve their own problems in real time.

5. Although it may not be a limitation in the technical sense, the methods I used was borrowed from the schools of TQM, reengineering, STS, change management and were modified to extend their use in my research. These extended and modified versions were *camouflaged.* It worked well for my situation because they did not intimidate anyone and allowed for open and trusting relationships over time. If I had used the methods without modifying them for my context, they would probably be sensed as threatening situations. The whole purpose of participation, ownership of responsibilities and openness would have been lost and my purpose of developing a learning culture would have been defeated even before I undertook any interventions.

Finally, action research can be an effective intervention process in a Singaporean engineering organisation, if disguised to fit the organisational culture. The incorporation of explicit action research and action learning methodologies in a managerial function is an important original contribution to literature on action research and organisational change. This research is also an extension of Lewin's model of change management in the context of an engineering organisation.

Action research, under a different label, was successfully introduced to the team members as an actual work process. In the fields of production engineering and project management, my research provides a significant contribution to the knowledge in effective organisation and management of engineering projects.

Bibliography

Keffeler, JB (1991) 'Managing Changing Organisations' in *Vital Speeches*. 58 (3), pp92–96

Kerr, S (1991) 'Managing Change Successfully' in *Leadership & Organisation Development Journal*. 12 (1), ppi–iii

Lee, Q (1997) 'Workcells design: An important step in achieving total quality' in *IIE Solutions*. 29 (4), pp22–31

Lewin, K (1951) 'Field Theory in Social Sciences' in Cartwright, D (ed) *Selected Theoretical Papers*. New York: Harper

Manz, CC & Stewart, GL (1977) 'Attaining flexible stability by integrating total quality management and socio-technical system theory' in *Organisation Science*. 8 (1), pp69–70

Perry, C & Zuber-Skerritt, O (1991) Action research for Change and Development. Brisbane: CALT, Griffith University

Purser, RE (1992) 'Sociotechnical Systems Design Principles for Computer-Aided Engineering' in *Technovation*. 12 (6), pp379–386

An Action Learning Experience to Change a Work Model in Yokogawa: Real Management Development Through a Real Project

Shankar Sankaran & Sng Hee Meng

Abstract

This case study, written by an action researcher and his co-researcher, describes an action research study of introducing change in a new engineering operation in a Japanese multinational company in Singapore. At the time of this intervention the engineering operation was dependent on younger managers taking on higher responsibilities rapidly to achieve challenging objectives set by the top management. To do this the action researcher had to help his managers 'learn to learn' by using challenging opportunities arising in the workplace to develop their management skills in addition to their technical skills.

Traditionally, the hierarchical organisation did not use a systematic method of introducing change. The action researcher wanted to introduce change in a more systematic way with the help of the very managers who would be affected by the change as his co-researchers. The action researchers used collaborative techniques such as a *search conference* to develop a vision for the operation, *action learning* for manager development and *action research* to introduce change.

The Situation

YES is a fully owned subsidiary of a Japanese multinational company located in Singapore and supplies high technology products to the process industry that includes industrial computers, instruments, control systems and associated services. It was established as a sales and service organisation in 1975 with 25 people (or *members* as Japanese refer to their employees). In 1986 the parent company in Japan set up a large engineering organisation in Singapore as part of its business strategy adding 150 members in Singapore – predominantly fresh, local engineering graduates. The parent organisation also had an independent manufacturing operation in Singapore. In 1990 the parent company decided to integrate all its operations – manufacturing, sales, engineering and services into one large operation bringing the total number of members to nearly 600.

The engineering operation ofYES acted mainly as a subcontractor to the engineering division of the parent company in Japan to do various tasks such as project engineering, system engineering, software engineering for large projects secured from Japanese contractors. This was essentially done to reduce the high manpower cost of engineering in Japan. In 1994 the parent company started a project called 'global engineering', to reduce the cost of engineering further, whereby the engineering operation in Singapore was now expected to undertake total responsibility for major projects including project management, design, engineering and execution.

At this time the Singapore dollar was also getting stronger and the cost reduction targets set by the parent organisation would have been difficult to achieve if the entire job was performed in Singapore. Therefore the engineering operation in Singapore decided to subcontract parts of the work to engineers in India and the Philippines just as it had been a subcontractor to the Japanese parent in the past.

To manage this conceptual change all the engineering personnel in Singapore were brought under a new operation called ATC (Asean Technical Centre) under the leadership of the action researcher. The total members in this centre were nearly 200.

Since ATC was now taking over the role of the engineering operation of the parent company it had to change its engineering method or 'work model' to take on full responsibility to execute jobs and not just be a mere subcontractor.

The action research intervention was used to change the work model of ATC in a systematic manner and simultaneously develop young first-line managers (who had joined as fresh graduates in 1986-87) to take on higher responsibilities so that ATC could successfully handle larger projects.

What did we do?

Prior to the formation of ATC the engineering operation in YES operated on the lines of 'scientific management' whereby the total engineering work in Japan was finely divided into various disciplines of engineering such as project engineering, system engineering and software engineering and local engineers were trained to do these jobs by doing them repeatedly to enhance both quality and productivity. This suited a subcontract model.

When ATC was formed it could not afford to have its engineers do only specific tasks; specialisation at high cost. Therefore some engineers had to take on multidisciplinary responsibilities and their detailed work was 'outsourced' to subcontractors outside Singapore. These engineers were now called 'system integrators'. However some 'experts' were also required to solve problems and do specialised tasks. This also suited the nature of some engineers of ATC and they were now called 'specialists'. To help this transition ATC set up a task force to oversee the conversion to the 'new work model'.

To set this up as an action research study the researchers used the Perry and Zuber-Skerrit model suggested for a post-graduate action research study (1991 p76). See Figure 22.1.

Using this model the 'new work model' intervention was a 'core action research' project to benefit the organisation (YES and ATC). The rapid development of the young managers was the 'thematic concern' and became the 'thesis action research' project for the action researcher.

Fig 22.1 Initial Action Research Model

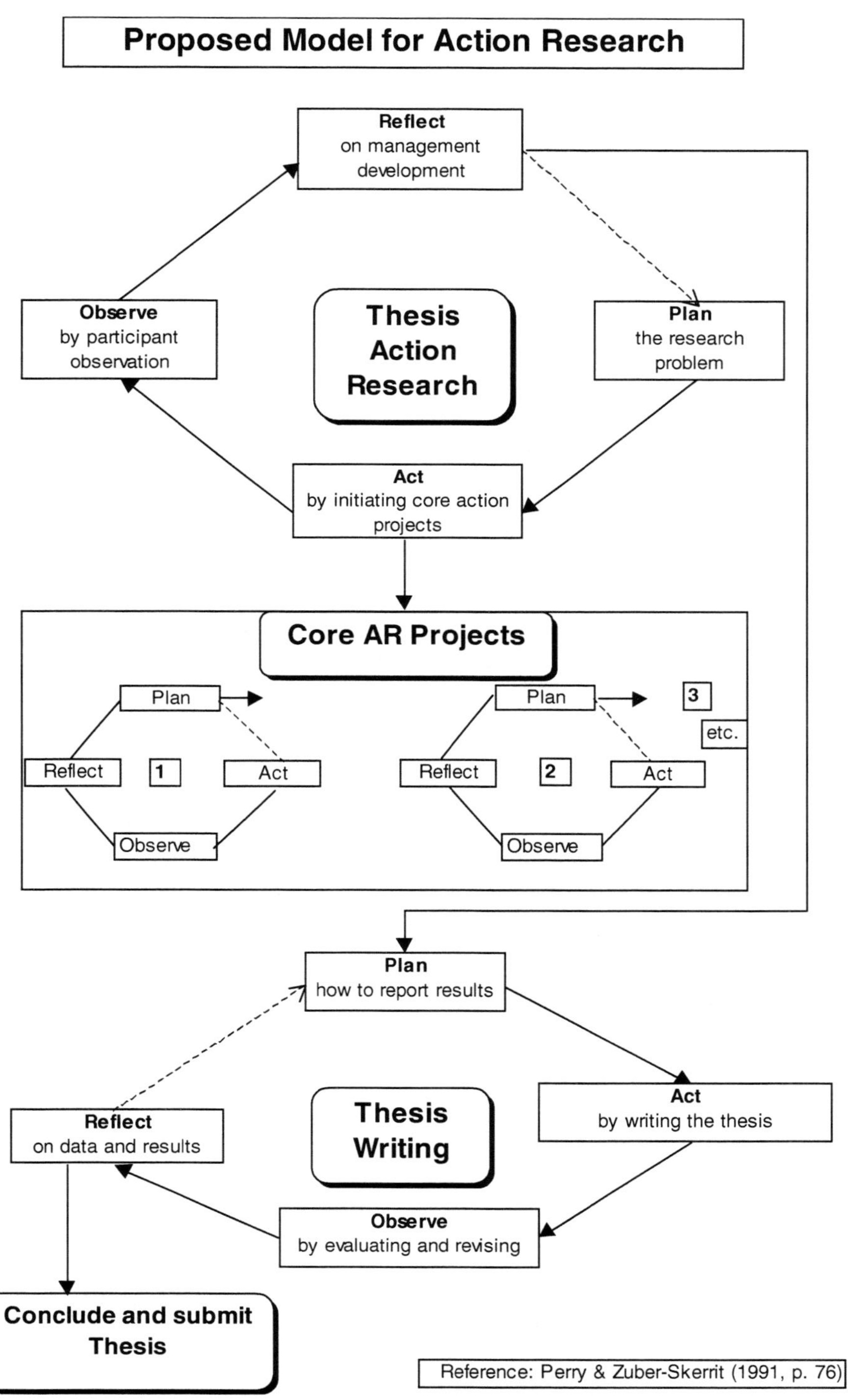

During this action research study the action researcher was also involved with two other 'learning sets'. One was a 'learning set' formed between him and three other action researchers in Singapore – professional managers like him who were doing their doctorates along with him. Another was an electronic learning set called Elogue with whom the researcher set up a virtual consultancy later on. This set was formed when the researcher joined an online course called AREOL (Action Research and Evaluation On-Line) conducted by Bob Dick from Southern Cross University in Australia. He joined this course to learn more about action research.

The interactions between him and the external 'learning sets' also helped the action researcher to carry out his intervention. Thus the action research model that he used was as shown in Figure 22.2.

Fig 22.2 Final Action Research Model

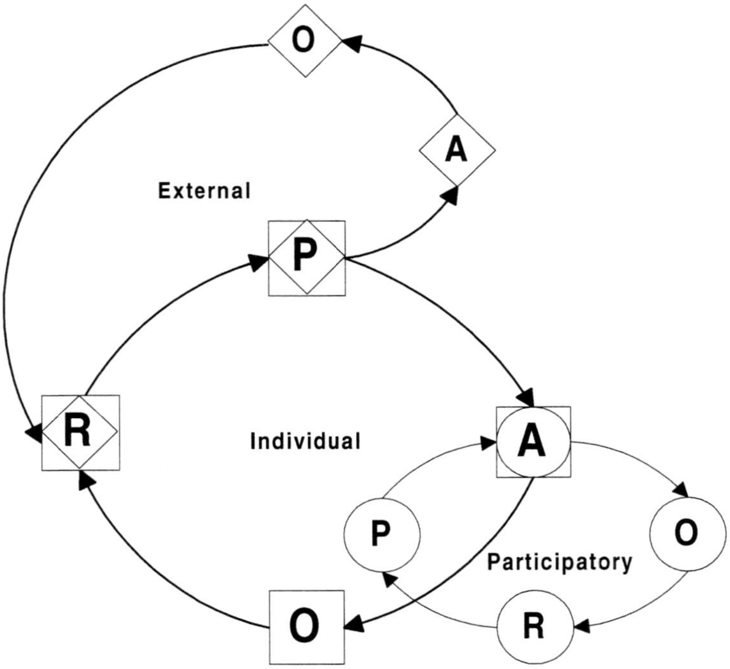

External

Individual

Participatory

Legend:
P – Plan
A – Act
O – Observe
R – Reflect

The revised model was arrived at due to the following reasons:

- The research included only one 'core action research' project.
- The external 'learning sets' were required to answer some of the research questions of the study.

In this new model the planning phase of the 'individual cycle' drove the 'action phase of the 'participatory cycle'. The reflection phase of the 'individual cycle' was carried out with the members of the external sets in Singapore and Elogue. This led to changes in the planning phase of the 'individual cycle' that then acted on the action phase of the 'participatory cycle'. The symbols in the model have been combined to show this effect.

The steps that were taken to carry out this study were as follows:

1. The researcher and a co-researcher (who is also the co-author of the paper) held a 'search conference' based on a model that he learnt from Emeritus Professor Alan Davies who later became his supervisor for his doctoral program. They used a professional consultant to facilitate this conference to give the members of ATC a chance to express their opinion freely.
2. The researcher, the co-researcher and a member of the human resource division of YES learnt about action learning through the literature and also sought the assistance of Scott English, a consultant from the UK, whose book they read (Inglis 1994). He provided them with overheads to conduct an initial action learning workshop.
3. All the managers of ATC were invited to this start-up workshop and introduced to the power of questioning and reflection through exercises. Then managers were asked to voluntarily form 'learning sets' to use action learning. Table 22.1 shows the agenda for this workshop.

Table 22.1: Action Learning Workshop

Program Outline	Facilitator	Duration	Time
Welcome and Ice Breaker	Lily*	15 min	9.15 9.30 am
Introduction and Program Objective	Shankar	10 min	9.30 - 9.40 am
What is Action Learning Part 1	Shankar	20 min	9.40 10.00 am
What is Action Learning Part II	Sean*	30 min	10.00-10.30 am
TEA BREAK		15 min	10.30 10.45 am
Action Learning Activity	Sean/Lily*	45 min	10.45 11.30 am
Learning Styles	Lily*		
Questionnaire		20 min	11.30-11.50 am
Using your Learning Styles		20 min	11.50 12.10 am
Learning Logs		20 min	12.10-12.30 p.m.
LUNCH		60 min	12.30-1.30 p.m.
Team Effectiveness	Lily*		
Stranded in the desert		45 min	1.30 2.15 p.m.
Team roles		20 min	2.15 2.35 p.m.
Traffic Jam		45 min	2.35 3.20 p.m.
Characteristics of an effective team		10 min	3.20 - 3.30 p.m.
TEA BREAK			
Action Learning in Action	Shankar/		
Project identification	Sean*	75 min	3.45 5.00 p.m.
Next steps		30 min	5.00 5.30 p.m.
Summary and Closure	Shankar	15 min	5.30 5.45 p.m.

(*Note: For confidentiality, pseudonyms have been used.)

Four managers from ATC decided to try out 'action learning' by forming a learning set with the researcher.

The authors would like to point out that although they were using 'action research' they called the 'core action research' project as an 'action learning project' so that it would be *politically acceptable* in a Japanese organisation steeped in 'quality control circles' (QCCs). The term 'research' would have sounded too academic. The Plan-Act-Observe-Reflect cycle bore close resemblance to the Plan-Do-Check-Act cycle of 'quality control circles'. The term 'action learning' also appealed to the engineering managers educated in a Western model who thought QCCs were more suitable for a factory environment. QCCs were very popular in the manufacturing operation of YES but did not take off in the rest of the organisation, such as sales, engineering and services.

Action Research Cycles

This study spanned three years from January 1994 until January 1997 with the following cycles:

- -A prelude phase (January 1994 to February 1995) that was devoted to setting up the 'action learning' program in ATC after a literature survey, attending workshops and a search conference and getting advice from 'practitioners'. ATC was formed in October 1994. The ATC search conference was held in November 1994 which set the ball rolling.
- -Cycle 1 (February to March 1995) Awareness cycle where the researchers agreed upon what they planned to achieve through this study.
- -Cycle 2 (March to December 1995) Framework phase where the researchers set up an action learning framework that suited their environment.
- -Cycle 3 (December 1995 to March 1996) Empowerment phase when the power relationship between the researcher and co-researchers were neutralised within the 'action learning' framework.
- -Cycle 4 (March to May 1996) Tackling a problem phase when the 'learning set' decided to work on the 'new work model' project.
- -Cycle 5 (June to August 1996) 'Learning to learn' cycle where the set finally established a process that helped them learn form the experience in addition to solving the problem.

The four managers who were the co-researchers in the 'learning set' were also members of the 'new work model task force' that was responsible for establishing the new work model in ATC. While the work of the task force was going on the co-researchers met separately as a 'learning set' to learn from what had happened due to the actions of the task force, reflect upon it and plan for the next action of the task force. As the 'learning set' progressed it set some 'learning goals' as well.

One problem faced by the co-researchers was how to record their reflections. While all the co-researchers were familiar with English they did not like the forms that were derived out of the literature that required them to write 'journal like' reflections. So they decided to devise a one-page form that would help them record their activities using plan, act, observe and reflect. The organisation was an ISO 9001 certified company that used a lot of forms and a Japanese Managing Director who promoted 'one page' reporting. Using this one page form worked out well. In fact others have used this form and you can find an improved version of it in the chapter written by Bob Williams and Bill Harris in this book. Table 22.2 shows the 'action learning guide' developed during this research.

Table 22.2: Action Learning Guide

<table>
<tr><td colspan="3">Project:</td><td colspan="3">Date:</td></tr>
<tr><td colspan="3">By:</td><td colspan="3">Div./Dept.:</td></tr>
<tr><td colspan="6">PLAN:</td></tr>
<tr><td colspan="2">What action will be taken?</td><td colspan="2">By whom?</td><td colspan="2">By when:</td></tr>
<tr><td colspan="2"></td><td colspan="2">1.</td><td colspan="2">1.</td></tr>
<tr><td colspan="2"></td><td colspan="2">2.</td><td colspan="2">2.</td></tr>
<tr><td colspan="2"></td><td colspan="2">3.</td><td colspan="2">3.</td></tr>
<tr><td colspan="2"></td><td colspan="2">4.</td><td colspan="2">4.</td></tr>
<tr><td colspan="2"></td><td colspan="2">5.</td><td colspan="2">5.</td></tr>
<tr><td colspan="6">ACT:</td></tr>
<tr><td colspan="3">Were any changes made to my plan?</td><td colspan="3">Why did we have to make these changes?</td></tr>
<tr><td colspan="3">1.</td><td colspan="3">1.</td></tr>
<tr><td colspan="3">2.</td><td colspan="3">2.</td></tr>
<tr><td colspan="3">3.</td><td colspan="3">3.</td></tr>
<tr><td colspan="3">4.</td><td colspan="3">4.</td></tr>
<tr><td colspan="3">5.</td><td colspan="3">5.</td></tr>
<tr><td colspan="6">OBSERVE:</td></tr>
<tr><td colspan="3">What Happened?</td><td colspan="3">Was there any feedback from parties affected?</td></tr>
<tr><td colspan="3">1.</td><td colspan="3">1.</td></tr>
<tr><td colspan="3">2.</td><td colspan="3">2.</td></tr>
<tr><td colspan="3">3.</td><td colspan="3">3.</td></tr>
<tr><td colspan="3">4.</td><td colspan="3">4.</td></tr>
<tr><td colspan="3">5.</td><td colspan="3">5.</td></tr>
<tr><td colspan="6">REFLECT:</td></tr>
<tr><td colspan="2">What happened as per plan:</td><td colspan="2">What did not happen as per plan?</td><td colspan="2">What did we learn?</td></tr>
<tr><td colspan="2">1.</td><td colspan="2">1.</td><td colspan="2">1.</td></tr>
<tr><td colspan="2">2.</td><td colspan="2">2.</td><td colspan="2">2.</td></tr>
<tr><td colspan="2">3.</td><td colspan="2">3.</td><td colspan="2">3.</td></tr>
<tr><td colspan="2">4.</td><td colspan="2">4.</td><td colspan="2">4.</td></tr>
<tr><td colspan="2">5.</td><td colspan="2">5.</td><td colspan="2">5.</td></tr>
<tr><td colspan="6">What shall we do next?</td></tr>
<tr><td colspan="6">1.</td></tr>
<tr><td colspan="6">2.</td></tr>
<tr><td colspan="6">3.</td></tr>
<tr><td colspan="6">4.</td></tr>
</table>

A post action learning phase (September to December 1996) where the researchers were able to go public about their learning by making presentations within ATC and holding a public workshop on 'action learning'.

Lessons Learnt from the Case

The case study had management, research and personal outcomes. Some of these are listed below.

Management outcomes

1. The 'new work model' was well established.
2. ATC exceeded the performance targets set by the top management part of which could be attributed to the 'new work model'.
3. The managers belonging to the 'learning set' grew to higher positions in the organisation due to their performance.

Research outcomes

1. ATC established a new way of developing managers.
2. Action learning and action research were successfully applied to an Asian culture with local adjustments.
3. The researcher was able to transfer his 'tacit knowledge' to his younger managers through the 'learning sets'.

Personal outcomes

1. The researcher had a 'smooth transition' to become a consultant and later on an academic.
2. The researchers became reflective practitioners.
3. The researcher also learnt how to analyse dilemmas by applying 'action science' tools to investigate the 'power relationship' that existed in the 'learning set'.

Some surprises from this experience

1. The researcher became aware of his weaknesses as a manager.
2. The researcher did not realise that he could use the external learning set comprising of Singaporean managers to triangulate his findings.
3. Camouflaging 'action research' to suit the 'language' of the organisation was effective in avoiding any political issues. This was also the case with the members of the external 'learning set' from Singapore who had to use different terminology to introduce 'action research' smoothly.

While the new work model worked well with the setting up of the 'system integrator' function of the new work model, the 'specialist' function was still not well established when this study was concluded.

The 'action learning' process itself faded as the organisation was restructured in 1998 and the 'researchers' became dispersed through the organisation. However the spirit of 'action learning' was retained, as these managers became 'reflective practitioners' in their own functions. There is also a possibility and hope that 'action learning' will be used again in this organisation when the co-researchers assume positions of power and influence in the organisation in the future. A major intervention does require 'top management' initiative and support to be successful.

Further details of this study are available in the PhD thesis submitted by the author that is also placed on a website (www.actionresearch.net) to be located within the resources of the Graduate College of Management of Southern Cross University. (Sankaran 1999).

Bibliography

Dick, B (1998) *Action Research and Evaluation On-line (AREOL) Course* (available online: http://www.scu.edu.au/schools/gcm/areol/areol-home.html)

Inglis, S (1994) *Making the Most of Action Learning*. Gower: Aldershot

Perry, C & Zuber-Skerrit, O (1991) 'Action Research in Graduate Management Programs' in *First World Congress on Action Research and Process Management – Conference Proceedings*. Brisbane: 1, pp67–83.

Sankaran, S (1999) An Action Research Study of Management Learning: Developing local engineering managers of a Japanese multinational company in Singapore. PhD thesis. Adelaide: University of South Australia.

Is My Teaching and Learning Practice in Environmental Education Action Research?

Bill Boyd

Introduction

This paper represents the reflections of a putative 'action researcher'. I am an established and productive academic research scholar concerned with studies embedded in the scientific approach. However, while science can be (very) broadly characterised by the expert professional, providing for society rather than with society, my interests have strayed beyond the strict limits of scientific inquiry. First, I am increasingly interested in cultural theory and its application in understanding human behaviour. Secondly, I am increasingly interested in the involvement of the subjects of my research with that research. These moves reflect both current scholarship in cultural studies (eg. Furey & Mansfield 1997; Fiske 1989) and an underlying personal politic of popular democratisation of authority and social responsibility.

With this background, the notions of action research offer some appeal. It is now helpful to reflect on my previous work, especially to consider whether some of it may fall within the rubric of action research. My question is relatively simple: in retrospect, has some of my work been action research, and if not, how close has it come? There are four parts to my answer.

- *What is action research?* I will provide a brief summary of action research, derived from the works of others currently involved in action research.
- *Case studies:* I will describe four case studies from my work (published in detail elsewhere), reflecting my interest in fostering cultural awareness and improved student skills. They are teaching exercises developed to increase awareness and sensitivity of university environmental science students to cultural diversity and difference, and self- and peer-guided exercises addressing issues of numeracy and literacy.
- *Evaluation of the cases studies:* I will follow the case studies with description of their evaluation.
- *Reflection on the case study activities as possible action research:* I will close by examining the case studies, assessing them against the definition and salient characteristics of action research.

Action Research

Action research means many things to many people (Kemmis & McTaggart 1988; McNiff et al 1992). Greenwood and Levin (1998) describe action research as 'a form of research that generates knowledge claims for the express purpose of taking action to promote social change and social analysis' (p6). The social change they refer to is the increased ability of community or organisation members to control their own destiny and to improve their capacity to do so. This reflects these authors' admitted social and workplace situatedness of their work. The core of action research is the goal of creating participant learning capacities, put into practice through continuous and participative learning process rather than by short-term intervention. The intellectual rigour of the process is grounded on a nexus between theory and practice, articulated in Lewin's slogans, 'Nothing is a practical as a good theory' and 'The best way to understand something is to try to change it' (Greenwood & Levin 1998 p19).

Action research, Greenwood and Levin (1998 p75) suggest, 'aims to solve pertinent problems in a given context through democratic inquiry where professional researchers collaborate with participants in an effort to seek and enact solutions to problems of major importance to the local people', and has the following core characteristics.

-Action research is context-bound and addresses real-life problems.

-Action research is inquiry in which all participants co-generate knowledge through collaborative communication. All contributions are valued, and the 'immense importance of insider knowledge' (Greenwood & Levin 1998 p50) is recognised.

-Action research treats diversity of experience and capacity as opportunity for enriching the process.

-Meanings constructed through action research should lead to social action and new construction of meanings.

-Credibility and validity of action research is measured against actions or increased participant control of situations arising from the process.

-Action research represents a practical, successful and disciplined version of the repeated cycles of testing relationships between thought and action, and values reflection as well as action.

Case Studies 1, 2 and 3: The Significance of Significance in Cultural Heritage Studies

These studies are teaching exercises designed to develop awareness and sensitivity of university environmental science students to cultural diversity and difference (Boyd 1996, 1999). The context was simple: third year university units on cultural matters presented to students in an environmental science and management degree program. The exercises support the unit curriculum by addressing issues of personal attitude and philosophy regarding cultural processes amongst students with an essentially scientific outlook. To that end, my intention was to find ways to encourage cultural and philosophical shifts students' thinking, and for them to be more aware, accepting and flexible in their assumptions about knowledge. This reflected my own presumptions and understandings of the differences between the ontologies and epistemologies of science- and humanities-based knowledge.

A role-play exercise was based round a simulated discussion at a public meeting in a small country town, where the issue of protection of an important Indigenous archaeological site had arisen. The role of the staff member throughout this exercise was to set the scene, establish the game rules, manage the process, keep time, co-ordinate progress through the exercise, and facilitate discussion. The students received a written statement of the situation, a sketch of a small Australian rural town with a 'typical' European history and a strong, self-identifying and conservative tradition of land clearance and farming. The accidental discovery, by an outsider university group, of unexpected archaeological remains of pre-European presence in the area stirs local concern.

Excavation yields a site of considerable regional importance. While the academic community was suitably impressed, the local farming community were unimpressed to uninterested, until a proposal was made to gazette the site as a 'Protected Heritage Site'; local residents began to talk about land rights, and general indignation arises. Concerned citizens called a public meeting to stop gazettal of the site, but the meeting was also attended by other groups, each with their own agenda. It is these various groups the students are required to simulate, with the intention of working their way into the particular culture of each group, to begin to appreciate the cultures of their and the other groups and differences between them. Each group has its own views on this site, based on the culture of its position, and each group hopes to convince the meeting of their position.

Student groups each took the identity of one lobby group, and received a written description outlining their group's attitudes, relationships with other groups, and specific issues of concern; each group only sees their own description. A week allowed the students to prepare a submission at the public meeting, and each group needed to agree on a common and unified approach; group responses were varied, most finding little difficulty in agreeing, but some finding it harder. The simulated public meeting started with five-minute outlines of each position, followed by a group discussion. During this session, additional information was introduced in the form of 'press cuttings' with stories that may bear on the events, and may alter the groups' perspectives. A second session allowed the groups to present responses, answer questions, and further support their own position or, if appropriate, develop compromise positions. Following summing-up, each student was asked to shed his or her *alter ego*, and to discuss amongst themselves how they thought the issue could be resolved.

A simulated decision-making exercise used a common cultural heritage management context, the need to evaluate the significance of a heritage place and to make critical decisions about its protection. Non-Indigenous cultural analogues (fictitious historical places and items) provided self-referencing and culturally familiar icons for non-Indigenous students, and served as a springboard for students to consider their response to cultures other than their own. Again, the lecturer's role was in establishing the exercise context and rules, and managing the progress of the exercise.

The focal idea was the concept of significance: heritage evaluation and management often hinges on the assessment of significance. Although significance is often difficult to define, it is enshrined within protective legislation, and forms the political basis of Indigenous self-determination and claims to Indigenous and community-based land management. A source of conflict in cultural heritage management is the many ways significance may be defined and the many perceptions of any one definition; a core concern is the role of cultural ethnocentrism.

The exercise required students to evaluate the significance of icons of the European settlement of Australia, chosen to relate to local history. The students were required to rank the icons according to their perception of cultural significance. This assumed that students had a sense of national and regional identity and history. Six of the thirteen icons were then to be chosen for a 'consent to destroy' permit. In New South Wales, one duty of the National Parks and Wildlife Service is to issue permits for the destruction of heritage sites. The exercise ran in six stages, guiding students through an assessment of the qualities of heritage objects and places, discussion of Eurocentric perspectives of Indigenous site significance and management dilemmas, and progressing to a point where students are placed outside the culture being assessed by asking them to attempt to imagine themselves into another culture. This naturally led to discussion of the situation where non-Indigenous people assess Indigenous heritage.

A value challenge exercise, rather than placing students into a role, directly challenged students' understanding of a concept, the cultural or ethnic stereotype, that is central to issues of cultural diversity and the resolution of intolerance of diversity. This exercise was linked to a home exercise requiring students to collect and examine examples of press reporting of social, cultural, ethnic and national identity. The exercise aimed to increase awareness of public images and stereotypes of people from different social groups, introduce analysis of popular social, cultural, ethnic and national imagery, and consider the role of the press in reporting social and cultural issues.

The exercise commenced with a minimal introduction to the term 'stereotype', and the class provided definitions in a 'brain-storming' session. Once no new definition emerged, discussion led to an agreed definition. It was important to confirm that the whole class agrees on this definition, and to adjust it until consensus was reached; this provided a common term of reference. Groups were then given a work sheet with the heading: 'Write down 10 popular images of [name of a national or ethnic group inserted] people which you think are now commonly held by Australians'. Once each group had written 10 images, all the work sheets were collected and redistributed, and the exercise continued through three stages.

First, the groups separated the images into three categories: positive, negative and neutral images. This often caused considerable debate. Listing these on the whiteboard was followed by class discussion in which students indicated degree of agreement. Those provoking disagreement were identified and considered in a discussion on subjectiveness and the diversity of the evaluation of stereotypes. Secondly, each group considered why the images may have arisen; the students were guided to avoid being judgmental, since the important output was insight into reasons behind the images rather than their 'correctness' or acceptability. Reporting their discussions to the class led to an attempt to draw together any common or dominant themes. Such themes tended to revolve round ideas such as the influence of the press, the influence of real or perceived histories, and concepts of superficial social and human qualities. Finally, the students took away and considered specific questions:

> Do you think that these images are correct? If you don't, how correct/incorrect do you think they are? What do you think the consequences of these images are? (Note the emphasis on 'Do you think...?'.)

Students were also asked to collect examples of ethnic/national stereotypes or images from the press, and for each, to consider whether it is positive, negative or neutral, what its origins might be, how correct an image it is, and what its consequences may be. Of course these were merely the same questions asked earlier, but dressed differently.

Case Study 4: A Response to Apparently Low Levels of Numeracy and Literacy Amongst Students

This case study deals with issues of numeracy and literacy amongst a diverse group of first year environmental students (Boyd et al 1998). The work responded to a perceived and widely articulated opinion that entering university students have unacceptably low levels of numeracy and literacy. This opinion is largely based on anecdotal evidence, but its widespread currency forces staff to consider a response; several are possible, mostly involving time, money and/or staff. My response was to invert the issue, and to use a devise that simultaneously evaluates whether there actually was an issue, and assists students to identify strength and weakness and thus commence self-education. The product was an activity labelled 'The Numeracy and Literacy Survey'. The intention of the survey was to provide guidance regarding levels of non-specialist numeracy and literacy skills, and was not an assessment of expert or specialist knowledge. The staff member's role throughout this exercise was to guide and advise (and in the trial stage, to assess the work), as well as to manage the process.

The survey comprised two parts. First was a numeracy test, with questions of varying difficulties, reflecting the immediate numerical requirements of the course, ranked according to difficulty. This part was prefaced with the statement:

> The following questions are designed to evaluate your mathematical skills. Try and complete as many questions as you can. Write your answers in the third column [of the table of questions provided]. A separate page has been supplied for working out if required. Calculators can be used.

Secondly, a short, non-technical article on scientific issues associated with the Chernobyl nuclear power plant disaster was used to reflect the types of issues that the students would encounter in their course. The students have to read this article and make written comment upon its content. The article is prefaced with the following statement:

> The following is an article from a chemistry textbook. Use the information in the article to write a response to the question below. Use your own words to describe and explain the explosion and its consequences in the Chernobyl nuclear power plant. What are we looking for in your answer? [Then a short list of requirements.]

The survey was trailed by staff from a learning assistance unit; it was considered important that the usual teaching staff were not involved in the immediate administration of this survey. Students were informed that the survey was unrelated to coursework assessment, and that teaching staff would have no access to results. The students were also told that learning assistance staff would assess completed surveys and report directly and confidentially to each student. Students were invited to visit the learning assistance staff to discuss results. Student performance was assessed in two ways. For numeracy, answers were marked (correct or incorrect), and a score and report on the range and types of correct and incorrect answers provided for each student. The markers were also able to indicate areas of strengths and weaknesses. For literacy, each student received a report of their strength in the four areas of paragraph structure, grammar, spelling and punctuation, with other comments.

Following the trial, evaluation (see below) indicated the need for changes: the survey was overly resource-intensive, cumbersome to administer, and not immediately beneficial for the students. It was, however, useful in informing staff and students about numeracy and literacy levels. A peer- and self-review process was identified as the appropriate replacement. It had the advantage that students became directly involved in assessing their work, and they were instructed in the assessment process typically used by staff. The survey was the same as the trial, administered by teaching staff. On completion, the students were issued assessment schedules. Numeracy was self-assessed, with students marking their answer sheets in a conventional manner and grading their work by scoring correct answers in each of the skills areas. Literacy is harder to mark, due to the nature of skills being tested; there is no specifically wrong answer. A procedure was developed to allow students to learn about assessment of written work, by using another student's work. This peer-review process allowed students to assess a peer's work systematically and to ask simple, non-specialist and easily answerable questions to arrive at an overall assessment of the quality of work. The assessment form contained spaces for students to either write comments or identify a ranking value for the work through four stages.

Evaluation of the Case Studies as Initial Reflection

The role-play exercise was not originally planned to be evaluated, and thus specific criteria were not identified. Nevertheless, in retrospect, following the use of this exercise in several small classes (around 30 students per year), some observations from the lecturer's perspective seem apt. The exercise was overtly a role-play of a situation that students, upon future employment, are likely to encounter; the broad mix of cultural values expressed here were reasonably representative of real situations, and, by using a familiar set of cultural groups, it was possible to focus attention on cultural difference. At the educational level, active engagement in such an exercise should be educationally enhancing (eg. Gold et al 1991). Student evaluation questionnaires certainly recorded positive levels of satisfaction for the subject as a whole. Secondly, the teaching effectiveness was reflected by the opportunity for the staff to convey information by making comment and observation without the limitations of lecturing. As information transfer, this appeared to work by providing alternative communication between teacher and student.

Finally, degree of student involvement in the exercise may provide indication of success. A serious impediment, however, arose from the context of this activity: the culture of science education, it appears, does not encourage role-play, and making the transition from fact to fiction, and from rational grounded debate to apparently playful interaction, proved difficult for some students. After all, what *is* the answer? While disappointing, this should not have been surprising, and reflects a science-based and non-humanist view of the world. While some professed enjoyment and educational benefit, many students found the exercise to be an unfamiliar form of learning. In retrospect, it is unfortunate that there was no formal evaluation, since despite this rejection of the method by some students, the exercise may have achieved its aims of fostering an enhanced appreciation of cultural diversity. The logistical difficulties of maintaining interest, however, eventually resulted in it being abandoned.

The simulated decision-making exercise was developed with the experience of running the previous exercise. Its structure and content reflected an effort to avoid the difficulties encountered previously. Assessment of the subject in which the exercise was used focused on specific teaching and learning outcomes. However, it was difficult to gauge the success of students in developing of a sense of cultural sensitivity and empathy. Nevertheless, three outcome measures do provide assessment of the exercise. First, class enthusiasm and the level and type of discussion varied from matter-of-fact responses to long and animated discussion. Secondly, long-term effectiveness was identified in later student interviews: several students had explicitly adopted the methods in further educational and professional activities (eg. Dutton et al 1997). Thirdly, a discussion of the results arising directly from the exercise (Boyd 1996) has indicated the successful completion of the exercise.

Assessment of student response to the exercise suggested it served its purpose in increasing awareness of cultural significance issues and of cultural heritage management difficulties. Furthermore, students viewed it as an appropriate and applicable device for cross-cultural studies. In contrast to the role-play, this exercise did not present concern to the students. The exercise was probably more readily identified by the students as an analytical activity, and so appealed more to both the students' scientific culture and to their experience: reflection and personalisation of inquiry do not feature highly in much environmental science. Both personality and practical experience were thus better catered for in this exercise. Secondly, in terms of expectation, the students probably recognised their future roles in decision-making positions, rather than as group facilitators at public meetings.

The value challenge exercise was not evaluated formally, but several observations indicate success. Student engagement was always positive, and there has been no hesitation in involvement. If anything, the contentious nature of the subject and the opportunity for increasingly public expression of opinions frequently led to reasonably heated discussion. On one occasion an Aboriginal student received the 'Write down 10 popular images of Aboriginal people...' list, which contained some potentially offensive material; he took it well and in the spirit of the discussion, but this caused some concern among other students. This raises ethical issues of personal sensitivity and behaviour that need to be considered carefully.

The exercise also tended to encourage active class response and debate, especially where an individual chose to be obstructionist (electing, for example, offensive comments as neutral, or asserting that these statements were true facts), when the more sensitive or insightful would become most vocal. Although encouraging such debate must be considered positive, a degree of classroom management was required. It was not clear whether obstructionist students gained much other than reinforcing their own views. Again, this raised ethical considerations.

The numeracy and literacy survey: Evaluation through gauging changes in student behaviour was limited by confidentiality issues. However, assessment of staff response to the survey reflected the availability of data regarding levels of numeracy and literacy, and discussion could use real information – that levels of numeracy and literacy were reasonably high, and details of significant weaknesses – rather than anecdote. Identifying patterns clearly has implications regarding both staff expectations and skill development strategies. To assess the survey's impact and effectiveness, several indicators were identified prior to its implementation (Boyd et al 1998), although when these were later found to be difficult to use. Nevertheless, their consideration yielded some outcome. The survey seems to have been a worthwhile instrument contributing to reduced difficulties in numeracy and literacy, and providing a morale boost for many students. The review also highlighted administration problems, resulting in a simpler procedure.

Indicators of the revised version noted some reduction in numeracy and literacy problems, an increased willingness for students to attempt difficult problems before seeking assistance, improved awareness of numeracy and literacy issues, morale boost for students, increased student involvement and opportunity for further learning, and more effective survey administration. Finally, students were provided formal opportunities to respond to the survey, from which some evaluation was possible. Responses tended to be positive, and some students provided further comment, reflecting views that the survey had been useful in identifying weaknesses, giving an indication of expectations throughout the degree, providing motivation to study, and encouraging confidence in students' abilities. Negative comments focused on perceptions that peer review is essentially flawed or that the entire exercise was not useful. This response indicated the need to discuss more fully the importance of clear communication and need for basic numeracy.

Are These Teaching and Learning Activities Action Research?

Taking action research to be 'a form of research that generates knowledge claims for the express purpose of taking action to promote social change and social analysis' (Greenwood & Levin 1998, p6), two issues need to be resolved. First, can these types of exercises be viewed as a form of *research*? In the simplest sense of forms of investigative activity, then perhaps they can. The cultural significance exercises certainly are: they pose questions to be solved, and provide a method through which solutions may be found.

The numeracy and literacy survey, however, is less clearly research, although the knowledge-seeking and evaluative process embedded in the self- and peer-review processes are effective forms of research. Secondly, do the activities take action to *promote social change and social analysis?* In this case, the intention of the cultural significance activities clearly do. They are designed to influence and develop cultural understandings of particular groups, and to provide an enhanced ability to deal with ideas. These notions sit comfortably in the version of action research embraced by Greenwood and Levin (1998).

Elaborating on definitions, we find that 'AR aims to solve pertinent problems in a given context through democratic inquiry where professional researchers collaborate with participants in an effort to seek and enact solutions to problems of major importance to the local people' (Greenwood & Levin 1998 p75). We need, therefore, to consider issues of the *pertinence of the problems* (matters of cultural awareness and sensitivity and of literacy and numeracy seem entirely pertinent in modern Australia) and *context* (the structures reflect the specific contexts and demands of a particular model of higher education). We also need to consider *democratic enquiry* (the intentional involvement of all students is key to this), and the *collaboration between researchers and participants* (the design of these exercises recognises specific roles for staff and students). The fundamental effort in all the examples is aimed towards the seeking and enacting of *solutions to problems of major importance to the local people.* Are the problems, however, either identified by the 'local people' (ie. the class of students), or considered by them to be of major importance? Given this broad correlation between action research and the activities described here, let us return to the more specific parameters of action research.

-*Action research is seen as a continuous and participative learning process rather than short-term intervention.* While, the role of staff (the 'researcher') and students is designed in all the cases to be a structured collaborative one, and there is a necessary interaction between staff and students, it is questionable whether this is simply reflects a well-designed interactive and engaging teaching and learning environment. Certainly, although there was longer-term informal interaction with (some) students, the specific activities were relatively short-lived. The continuity embedded in these activities was largely one for the students, who were encouraged and supported to undertake follow-up activities. Is this an inherent weakness as a piece of action research, or does it reflect the appropriate needs of the learning being addressed? There is an element of both: there may not be a specific need to draw the activities out over a long period, although more active continuing and structured engagement with the issues may have been beneficial.

- *The core goal of action research is the creation participant learning capacities.* The intention of all the activities is clearly that. However, whether this differentiates these as action research or simply as good skills-based teaching (cf. Shepherd 2000; Livingston & Matthews 2000) is unclear.
- *Context and real-life problems.* These activities are all contextualised as classroom-bound, higher education teaching and learning. All address core curriculum, all with an eye on the 'real world'.
- *Inquiry co-generating knowledge through collaborative communication.* All the exercises meet this characteristic. The cultural significance activities require a facilitator, whose role is clearly defined; that person needs to do certain activities at certain stages to ensure satisfactory progress. In the numeracy and literacy survey, the facilitator's role is more limited; that person largely sets the context and provides the materials, offering guidance at the start and (optional) assistance and follow-up as required later. Likewise, there is some difference in level of use of 'insider knowledge' between the case studies. The cultural significance exercises rely considerably on insider knowledge (or opinion) and, especially, on the participants' willingness and/or ability to express that knowledge or opinion. The numeracy and literacy survey relies more on the participants' analytical ability to address criteria and questions structured to assist them through the work. Does this equate to a recognition of 'immense importance of insider knowledge'?

-*Diversity of experience and capacity as an opportunity to enrich the process.* The notion of diversity of experience is central to the success of these activities, both for the cultural significance case studies, and, perhaps less so, for the numeracy and literacy survey. Whether this is important in the latter may be questionable.

-*Constructed meanings should lead to social action and new construction of meanings.* All the case studies are intended to develop participants' ability to engage social action previously not possible, and to become open to new constructions of meanings. Any cultural process exercise must, by definition, have such outcomes (Kemmis & Wilkinson 1998). Evaluation, however, is harder to pin down, especially where formal recognition of credibility and validity is measured against actions or increased participant control of situations arising from the process. Issues affecting the success of culture shifts for some of these examples are discussed elsewhere (Boyd 1999). It is particularly difficult to assess the success of exercises with an aim to enhancing empathy to other cultures, since both performance indicators that reflect attitudinal change and criteria to evaluate the level of change are hard to identify. Level of change must be context-dependent, and change may occur over a long time. Furthermore, such exercises are run within a whole teaching program, and any indication of attitudinal change may be difficult to ascribe specifically to the exercises.

-*A practical, successful and disciplined version of repeated cycles of testing thought-action relationships.* The descriptions above reflect my inclination to reflect upon the activities, and, where appropriate, modify and develop activities (cf. McNiff et al 1992). However, is this simply not good teaching practice? Greenwood and Levin (1998) acknowledge that such reflection and cyclicity of thought and action is a hallmark of good science, but lay claims of structure and deliberation as hallmarks of action research. I suspect it is this latter level of reflective engagement that distinguishes my work as teaching practice yet to be labelled as action research.

Conclusions

It appears that the exercises and their evaluation meet many of the characteristics of action research. However, questions remain. How much do these approaches truly represent 'research' (cf. Kennedy, 1997)? Is the role of the staff member appropriate to action research (Kemmis & McTaggart 1988 pp21–22)? Is the cycle of thought-action interaction structured and continuous enough? At the root of this uncertainty is a concern that the case studies are difficult to differentiate as action research, as opposed to being structured, engaging, skills-based teaching and learning. Despite the answers to these questions, at the very least the opportunity to write this paper has encouraged continued consideration and reflection of my own teaching practices, an activity that some seem to be central to educational action research (Chapter 1, McNiff 1996).

Bibliography

Boyd, WE (1996) 'The significance of significance in cultural heritage studies: a role for cultural analogues in applied geography teaching' in *Journal of Geography in Higher Education*. 20, pp295–304

Boyd, WE (1999) 'Teaching cultural diversity to environmental science university students: Humanities-science culture clash and the relative effectiveness of three exercises confronting socio-cultural images and values' in Kesby, JA, Stanley, JM, McLean, RF & Olive, LJ (eds) *Geodiversity: Readings in Australian Geography at the Close of the 20th Century*. pp213–223 Canberra: School of Geography & Oceanography, Australian Defence Force Academy

Boyd, WE, Cullen, M, Bass, D, Pittman, J & Regan, J (1998) 'A response to apparently-low levels of numeracy and literacy amongst first-year university environmental science students: A numeracy and literacy skills survey' in *International Research in Geographical and Environmental Education*. 7.2, pp106–121

Dutton, IM, Derrett, R, Dimmock, K, Luckie, K, Boyd, WE & Knox, S (eds) (1997) *'Images from the Edge!': Landscape and lifestyle choices for the Northern Rivers Region of NSW*. Final report of a 'Coastwise' project. Lismore: Southern Cross University

Fiske, J. (1989) *Understanding Popular Culture*. London, New York: Routledge

Fuery, P & Mansfield, N (1997) *Cultural Studies and the New Humanities: Concepts and controversies*. Melbourne: Oxford University Press

Gold, JR, Jenkins, A, Lee, R, Monk, J, Riley, J, Shepherd, I & Unwin, D (1991) *Teaching Geography in Higher Education: A manual of good practice*. Oxford: Blackwell

Greenwood, DJ & Levin, M (1998) *Introduction to Action Research: Social research for social change*. Thousand Oaks: Sage

Kemmis, S & McTaggart, R (eds) (1998) *The Action Research Planner*. Waurn Pond: Deakin University

Kemmis, S & Wilkinson, M (1998) 'Participation Action Research and Study of Practice' in Arweh, B, Kemmis, S & Weeks, R (eds) *Action Research in Practice Planner: Partnership for social justice in education*. pp21–36 London: Routledge

Kennedy, M (1997) 'The connection between research and practice' in *Educational Researcher*. 26/7, pp45–12

Livingstone, I & Matthews, H (2000) *Assessing and Recording a Skill-based Curriculum*. Cheltenham: Geography Discipline Network

McNiff, J (1996) *Action Research: Principles and practice*. London: Routledge

McNiff, J, Whithead, J & Laidlaw, M (1992) *Creating Good Social Order Through Action Research*. Poole: Hyde

Shepherd, I (2000) *Key Skills: Teaching & learning for transfer*. Cheltenham: Geography Discipline Network.